Advance Prai

"It's because of the passion, ingenuity, and hard work of Trathen and Daily Acts that I have hope wc as a society can tackle one of the biggest threats to humankind: the climate crisis. Daily Acts is leading the way to a more sustainable climate-resilient future here at home and across the nation."
- Mike McGuire, California State Senate Majority Leader

"With political divisiveness and a worsening climate crisis, Trathen's leadership and the work of Daily Acts are shining examples of the power of community, collaboration, and local solutions. Such local models of addressing our environmental and social crises are critical to spread far and wide. His unwavering commitment to lead on climate change, combined with his enthusiasm and vision, is inspiring."
- Jared Huffman, US Congressman

"Amid the necessary work of national and global organizing, it's important and refreshing to make an impact locally. You'll get some great ideas here about how to help and be inspired."
- Bill McKibben, author of *The Flag, the Cross, and the Station Wagon*

"Often, it's the small community-led efforts, actions, and connection to Earth and its elements that amount to the bigger transformation we are needing and seeking. They can contribute to the catalytic moments and movements beyond our wildest imaginations and dreams. This book illuminates this spirit and reverence through a journey of what's possible from a leader who authentically embodies and radiates what 'take heart, take action' can look like as a way of being."
- Corrine Van Hook-Turner, Director of Climate Innovations at Movement Strategy Center

"Trathen Heckman is an exceptional visionary leader who has created one of the most effective and transformational organizations I've ever seen. The work of Daily Acts is among the most important models in the world today. It needs to not only expand locally but to spread nationally and globally. This remarkable book tells this inspiring story and provides a field guide for how seemingly small acts can add up to transformative impacts."
- **Kenny Ausubel, CEO and Co-Founder of Bioneers**

"If we are to find a way through the next ten years that results in a livable climate and a more just and equitable society, it will have felt like we lived through a revolution of the imagination. What would it feel like to live through a revolution of the imagination? I have no idea. But Trathen Heckman's book will give you a strong taste of some of the tools and the thinking that we'll need in order to create that. Be inspired, and then go put it into practice."
- **Rob Hopkins, founder of the Transition movement and author of *From What Is to What If?***

"In times of crisis, humans in small groups rise to the occasion. Foxhole mates. Neighbors after fires or floods. The 'helper's high' can fade when normal returns, but these are not normal times. Trathen Heckman's book provides a roadmap for you to live a life of camaraderie, meaning, and kick-ass regenerative actions with people in your 'foxhole'— your neighbors, neighborhoods and towns—during the wild ride of climate disruptions."
- **Vicki Robin, co-author of *Your Money or Your Life* and author of *Blessing the Hands that Feed Us***

"Big governments and corporations, even big environmental organizations, seem incapable of halting our species' juggernaut toward eco-doom. Can daily acts of small cooperative groups of ordinary people turn things around? Don't scoff if you haven't tried. Trathen is the right messenger at the right time: he's been showing what's possible for the last couple of decades, and the results are stunning. If you need a dose of inspiration, here it is."
- **Richard Heinberg, Senior Fellow at the Post Carbon Institute and author of *Power: Limits and Prospects for Human Survival***

"Trathen and Daily Acts have perfected a recipe for transformative community action that blends equal parts heart (hope, inspiration, and leadership), head (strategy), and hands (in the soil). I have been deeply inspired by the impact and evolution of Daily Acts over the past two decades, as have countless other community leaders across the country. *Take Heart, Take Action* is a must-read for anyone who is ready to rise to the calling of our time and make their community a more just, regenerative, and resilient place to live."
- Marissa Mommaerts, National Network Organizer at Transition US

"Delicious! I've long been inspired (rippled) by Trathen and Daily Acts. I've gorged on the mouth-watering fruits from his family's abundant garden freely irrigated by harvested rain and other household waste waters-turned-resource waters and then stepped across the street to soak up the wonder of oasis-like rain gardens spreading throughout his city—all lovingly planted and stewarded by Daily Acts-sparked community volunteers/enhancers. Life grows from their actions—life that you want more of. And thus, it pollinates me and a great many others in a way that we start planting more such life where we live. Deep life. Life that nourishes the soul, brings people together, and grows community resilience, health, and joy."
- Brad Lancaster, author of *Rainwater Harvesting for Drylands and Beyond* and Co-Founder of NeighborhoodForesters.org

"From training leaders to mobilizing collective action and helping drive bold community-scale climate policy, Trathen and Daily Acts are helping create a roadmap to the kind of transformation communities need and are capable of when working together across scale and difference toward a shared vision."
- Tanya Narath, Director of Climate Programs at Regional Climate Protection Authority

"This book is an open-hearted invitation to be inspired and informed. Trathen's empowering worldview—where each of us can express our unique agency every day to act on behalf of the whole—supports us in moving beyond our individuality to being greater than the sum of ourselves. Bring it home and read a page or two each day as your Daily Act. His words will speak to you as loudly as the actions you choose to take."
- Brock Dolman, Co-Founder of the Occidental Arts & Ecology Center

"If science was the foundation of saving this planet, we would have solved climate change, biodiversity loss, and a host of other existential problems a long time ago. While this technical knowledge is important, it has also disempowered and disenfranchised us by making us think only big-scale, big-tech, big-investment efforts will make the difference. Through decades of quietly growing a local movement, Trathen Heckman and his many partners have demonstrated that real change always starts with daily acts grounded in intention, motivated by love, and exercised with compassion, humor, and joy. He and his colleagues show us we still have the power to create constructive change—one daily act at a time!"
- Brett KenCairn, Senior Policy Advisory for Climate and Resilience for the the City of Boulder and Director of Nature-Based Climate Solutions at the US Sustainability Directors Network

"For over two decades, Trathen and his organization, Daily Acts, have been leading communities through climate action that builds social cohesion. We need those twenty-plus years of lessons learned from those efforts more than ever right now. Our issues are as social as they are physical, and Trathen and Daily Acts have seen it all and then developed programming and solutions to address everything they have learned into the next project. What we need to do now is rapidly accelerate social change at a local-global level. Trathen provides a unique experience and voice in this journey that every community leader should hear."
- Panama Bartholomy, Director at Building Decarbonization Coalition

"If you are wondering, 'What can I do?' or 'How might my actions contribute to a healthier community, town, or region?' then this book is for you. If you're concerned that your actions are too small to make a difference, read this for insight, encouragement, and grounded guidance. Trathen Heckman's Daily Acts has illuminated pathways to reclaim the power of anyone's actions to regenerate self, nature, and community. Daily Acts' models are an antidote to our bias towards bigness and show over and over again how small changes done with conscious care in community can grow into lasting change, from the grassroots to policy levels. Trathen's irrepressible spirit infuses this book with honest and contagious inspiration and joy in the work, and his work with Daily Acts organizationally demonstrates the power of a whole-system approach to effect resilience, change, and growth. This is as timely, relevant, and accessible a book as you'll find, and it's likely to renew your vision, nourish your heart, and catalyze you into action."
- Nina Simons, Co-Founder and Chief Relationship Officer at Bioneers

"Trathen Heckman is a walking, talking, digging, planting ball of contradiction and inspiration. His capacity to look squarely at the enormous human and environmental challenges we face with love, and passion, and positivity; his bold vision for a world transformed through daily acts of dedication to the people, soil, and water right around us; his proven ability to motivate and mobilize dozens, hundreds, and then thousands to practice the same heart, the same action. These are just some of reasons *Take Heart, Take Action* can serve as a much-needed inspiration for anyone who wants to engage in the task of our time: building personal and community resilience."
-Asher Miller, Executive Director at the Post Carbon Institute and Resilience.org

"Daily Acts is one of the most effective organizations I've seen at galvanizing a wide variety of community partners to take collaborative action. They are an essential partner for the future of sustainability in Sonoma County. As Chair of the Resilient Counties Initiative for the National Association of County Governments, I am excited to partner with Daily Acts and other communities to spread such government and grassroots collaborations in addressing our most pressing environmental and social issues."
- James Gore, Supervisor of Sonoma County and Chair of Resilient Counties Initiative for the National Association of County Governments

"In this book and their work, Trathen and Daily Acts provide a beacon of what's possible, with the vision and experience to help spread collaborative resilience-building models across California and beyond. The only thing more inspiring than Trathen's leadership and Daily Acts' many impacts is their potential to inspire and drive bigger change relative to the crises our communities face."
- Tia Fleming, Executive Director of External Affairs at the California Water Efficiency Partnership

"If you are reading these words, this book was written for you. If you care about Earth, trees, critters, your family, other people, or just yourself, this book was written for you. You have been raised, shaped, trained, and continuously fed by the family and community of life on Earth to be a sensing, conscious participant. We need you. This book contains simple recipes for making what appear to be miracles. Whether it's a successful recycling program for a megacity or massive rescue operations during extreme climate disasters, the critical success factor is diverse individuals responding to an invitation to work as a community to save lives, change policies, or build long-term change. Over my career, I have witnessed millions of people choose to engage in actions that prove Trathen's words to be true: small change is the game-changer."
- Andy Lipkis, Founder of TreePeople and Accelerate Resilience LA and co-author of *The Simple Act of Planting a Tree: A Citizen Foresters' Guide to Healing Your Neighborhood, Your City and Your World*

TAKE HEART
TAKE ACTION

The TRANSFORMATIVE POWER of SMALL ACTS, GROUPS, and GARDENS

TAKE HEART
TAKE ACTION

The TRANSFORMATIVE POWER of SMALL ACTS, GROUPS, and GARDENS

TRATHEN HECKMAN

"Tell me, what is it you plan to do with your one wild and precious life?"

- Mary Oliver

For Mary and Ella, you are the beat in my heart.

*For the indomitable Daily Acts team and community, you have
shown me again and again that amidst heartbreak and hard
work, radical transformation can be a ridiculously good time.*

*For the people and places that have cracked open my heart
and mind and exposed what's possible.*

*For you who boldly choose to step into this big planetary moment,
to live and give your best and regenerate the hell out of it all.*

*For the magic and mystery of a world made of the dust and stuff
of stars, in a galaxy that spirals like your blood and bones.*

Use your stardust well.

Take Heart, Take Action

Rural street sign hack on Lone Pine Way.

Introduction

In a world on fire with overwhelmingly large crises,

what if the power of small could change it all?

Three days into the historically devastating Tubbs Fire of California in 2017, I can barely comprehend it when the state fire chief says, "It's gonna get worse before it gets better." Years later, with an endless procession of more devastating fires, floods, droughts, hurricanes, a pandemic, and the unrest of injustice boiling over, many are coming to grips with the hard-to-swallow truth that it's gonna get worse before it gets better.

But what if the power of *small* could change it all? What if small daily acts of courage and conviction, small groups of unstoppable world changers, and even small gardens of regenerative delight could transform your life and your community and help grow a movement big enough to change the world just when it's needed most?

Of course, it all seems so daunting that it's hard to fathom how one person's actions can have any real impact. Our small efforts and groups feel woefully insufficient to the task at hand. When we're fueled by fear and urgency, it's easy to burn out or push others away, frustrated at a lack of concern.

Full of beauty, inspiration, and practical ideas, *Take Heart, Take Action* is an ode to the reverent, resilient, and irrepressible spirit in each of us. Every day there is a better world being born, and a world that is rapidly unraveling. Which do your actions feed? Are you ready to rise up and reclaim your joy and greatest contribution?

This book is for grassroots activists, leaders, and everyday people who seek a new path to personal and community transformation by being the change they wish to see. When you start changing yourself, and transform your hurt into positive action, the world around you starts to change; though individual efforts alone won't do it. We need collective action and collective will to rapidly spread climate solutions, models, and policies that are just and regenerative.

Twenty-five years ago, as I was waking up to the painful state of our people and planet, I felt somewhat overwhelmed and alone in my concerns, with little hope or vision for what could be different. But then I started to come across people who seemed more alive and passionately connected to a deeper purpose. They were regenerating gardens, farms, and even forests. This landed me at a conference with thousands of such changemakers, who cracked open my heart, mind, and paradigm to how rich we could live while solving our most pressing planetary problems. It set me on a path.

That path led me to start Daily Acts, an educational nonprofit that inspires transformative actions that create connected, equitable, climate-resilient communities. Twenty years ago, Daily Acts was founded on the belief that to transform our communities and world, we start with ourselves. We must be the change we wish to see. By unleashing the power of community and through a wide array of partners, Daily Acts has shown again and again the incredible power of small, passionate, committed groups of changemakers.

Many years later, I was strolling through the Solar Living Institute gardens, finalizing details for a workshop at another gathering of changemakers when my phone rang. It was one of our speakers. As I answered, I heard this sprite-like voice burst through the line, "Hot damn, Mr. Heckman! How the hell are ya?" I smiled and laughed, thinking, *I can't believe this is my senator.*

A decade before, I couldn't have imagined knowing who my senator was, let alone that he'd be so damn real, funny, and inspiring. At best, government seemed not to be stepping up to the problems we face. Not to mention the broken, divisive politics. So, I didn't yet see government and grassroots collaboration as a pathway to transformative change.

I didn't yet know the power of small, the power of community, the power of simply taking heart and taking action. I couldn't have imagined going from installing one greywater system to five in a day, thirteen in a weekend, and then the one hundred Greywater System Challenge, helping shift local and state policies along the way. Or that we could go from transforming one landscape to the scary-to-mention goal of mobilizing 350 gardens in a weekend and later to catalyzing tens of thousands of resilience-building actions and projects. Or that a small group could be a big catalyst in shifting a city from climate laggard to national leader.

The simple truth is that there has never been a time when our small acts and small groups have mattered more. But we gotta believe and lean in, and sometimes let our hearts break. Because this is how the light gets in. It's finding where your heart's inspiration meets the hurt you are called to heal.

In this big planetary moment, *Take Heart, Take Action* is about the journey of finding your path, your people, and a good compass to guide you. Through a series of inspiring stories, you'll learn about three things: how to transform yourself, your garden, and your group as a pathway to transforming our communities and world. Such stories provide a road map—a secret formula to success.

As you read through these pages, you'll:

- Discover a set of steps for how to find and live your inspiration. This includes creating a personal compass that helps you stay awake, engaged, and sustained.

- Learn how growing a garden filled with food, medicine, and wonder can teach you about community and nature's operating instructions. Whether you garden or not, the lessons you learn in a garden about how nature works apply to most everything.

- Build on the lessons of personal change and gardening to see how small groups can become ecosystem catalysts, aligning many people and partners to act as a larger force for good.

Importantly, you'll learn a simple formula to do it all, a time-tested set of values and operating principles that form the structure and flow of this book: Reverence + Ripples + Relationships = Resilience. Reverence is about waking up and following our hearts. Once awake, Ripples are the actions we take to find our vision, voice, and power. Relationships is about creating and nurturing community because that's how our planet works. What comes of this is a Resilience we live and build by waking and taking action in right relation, day after day. And it doesn't matter if you are far along your path or just starting, super organized, or would never ponder such levels of geekery as pontificated in these pages. It's about finding what's right for you and keeping it close by.

In a dark and stormy world, we need bright beacons and a good compass to guide us. The stories and tools in these pages provide both, as well as some bread for the journey.

I wrote this book to help us gather reverence in our hearts, to reclaim the power in our actions, and to nurture life's relationships as an essential pathway to personal and community transformation. Long ago, exposure to people who used their voices to inspire others woke something in me: a desire to live my inspiration in a way that regenerates self, nature, and community, and to nurture this in others.

I also wanted to answer two questions I get asked a lot. How has a small group like Daily Acts created so much positive change, continuing to innovate, adapt, and evolve through all manner of crisis and difficulty? And how in the hell do I stay so inspired and engaged after decades of navigating such challenging terrain?

I've spent over half my life following my inspiration and twenty years helping grow grassroots organizations, networks, and collaborations that unleash the power of community. But given the urgency of now, we need quicker, more systemic change. Wherever you are on your journey in finding your calling and helping grow kick-ass groups, I want the hard-earned wins and losses of Daily Acts and myself to quicken the curve for you. I want government, business, and philanthropic leaders to quit focusing so much on big fixes and to invest in the world-changing power of small.

Nothing in these pages will excuse you from the difficult work of finding and following your North Star or from dealing with the messiness of being human and working with humans. But that doesn't mean we can't have a damn fun, inspiring time and build great relationships as we heal our hurt and the hurt of our world.

This is not a "How To" for self-help, permaculture gardening, or running grassroots organizations. It's a heart-centered "Why To" sharing my experience and Daily Acts' success to inspire readers and leaders to change their lives, organizations, and communities, and to support others to do the same. We do this by claiming the only power we have—our daily actions—and by following nature's operating instructions to nurture community and regenerate life on this planet.

As people, organizations, and movements rise to this moment and prioritize nurturing networks, regenerating ecosystems, and unleashing the power of community, the small, engaged groups in every place are essential. Your daily acts are essential. And the power of small is bigger than you think. It's time to rise. As we say at Daily Acts: **take heart, take part, take action.**

STOP
breathe
listen
Photo: Gavio

Reverence

Start with Your Heart

Heaven on earth for snow lovers.
What's yours? How can you spend more time in it?

Chapter 1:

Finding True North

"Awakening is the foundation of every kind of change…
you have just this one moment, and you can make a choice."
—Thich Nhat Hanh

It took some time to realize that *reverence* for me was true north—in life, leadership, and driving transformative change. There's such a depth and levity to the word, how it sits on your tongue, and moves through your insides like wind chimes in a soft breeze. Reverence is that state of awe, where for a moment you are timeless and mindless…yet fully present and connected to that sunset view, patch of dappled forest light, or a newborn baby's eyes. It's the quiet, peaceful center that connects you to something larger in times of crisis, that moment when it's all on the line. Of the many ways to define reverence, what has acted as a compass and guide in my life and leadership, are the words of Deng Ming Dao: "The stately determination to make something worthy of the materials and the moment is reverence." The first time I read this, sitting on a small wooden stool in a garden, I felt a spark.

Here in this moment, reverence is intimately small.
It's you and I intertwined through words on a page.

Words have the ability to connect us to the state from which they came. These come from a sense of sanctity, wonder, and the nervous excitement of embarking on a journey. Ahead of us is a long, difficult path, full of beauty and hurt. Your full presence and attention are needed.

With a reverent intent, we gain the space, grace, and insight to make the most of the materials and the moment. This ranges from big to small, from holding the hurt of a world coming apart at the seams to reclaiming the only power we have, which is our daily actions. For both, it's about transcending the unconscious conditioning consuming us and this precious planet whole.

Waking Up

The essence of reverence lies in waking up and learning to live well in place. This is no small task in a time of such painful personal and planetary upheaval. Waking up is living in the present moment, becoming aware of our thoughts, emotions, and experiences, and to the truth of our interconnectedness. It's taking in more of the beauty and hurt in our lives and in the world. It's ultimately about living your inspiration in a way that nurtures community, regenerates nature, and stabilizes our climate.

Yes, we need all of the climate-saving, decarbonizing, carbon-sequestering, resilience-building solutions and policies. But I believe that a reverent intent is a strategic imperative for how to create our world anew. The root of our problems lies in who we consider to be "our relations" and who we consider to be "other." We must start with our hearts and wake to the truth of who "we" are, on this little blue marble of marvel and relationships.

Beauty and hurt are intimately intertwined with each deepening our capacity to experience life. When we're not fully present, it's easy to miss what is significant in the moment-to-moment unfolding of our lives and world. Being awake and heartfully engaged is a meaningful, enriching way to be, with endless opportunities for positive impact. This is how we build a waking momentum that can transform our lives, organizations, and communities. This ranges from the easy-to-overlook minutia of daily living to complicated problems like reinventing most everything to avoid climate collapse. And then there's addressing the elephant in the room by composting systemic racism. We definitely need a lot of heart to heal that which we didn't create but has shaped us nonetheless.

Once we awaken to the larger truths of our time, it's about finding our small but essential part in caring for our places and relations. This includes the families and forests across the planet that our decisions impact each day, and the future generations whose lives depend on the choices we make now. While individual action is essential, it's not enough. Given the scale and urgency of the crises, we need collective power to drive wider transformative change.

A Path Laden with Juicy Opportunities

As Thich Nhat Hanh has written, the best way to care for the future is to sit skillfully with the present moment. This helps us make the most of our current choices and challenges. Solving the problems before us builds awareness, agency, and resolve. It grounds us in our power and aliveness so that we can see, hear, and think more clearly. When present, we can better sense and be guided by the intrinsic pulse of this precious planet, which is to help life flourish. Committing to finding your path and larger purpose is ripe with opportunities for healing and service. Recognizing it as a path provides focus and direction, calling in the guides, mentors, and beacons we need. This lends itself to the difficult but rich and vital pathfinding with others to effect widescale change.

From our cells to macro ecosystems, we both shape and are shaped by our perception and reality. A key challenge is that the structures we operate in are invisible and controlled by forces we have yet to perceive. This ranges from limiting beliefs like not believing we have the power to achieve what we want or feeling we deserve what we want to the discomfort and defensiveness of white fragility that furthers societal systems of injustice, continually concentrating wealth and power. We are being shaped by and are shaping experiences and beliefs that disempower and devalue us while destroying the life systems we depend on for clean air, fresh water, and wonder. It comes down to our relationship with self, community, and planet. As Indigenous cultures have long known, we are the earth, air, water, and trees.

This issues forth the opportunity to rediscover and explore with WONDER the unseen patterns and structures in our lives and world. As science confirms, we are wired for the wonder of exploration and a desire to contribute to others, to something larger than self.[1] In the book *Buddha's Brain*, author Rick Hanson speaks to the practices that help transform these unseen patterns and structures and that are central to every path of psychological and spiritual development. It comes through small, positive, and mindful actions and practices like meditation, yoga, and journaling. These add up through time, encouraging what is beneficial and uprooting what is not. From a Buddhist neuroscientist's perspective, Hanson writes that using this ability to reduce stress, increase well-being, and support spiritual practice is the central activity of what could be called the path of awakening.

There has been an upwelling of evidence providing a scientific basis for how the heart positively affects mental clarity, creativity, emotional balance, and personal effectiveness.[2]

Being heart-centered is also a critical strategy to feel and function better. This simply means practicing heart qualities like love, compassion, forgiveness, and kindness. By changing our minds, we can resculpt our brains and transform our lives, making us more mindful, compassionate, focused, resilient, and resourceful. Engaging in consciousness-building practices changes our brains. The circuits of kindness and well-being are strengthened moment by conscious moment, one person, one relation at a time. These small, positive, daily actions add up to large changes over time as we gradually build new neural structures. Living in such a pivotal time, these changes in the brains of many people could help tip the world in a better direction.

Why not create new habits and practices that help transform you, your place, and your relations? This is reverence as a state of being, a compass, a playful and curious companion in waking and learning to live well in place. It feels better, has a lasting positive impact, and gives you the inner resources to not just transform internal structures and patterns but your home, garden, relations, and all of it. For world-changing groups, what better guide to dealing with stress, burnout, and a larger-than-life mission than centering in your collective hearts, your joy, and your shared wisdom?

Here are a handful of ways to get more present in daily life:

- **Follow your breath**—slow, deep breathing brings us into our bodies and the moment.

- **Focus on your heart**—breathe more deeply with your attention on your heart.

- **Listen more closely**—listen to your body, your emotions, the people you're with, the chirps, buzzes, and sounds of life around you.

- **Savor and celebrate the small stuff**—each moment of life is worth treasuring.

- **Simplify**—reduce distractions and take breaks from technology.

- **Practice forgiveness**—be kind and compassionate to yourself and others.

Becoming Aware

Before I had a sense of reverence as a center or much planetary awareness, I was all about passion. My main connection to nature was flying off snow-covered cliffs and through trees on a snowboard. It's all I wanted to do. But with college graduation and the pressure to get a good job, the next thing I knew I was a computer programmer in San Francisco.

I was also becoming aware of environmental issues and doing what I could but growing disillusioned by the material and consumer values of our culture. Then I reached out to a long-lost friend who landed back in my life at just the right time. Stephanie embodied a fun, free, lightness with how she lived. She conveyed a kind, shining altruism that left me with a warm glow and a subtle desire to be and do better. It was the spirit with which she approached life combined with her strong environmental and social values. It was how she lived; the things she bought or didn't; and just how she thought about the world. She's also a great listener, so much so that I began to feel the absence of this quiet, receptive presence in my interactions with others.

Then a visit to Stephanie cracked open my perception about how I experienced life. As I walked into her room, a page of brightly colored words pinned to the wall grabbed my attention. It read, "How to Be Really Alive" by Sark. Reading it was like plugging my finger into a light socket. The words and ideas oozed a freedom and vitality, talking about living juicy, stamping out conformity, eating mangoes naked, and living life as a miracle. A surge of verve electrified me as an intoxicating barrage of feelings flooded my insides. It was an extrasensory, technicolor *holy shitness* that sparked in me the possibility of being alive in a whole different way.

I didn't have an inkling of being that free until I felt it. Then came the sinking feeling of being aware but not "there," of feeling *less than*. As they say, ignorance is bliss. In the span of a moment, I dropped from euphoria to intrigue, insecurity, and insufficiency. It can be easy to not notice that we are just getting by and that life can be far richer and more enjoyable than what we are living or what surrounds us. I suddenly had a new, high bar for how life could be that made my current situation all the less satisfying. Not only was I waking to our environmental woes and feeling boxed in by my job, but now there was this whole other level of discomfort from becoming more aware of how inspired and alive I could feel and live.

To follow your heart is wise, timeless advice that's easy to say and not so easy to do. As we accumulate insightful encounters and get exposed to other ways to be, we are creating conditions conducive to change. From not following my heart to becoming more environmentally aware, I was uncomfortable in a range of ways. That is until I chose my passion over the trappings of a good job. I packed my stuff and moved to my friend's studio outside of Truckee, California, to spend that spring snowboarding.

Breaking Free

I had never felt so free and alive as those first mornings. It was like waking up in a dream, just opening my eyes and staring out at a vast, serene expanse of snow-covered open space, my life an equally free, open slate. It was the first time since I was a kid that there wasn't something I was supposed to do. No school, career, or agenda but one: follow my inspiration. I just woke each day and snowboarded, flying through trees, hitting jumps, and having fun. My sense of freedom, joy, and connection was off the charts. It was that unbridled aliveness I felt from Sark's words. It woke something in me.

It's difficult to push past our fears to find and follow what makes us come alive. Our deep-seated need for security and belonging combined with the pressure of how success is defined by society are powerful forces. This is especially true in our Western culture, which is so disconnected from nature and healthy relations, with profit-driven consumption a compelling force. But how rich and affirming it is when you do break free. It's this deep-in-your-bones rightness that reverberates

The author floating high above a catwalk, before gardening and grassroots organizing became his primary action sports. Whistler Mountain, British Columbia. Photo: James Cole

through each ounce of your being, shouting HELL YES!

Amplifying this feeling was the subtle serenity of being immersed daily in the presence of the Sierra Nevada Mountains. Picture a glacially sculpted granite wall that gets covered in white by the waters of the Pacific, as the ocean cycles from sky to snow. I just sat in awe each day as I rode up the chairlift. It was moving down the mountain in rhythm with place, the aliveness of chutes, cliffs, and steep snowy slopes. In such moments, my body and mind were acutely attuned and in harmony out of necessity, as is the case when consequences are high. Without knowing it, a more subtle accumulation of awareness and connection was growing in me.

My plan was to follow the snow—to move to Tahoe until the spring snow was gone. Then I'd go to New Zealand, where seasons were opposite, to catch their winter. When we take a leap to find and follow our paths, all sorts of things get set in motion, and in these moments, the strength of your signal can draw in who and what you need.

Grow Aware, Do Less Bad

The freedom of travel is a potent thing, especially when seeking a new perspective. It's the space to soak life in, to see that there are lots of different cultures and ways to be in the world. Moving to the snow led to meeting a girl, which led to a month-long stop in Thailand before following the snow to New Zealand. Shortly after landing in Thailand, while euphorically ambling down a trail, enveloped in lushness and beauty, I came face to face with a giant heap of plastic water bottles. With the bliss of the moment and my growing environmental awareness, the pain left a lasting impression, feeding a growing fire in me to take action.

Then on my flight home, I became absorbed in conversation with a Japanese businessman. We talked from takeoff until landing hours later as if only moments had passed. While he seemed normal, his warm, peaceful presence and deep belief in unconditional love stood out, as did some sort of otherworldly quality. He didn't come across as overtly spiritual or seem to be preaching or teaching. It was simply his way. The love he spoke penetrated because of how he seemed to embody it. When we are with a deeply present person, it can awaken a higher level of awareness in us. When we feel really seen and heard, we can begin to notice the absence of this elsewhere.

Shortly after the flight, I realized I had left from gate nineteen. Weeks before, while on a small island, I was reading psychoanalyst Carl Jung's writings about dream symbolism and synchronicity or meaningful coincidences, when I had a vivid dream about meeting an important person at Pier Nineteen. There was barely one pier let alone nineteen, but I was struck by how real the dream felt. As we wake and start to find and follow our path, the universe can respond in surprising and mysterious ways, letting us know that we are connected in ways beyond our understanding.

Reconnecting Nature and Need

After another year of travel, snowboarding, and waking up to the world, I landed in the Ecuadorian village of Vilcabamba. After walking for several hours outside of town, in the famous "Valley of Longevity," there's a small, rustic hut on a beautiful plateau. The meadow in front steeply drops away into dense, lush rainforest. The whole place feels imbued with enchantedness. But what struck me most was when, just before sitting to watch the sun sink into the horizon, a peaceful, young, Swedish traveler offered me tea. When I glanced down at the old, dented pot on the stove, I froze, perplexed by what I saw. It was a swirl of flowers, and bright green leaves floating in the water.

Before that moment, tea meant little bags of some unknown substance I had never considered, much like the rest of the food, clothing, and things that sustained me. While I had become more aware of waste, organic food, and such, I still had no real connection to the sources of my sustenance and the countless goods that made up my world or the people who grew and produced them. Here I was surrounded by beautiful nature but disoriented when nature was in my tea. The depth of disconnection is sadly comical. It would be years before fresh-picked tea became a daily ritual, but like my encounter with the Japanese businessman, the wholeness of the experience showed me a different way of being. It transformed my perception of tea and began rewiring my connection to all sorts of things.

There was more to the moment than the tea. It was the right effort, in the right place, at the right time. There was the simplicity of the hut, the tea maker's presence, and greeting the evening with a warm cup of what grows just outside the door, sitting in silence on a grassy hill, as the sun sinks into the horizon. No unnecessary packaging or distractions, only the essentials, imbuing the moment with a subtle sense of belonging that was woven into the fabric of it all.

It was another direct transmission of a more alive way of living, like I'd expect to find on a page of Sark's words: "soak in sunsets with fresh flower tea." But this wasn't sticking my finger in a light socket; it was more being steeped in a serenity that gently seeps into your pores.

A page on a wall, a chat on a plane, a cup of tea. While each encounter was different, they were all deeply moving glimpses into a more alive way of being. Each embodied genius, which in Latin means *spirit of place*, or as poet David Whyte writes, "being unutterably yourself in conversation with the world."

Sometimes you don't know what you are missing until you experience it. Part of waking up is being exposed to this subtle but deep, natural sense of belonging and with it the discomfort of noticing its absence. To reconnect to people and nature in this way, there needs to be a receptivity in us, an awareness and desire to have a different conversation with the world, even if we don't know how just yet.

For a moment, tapping into this unbridled aliveness overrides any internalized culture of disconnection. Often our excuse for our problems and disempowerment is a lack of some resource—time, money, skill. I acknowledge that for those who face systemic racism and other historical forms of oppression and trauma, this may be the case. But for those of us with the advantages of the twenty-first century, it's not an issue of resources. It's about resourcefulness, relationships, and making the most of the materials and the moment. It's about the story in our heads and re-sourcing our power from the fullness in our hearts to live our dreams here and now.

Find and follow what brings you alive.

As we embrace the beauty and hurt and let it guide our way, paying attention to transitions is important. This means noticing when one is needed and being extra present when entering a new phase or territory. Whether from one big event or a more subtle accumulation, with enough waking momentum, there's a catalyst for change. It could mean quitting your job, ending or starting a relationship, moving, travel, or all of them. Such changes come with new lessons, relationships, values, and insights.

Like Confucius penned eons ago: "To put the world in order, we must first put the nation in order; to put the nation in order, we must put the family in order; to put the family in order, we must cultivate our personal life; and to cultivate our personal life, we must first set our hearts right."

We must begin with reverence,
with small acts of transformation
in our hearts, minds, and daily choices.

Banish uncertainty.
Affirm strength.
Hold resolve.
Expect death.

Make your stand today. On this spot. On this day. Make your actions count; do not falter in your determination to fulfill your destiny. Don't follow the destiny outlined in some mystical book: Create your own.

Your resolve to tread the path of life is your best asset. Without it, you die. Death is unavoidable, but let it not be from loss of will but because your time is over. As long as you can keep going, use your imagination to cope with the travails of life. Overcome your obstacles and realize what you envision.

You will know unexpected happiness. You will know the sorrow of seeing what is dearest to you cut down before your eyes. Accept that. That is the nature of human existence, and you have no time to buffer this fact with fairy tales and illogical explanations.

Each day, your life grows shorter by twenty-four hours. The time to make achievements becomes more precious. You must fulfill everything you want in life and then release your will upon the moment of death. Your life is a creation that dies when you die. Release it, give up your individuality, and in so doing, finally merge completely with Tao.

Until that moment, create the poetry of your life with toughness and determination.

365 TAO: Daily Meditations, Deng Ming Dao

Chapter 2:

Deepening into Self and Community

A couple of months before Ecuador, I competed in an X Games-like Big Air contest where thousands of people would come to hear music and watch snowboarders hurl through the air off a ginormous jump. Seared into my mind and emotions from that day was watching a rider hit the jump, spin through the air, and disappear. He was off in his rotation in the wrong way at the wrong time. Hearing later that he broke his back and wouldn't walk again, I thought of countless close calls I'd had. Was any of it worth dying or being paralyzed?

As much as I loved snowboarding and the mountains, it was time to step away. For two years, I immersed in nature and travel, following my inspiration and growing more aware and connected to myself and the world around me. Leaving the mountains to focus on my well-being felt linked to this growing question of my direction in life. Eventually I moved back to the San Francisco Bay Area to reconnect with friends and to focus on my health and a new relationship with Mary, whom I had a serious crush on since college, and would later marry.

Stillness in Motion

I had a lot of physical healing to do from two years of snowboarding, and I wanted to get more present in my body and life, which drew me to Tai chi. This created an entirely new foundation of health, healing, and awareness upon which everything else is now built. It's how I'm better able to center in my heart and make the most of life's moments while navigating whatever difficulty shows up in life and leadership.

Just as sports like snowboarding and being immersed in nature can wake something in us, weaving together a unique expression of connection to season and place, movement arts like Tai chi and yoga can deepen our self-awareness, opening up a whole new terrain of inner exploration. While it takes focus to twist, flip, and flow down a snow-covered mountain, tuning into how energy moves through your body and how your body moves through the landscape of life has its own flow-filled, joyful, and invigorating experiences. Training in mindfulness and concentration can help navigate the complexities of daily living with greater awareness, joy, and ease.

Having a mind/body/movement practice is an essential tool for finding and living your inspiration. It's vital support for health, self-care, and even processing the hurt in our lives and world. Movement arts teach us about the power of small, as even a modest external motion can penetrate deeply to unlock trauma via body work or physically launch a person across the room in a fight or training. Both examples are about what's happening below the surface—the level of integration and alignment in your body.

Near thirty years in to finding and living my inspiration and supporting this in others as a vehicle for bigger change, there is no way to overstate the importance of developing a daily self-renewal practice. Living in a time of rapid change, our physical and mental health is under enormous daily strain. From constant work and technological inundation to the toxic barrage of chemicals in everything, we are not equipped or skilled to stay healthy and sane, let alone contribute our best. It's tough for many to get through the day, let alone find and stick to routines that help us hear and embody our light and insights.

Simply begin with your breath. Whether your aim is happiness, spiritual insight, or leading well in tough times, everything starts with a breath. It's claiming that instant between life's harsh impacts and how we react. Do we respond to challenges with fear, contraction, and unconscious reaction, or do we breathe and mindfully choose our response? Having a daily practice that roots us in the present moment to process what is difficult and center in who we seek to be and how we want to respond to life's challenges is essential.

*"Between stimulus and response there is a space. In that space is our power to choose
our response. In our response lies our growth and our freedom."*
—Viktor E. Frankl

A favorite Gandhi quote that helps in this regard is: "I'm so busy today I'm going
to meditate TWICE AS LONG." Sit with this enough, and it will change you.
Taking the time to increase our awareness of body and breath anchors us in the
moment, strengthens our immunity, and makes us more effective at whatever we're
trying to accomplish.[3] Doing so daily creates the space to be, to meditate on life
and our motivations, and to look at what's working and what's not. It can provide
the fortitude to keep asking the big questions and relentlessly living the answers
that come, turning your inspiring references into reality. What once jolted me alive
through words on a wall and a cup of mountaintop tea have become daily routine
and ritual. As Thich Nhat Hanh writes, "Peace is every step." It must be continually
renewed.

Inspiration is what flows through us when we are tuned in to the materials and the
moment. Staying in touch with this animating force is fuel for the long work of
following our path. It's the paradox of finding freedom in focus, doubling down on
what grows us whole, especially when busyness takes hold. As one day leads to the
next, spring turns to summer, fall, and another cycle around the sun, it's reassuring
to know that every cell in our body is replaced every seven years.

With each day's waking, why not root into connection to nature and call in the wisdom of your references—the people and places that inspire you most? In a noisy, cha-
otic world, the subtle intoxication of long, deep breaths and fully felt steps is grounding and centering, bringing more flow and a richer experience to each moment. As
Zen Buddhist Shunryu Suzuki taught, follow your breath to not lose yourself.

It Takes a Village

In addition to following our passions and developing a practice, we need good mentors and models. Simply being repeatedly exposed to excellence, to others who are living their genius powerfully impacts what we hold possible. An easy way to elevate your joy, performance, and impact is community. It's having a place to show up for support and connection, to put what we've learned into action. On the healing front, groups can be powerful in holding and transmuting sorrow and despair and in helping us step into our power.

In the Sierra Nevada, I had an amazing community of folks, always pushing each other to the next level. With Tai chi, a similar network of friends evolved to provide support, learning, and encouragement. The same is true for each significant moment or success in this book, from personal action to growing regenerative gardens, high-impact groups, and city-scale transformations.

On the path from passion to purpose, our focus grows from self-interest to include the interests of others. While finding our path requires greater self-awareness and self-focus, it's about self as service, or selfish altruism. Though "selfish" and "altruism" seem like a contradiction, the more you give, the more you get. This means questioning our instincts about how we act in community and with things we value. In a culture that largely values personal accumulation and wealth, it's remembering the importance of valuing the collective over the individual.

Given our planetary situation, this is literally a matter of survival. Thankfully we are wired to share. The perks of sharing range from greater health to personal happiness, as oxytocin is released in our brains, which relieves stress, improves immune function, and increases feelings of well-being.[4] Sharing builds the trust and cooperation at the heart of flourishing communities, while invoking a feeling of gratitude and happiness.

We are deeply influenced by who and what we are surrounded by. Creating conditions conducive to following our bliss like traveling, learning, finding new reference points, and tuning into breath and body are vital to finding and following one's path. Who and what inspires you? Who embodies values or a way of being in the world that speaks to you? What steps do you need to take? What difficulties and discomfort do you need to pay attention to? Even the pain of breaking bones and breaking up can wake us to what's missing, to deepening our path and finding our greatest joy and contribution. We have teachers all around us. But we have to give up having all the answers and learn to look, listen, and ask for support.

Live for What Matters

What a difference a move and a few months can make. I was immersed in the movement arts, had insightful roommates, and was mending from broken ribs (one reason why I stepped away from snowboarding), and a recent breakup. At work, even in a more enlightened corporate culture, it didn't take long to be reminded that I didn't fit there. Having gotten used to the freedom of following my own path, waking to nature connection, and leaning into our planetary problems, making a better shopping experience as a software programmer was a far cry from whatever it was that I could contribute to the world. Like my first round in tech, I struggled with a growing knowledge that this wasn't right. Until Paige intervened.

I think Paige was the first person I met at my new job. Full of warmth and positivity, she was a coworker who quickly become a dear friend. Like Sark's words, Paige had a vitality to her that showed up in most everything she did. She was in her twenties, had recently gotten engaged to her long-time boyfriend, and was full of vision, verve, and things to do. Then she got sick. One minute she was full of life, and the next she was gone. I was crushed, confused, and suddenly felt vulnerable. I had never lost anyone my age. The last time I saw her, she told me to live for what matters, to do it now, and not to wait. With the urgency of suddenly recognizing that life was precious and fleeting, I quit my job, this time leaving the corporate world for good.

Tufted Poppies. Photo: Robb Hirsch

Chapter 3

Finding Freedom and Focus

Sometimes when we take a leap, we have something to guide us. Other times we just feel a need and have to create the space for opportunity. This time when I quit my job, I was pulled towards more purposeful service. I had no clear focus like snowboarding, just a strong interest in health and natural healing for people and the planet. This led to a chance encounter with an herbalist and a free ticket to an herb symposium back east. With no job or agenda, I said, "Sure, why not?"

There is an infinite potential for wonder when you consider that you never know which decision or set of events might shift your perspective or profoundly alter your world. Approaching life and our common encounters and choices with a sense of curiosity, wonder, and exploration alters the chemistry in our brains, resulting in a range of physical and psychological benefits.[5] We are literally wired to wonder because to make good decisions in an unpredictable world, our survival instinct helps us find fulfillment in the new as well as by embracing uncertainty. Time spent here can increase the size and number of neurons in our brains and the connections between them. Simply saying yes to more of what inspires and interests you does a body good.

Finding Your Key References—the Blueprint to a Better You

At the symposium, my senses came alive with the exotic sights, scents, and languages of this new world. It felt like I had been dipped and rolled in a field of wildflower seeds, with new inspirations sprouting like mad. I had this increasingly familiar feeling of somehow being more alive, connected, and intrinsically nourished.

While I didn't know it at the time, a similar pattern was playing out for the third time. It happened in roughly two-year increments—a life pain leading to leaving a job or place to follow my inspiration, then getting exposed to more transformed people and places along the way, further altering the contents and direction of my life and amplifying its richness, connection, and meaning. Once we recognize a pattern, we can learn from it, quickening our evolution. This is helpful to know given the urgency of the times, but upgrading our awareness, skills, and relational capacities can take a few iterations or be a lifelong journey.

I had no idea that the next couple years of encounters would shape my life and work for decades to come. Or that exposure to transformed people and places in wildflower fields and regenerated forests would lead to a gathering with thousands of purposefully alive humans resonating the beauty, inspiration, and healing we are capable of. Or that seven years of sniffing out this divine wind of inspiration would all lead through a backyard gate into another dimension.

But first there was another herb fest just months away, and I was ready to again immerse in healing plants and people, this time at the United Plant Savers Sanctuary on 370 acres of diverse native woodlands, restored prairie, and reclaimed mine lands. Throughout the weekend, my mind was blown by so much. Whatever this was, it seemed a distinct layer deeper than words on a wall, a mystical mid-air encounter, or a cup of fresh flower tea. With over 800 species of plants, trees, and fungi, this place was a multilayered forest sanctuary of food, medicine, and wonder. It was a living, breathing model of the transformation possible.

What made it even more intoxicating was how it was shared. Wise and skilled stewards educated and awakened people by immersing them in this regenerated natural system. You could tour, touch, and taste it, building skills and connections while learning a richer way of life. Being touched, poked, and inoculated in so many ways leaves one soaked in a stupor that furthers the rewiring of one's insides. This direct transmission breaks through our disconnection, touching a deeper, more ancient truth in our DNA.

Herbalist and forest farmer, Paul Strauss tended this land for decades before donating seventy acres to start the sanctuary. His reverential connection to the land and plants emanated a veneration and spirit of service for restoring a patch of the Earth while providing medicine for the people.

As I euphorically ambled about, I was pulled in by a small, engaged group listening to a talk on permaculture. While permaculture was new to me, I got the gist of it, that all of these elements of sustainability fit into a larger whole in regards to the design of homes, landscapes, and lives. The fellow giving the talk, Mark Cohen, had this alluring spark in his eyes and a stirring vitality for life that instantly came through. Like with Paul, the guy on the plane, and the mountain hut tea maker, there was this thing about him that didn't quite fit into words. It was like they were all tapped into something deeper and richer. Throughout the weekend I could feel this aliveness growing in me as new bits of knowledge, experience, and connection flooded in. After Mark's talk, we had lunch. I knew I had to spend more time with this guy.

On the last night of the conference, a small group gathered in the greenhouse for a slideshow by Kenny Ausubel, the founder of a conference and organization called Bioneers. It was full of inspiring solutions and passionate people, from next-level mushroom geeks to economists, energy experts, and justice advocates, all pioneering or "bioneering" solutions from the heart of nature. Even better, Bioneers' annual conference was in a few months near where I lived.

Bioneers—Glimpsing a Wider Community of Changemakers

Once at Bioneers, the profusion of solutions and empowered, insightful people packed into each nook and cranny of the gathering was astounding. There was organic farming, backyard food growing, natural building, green chemistry, Indigenous rights, and efforts to change the media, politics, and everything else. It was a whole community of folks putting heart and shoulder to the wheel on our biggest issues and doing it with joy, creativity, and fierce commitment.

My inspiration glands were about to burst. I had gone from exposure to individuals while traveling to a community focused on the healing power of plants to a weekend immersion with thousands of changemakers. A key insight that Bioneers, the herb symposiums, and related activities embody is this: **when we are exposed to and expose others to painful but necessary truths in the context of deeply empowering solutions and a supportive community, we are more receptive, able, and willing to take action.**

Exposure to a more alive way of being, full of inspiring solutions and people living their vision, provides the strength to peel back the illusion of our separateness and to reconnect to the sources of our sustenance. As we reclaim the power in our common choices, it starts to add up to living in a more relationally rich way, positively connected to people and places across the planet.

Once exposed to a vibrant ecosystem of Earth stewards, I wanted more. I wanted to soak it in and share it. When fresh and tender from the wounds of waking, such experiences can create a potent swirl of energies in us. It's sort of a bipolar swing between the world coming undone and the one being born. But once we break through our fear to follow our passion, find nature connection, and get a glimpse into a more alive, connected way of being, we can open to more of the hurt, too. With practice, we become less awkward in our navigation. Meeting more folks living their truth while using nature's wisdom to heal people and place shows us what's possible and what steps to take.

Belize—Experiencing a Culture of Connection

As if perfectly placed on some unseen breadcrumb trail, in the months following Bioneers and the herb fest immersion, a trip to Belize gave me a powerful next reference. It was the intact connection Belizean people had with the land. These weren't just eco-minded folks, special experts, or a gathering of Earth stewards. Nature connection and respectful use of plants and trees for food and medicine was common practice among most anyone you'd meet. As the Western world wakes to our disconnection and the damage this causes to nature and to us, it creates the space to learn the healing potential of plants and places and how to live well as we care for them.

Like a fish in water, culture is something we are so immersed in that we don't see it. Some cultures are conscious of this and others are not. Getting a glimpse into a whole culture of connection can grow an awareness in us of intimate, real relationships as a way of being. All of our ancestors were once indigenous to place. It was just how you lived, ate, and handled a stomachache. It's crazy that such a thing should even be a surprise; that many of us, particularly in the US, don't know how different being intimately connected to place is and why it matters so much. Historically, culture has been an evolutionary mechanism to protect us against the stresses and dangers of life. Modern-day consumer culture (and colonial capitalism) has instead infected the US and many other countries with affluenza, a powerful socially transmitted condition of overload, debt, anxiety, and waste, with an incessant drive for more. How many people travel to quaint villages, towns, and cities with narrow streets, corner markets, and neighborhood piazzas to experience a sense of place that our lives, neighborhoods, and towns lack?

Locally grown, hand-crafted
transportation, Belize
Agroforestry Research Center.

Belize Agroforestry Research Center (BARC)

A year after my first Belizean experience and still mesmerized by it, another piece fell into place. I had stayed in touch with Mark Cohen and learned more about the Belize Agroforestry Research Center (BARC), which he was involved with. A return trip seemed perfect. As my bus pulled into the village of San Pedro Columbia, something about the place just felt right. There were coconut trees and thatch-roofed huts woven from the palm trees that swayed above. Chickens and an occasional cow roamed the dirt roads as curious kids swarmed about. I found my way to the river where women were washing clothes on flat river stones. There my taxi awaited: a dugout canoe that locals pull up and down the river with a long-carved pole. Truly shaped by place, the Kahune palm was their main roofing material, and the inner rib of the Kahune was used as a guide for shaping their canoes from the giant cedar, teak, and mahogany trees above. The tropical forest buzzed with life, and brightly colored birds were chirping and zipping about as we made our way up river.

After my ride, a gently meandering path led me to a clearing with an open-air structure. Bunches of bananas and plantains hung from the beams while coffee beans and bright red hibiscus flowers dried on bamboo racks. I had arrived at BARC, a 170-acre jungle farm. Agroforestry is a land management system that integrates food crops with trees, shrubs, and natural forest systems. From the serene, milky green river and dense tropical forests to the elegant simplicity of thatched huts and dugout canoes, this place was a refreshing tonic for my growing knowledge of the woes of our world. The locals lived in simple huts with earthen floors and often spoke multiple languages, including English, the Mayan dialect Keck chi, Spanish, and Garifuna, the tongue of the Coastal Creole culture. Miles above BARC, the river bursts forth out of limestone rock at "the source," and a short walk below would land you at the ancient Mayan city of Lubaantun. All this imbued the place with some sort of otherworldliness and fed my desire for a more meaningful connection than just that of a visitor passing through.

Stepping out of the hot tropical sun into cool shade, the canopy above had just the

Carambola (also known as starfruit) and cacao beans

right blend and placement of species, pruned to let light and air flow through for habitat and disease prevention, which made it easier to enjoy the many different types of birds. It achieved all this even while growing food and life stuff, from boats and homes to coffee, chocolate, bananas, and more. Words like *presence* weren't yet in my vocabulary, but this place was penetrating and entrancing. As we deepen into the path of finding and living what brings us alive and what reconnects us to this precious planet, the circuitry of our mind/body/emotions is getting this continuous set of upgrades. Our connection to the vitality and complexity of life has so atrophied that it takes time to rebuild this muscle, gradually evolving our perception, understanding, and functional relationships.

How nice it was to pick coffee and cacao in the shade, carrying bundles of bananas past giant timber bamboo while watching brightly colored toucans eat Malay apples. Or cooling off in an enchanting milky green river, colored by the limestone, as folks in dories floated by. Eating apple bananas with their sweet, tart flavor ruined the blandly sweet cavendish bananas for me, which, due to a monoculture mindset, make up 99 percent of all bananas sold commercially for export. Then there was the self-reliant efficiency of learning which foods to use first to minimize waste and which ones can be fermented, roasted, or dried. Everything was dialed in to reduce waste and pollution, not just because of altruistic values, but because there was no corner store.

In addition to protecting biodiversity, a key aspect of BARC is teaching visitors how self-reliance skills can be used at home, applying nature's wisdom to the scale of your life. It was about modeling how meeting one's needs through living a more eco-centric rather than ego-centric life can be rich with incredible meals, laughter with friends, and a generally more nourishing, connected way of being.

We only care for and respect what we understand and feel connected to. It's easy to lose compassion when we no longer know where our things come from or how they were grown or gotten. Sweatshop labor is sewn into your clothes and child slavery your chocolate. Rebuilding one's home-scale self-reliance is an antidote to apathy, indifference, and a culture of consumption that destroys cultures that care for people and nature. Through simple tasks, BARC made the link between rapidly fragmenting cultures of place and where we are as a people and planet. Exposure to such solutions is an empowering, enriching path that reconnects us to our ability to effect change through our common choices rather than just being overwhelmed by the scale of it all.

Through meeting our needs with our own hearts and hands and by sharing in community, we can feed a life-serving economy and remove our support from an extractive, life-killing economy. When we support local farmers and businesses, we strengthen our food system and local living economies while caring for people who care for our community and for us. If we can't buy local, purchasing fair trade helps steward the people and places where products come from. This positively connects us to folks across the planet who are protecting the forests, families, and critters that live there. Like the chocolate from the cacao farms in this Belizean watershed, the difference of a few extra cents means a family has running water, or their kids can attend school to improve their lives and communities.

Changing the World in a Garden

Having been immersed in the richness of BARC, I started to understand how working with nature and building one's self-reliance was tied to a bigger picture. But what did it look like at home? When I arrived at the Permaculture Institute of Northern California, if there was any shred left of my paradigm of disconnection, it quickly got composted. As I walked through the gate into a suburban backyard, even with the profound experiences of recent years, nothing prepared me for what I saw—a once vast expanse of water-thirsty, chemical-intensive lawn had been transformed into a lush jungle of food, medicine, and wonder, dripping with fruit, herbs, and life galore. This wasn't a regenerated woodland or far-off tropical forest; this was someone's yard. It was a living lab rooted in billions of years of nature's wisdom.

It all started with Penny and James's love for strawberries. Penny Livingston-Stark and James Stark are co-directors of the Regenerative Design Institute and renowned permaculture and leadership teachers. First came the berries. Then ducks to protect the berries from pests. Then a pond for the ducks…and then a beautiful cob office because they had a pile of earth from the pond. Oh, and why not throw in some functional fun with a dragon head pizza oven built into the side of the office wall? The next thing you know, their lawn was a food forest with a fruit tree fence, greywater-fed pond, straw bale and cob cottages, and an endless supply of delectable, edible, multi-beneficial goodness.

Like dry earth soaking up the rain, this place seeped into my pores. It was a vibrant paella of colors, textures, and sounds, a direct transmission of life's vitality. More than sticking my finger in some light socket of aliveness, I got sucked into the circuitry and popped out in some brightly colored Willy Wonka wonderland. It was mind-blowingly exotic yet familiar and accessible. It was someone's garden.

It was also seven years of enriching glimpses, exposure to transformed people and places, and slowly being pulled forward on some invisible path. At the time, I didn't even know what in the hell it all was. I just knew that my life and our world were deeply deficient in this sort of aliveness. After a steady set of inoculations through time, this was it. I was fully infected, no turning back. I had to live and share this.

At the heart of life on this precious planet is an intrinsic force to help life flourish. Without being able to name it, I had been bumping up against this force on snow-covered mountains, in foreign lands, through art on a wall, and from folks who simply had a vitality to them. But most surprising and penetrating was coming across it in someone's backyard. How different this living, breathing, regenerative garden was compared to the average yard, the embodiment of our disconnected, destructive relationship with nature. When we see ourselves as separate from the natural world, we project this separation onto everything else and design things that take huge amounts of energy and effort to maintain, which creates toxicity and waste. We grow plants that provide little benefit while our food is shipped in, requiring lots of fertilizers, pesticides, and fossil fuels. Leaves are raked and burned or taken away from the plants and soil that need them. Water is pumped in for irrigation while runoff water and toxic residues on compacted lawns head to gutters, rivers, and streams. The difference between the average yard and a regenerative

At the heart of life
on this precious planet
is an intrinsic force
to help life flourish.

landscape is the same dissonance as between struggling to get by and feeling really alive. When we stumble across or seek out the intersection of where the regenerative forces of nature meet our deepest inspiration, this level of reintegration exudes a deep and tasty resonance.

Learning nature's operating instructions is like unlocking the keys to the universe. Decades later, I'm still astonished. You would think you have to do some crazy Indiana Jones shit to be handed the secrets to life's form and function. But it's all right there in the spiral of sunflowers, pinecones, and your blood flow, how the rivers of the Earth meander the same as the wrinkles in your gut and sutures in your brain, and how the splatter pattern disperses matter, be it dandelion seeds, a rain drop, a volcanic explosion, or falling glass.

If disconnection and divisiveness is ripping our world apart, the sense of relatedness from falling in love with this magic planet is part of the mending. We can be intimately connected to life by tapping into the intrinsic forces of nature, right in our own gardens. These are things we can live and apply here and now.

If disconnection and divisiveness
is ripping our world apart,
the sense of relatedness
from falling in love
with this magic planet is
part of the mending.

Dragon built into the side of cob building for fun, functional, and tasty eco art. Enthralled tourees sit on the dragon-tail bench waiting for someone to put a pizza in the dragon-mouth oven.

Photo: Permaculture Institute of Northern California

My sister placing flowers on my mother's grave.

Chapter 4:

Embracing Suffering and Loss

as a Catalyst to Act

While most of us want to be happy, loved, and to contribute something of worth, suffering and loss are part of the story of our time. Our loss of meaningful connection to this beauteous planet and the life we share it with has resulted in civilization-threatening devastation. While people try to avoid suffering, there is power in facing our fear, processing pain, and awakening our sense of care and connection to our world. Heartbreak is something to embrace, not shy away from. It can also be a vital catalyst for action.

> "The heart that breaks open
> can contain the whole universe.
> Your heart is that large.
> Trust it."
>
> —Joanna Macy

In crisis and loss, people need to grieve and make sense. Being overcome by our frustration and urgency can keep us from sensing the moment and the right action. It's important to meet people where they are. This isn't to say hold back on speaking truths that may make others or us uncomfortable. That's a survival imperative. But appropriately stepping to the moment in crisis requires extra presence and qualities of the heart, such as love, compassion, empathy, and connection.

Mom

A month after the national tragedy of 9/11, I was in Colorado following an inspiring natural building conference. Then the phone rang. My mom was in the hospital, and I had to get there. It was a long twenty-hour drive west. I watched the landscape change from big clouds and open spaces to the sprawl that had consumed most of the space between the Sierra Nevada Mountains and the California coast. Once I arrived, it was an intense, painful blur, and then she was gone.

Seared into my memory was listening to the most joyful, unconditionally loving person I've ever known look up at me before she passed and say, "I'm tired and ready to step off this cruel world." Given how she lived and loved, how my mom left this world was devastating. Misdiagnosed by her first doctor and given a "heroic" dose of chemo chemicals by her second one—an arrogant young oncologist who told me that diet, nutrition, herbs, and the like had nothing to do with cancer—my mom spent her last breaths in a sterile little room. Thankfully, she was surrounded by loved ones and not just pumps, monitors, and buzzing things. But it wasn't her cats or countless scraps of driftwood art, her crazy lion paintings and statues that were everywhere, or the other vivid bits of life that she infused into her home, family, and all she touched.

Moments after she passed, I was sobbing in shock. Just trying to breathe. I needed air. As I walked out the hospital doors, I stepped into another dimension.

There was a deafening quiet.

The glowing red stoplight and street signs felt larger than life. The rain-moistened pavement seemed alive and breathing. Everything amplified in its radiance, a vibrant stillness.

Years later, Eckhart Tolle's words helped it make more sense. He wrote about how when we experience a deep loss, part of us dies. Resisting this leads to more suffering. But if we accept it, a new level of consciousness opens up in us. In death, life is replenished; our bodies renew the soil. Our hearts break and grow. And apparently our awareness can, too, as some of our ego and attachments fall away, creating a sublime, open space.

It was difficult when my dad died days after my eighteenth birthday. But the two years he spent sick, and struggling to find a new sense of self in a physically diminished state was worse. When he passed, we were ready for him to be in a better place.

With my mom, the suddenness was a shock. It was a flurry of intense emotions and difficult interactions with her doctor, and then she was gone. I was in disbelief, torn by how bad it hurt, and angry at our broken medical system and culture. Then comes this startling quiet. A pain-induced immersion into a new reality, just below the surface of everyday stuff. It was the same world of clouds, trees, and sidewalks but amplified in its radiant quietude. For a moment, I felt more a part of the fabric of life than apart from it. I had no reference for that depth of loss nor for being plunged into such a profound peace and beauty.

Given the times, practicing love, gratitude, and acceptance are important muscles to develop. Embracing our heartbreak and struggle can get us to explore beautiful places, meet remarkable people, and start finding our way, changing our jobs, our situations, even ourselves. If you are going to suffer, why not suffer wisely, to learn and grow from what life throws your way?

"Ours is not the task to fix the entire world at once but to mend the part that is within our reach…one of the most calming and powerful things you can do in a stormy world is to stand up and show your soul…Soul on deck shines like gold in dark times… Struggling souls catch light from others who are fully lit and willing to show it…"[6]

—Clarissa Pinkola Estés

The deep sense of loss and pain from heartbreak can be a catalyst for positive action if we use it so. It can awaken a sense of connection to our own selves, to loved ones, or to the world. Hurt brings us into our hearts and gives us the choice to stay if we heal from and accept what has broken our hearts. The loss of my mom combined with the recent national tragedy of 9/11 acted as a catalyst for me to make a bigger change, leading to the founding of Daily Acts. Like many beacons and reference points, Clarissa Pinkola Estés's words acted as a simple set of operating instructions—

focus on what you
can positively impact;
take a stand
for what lights you up
and share this.

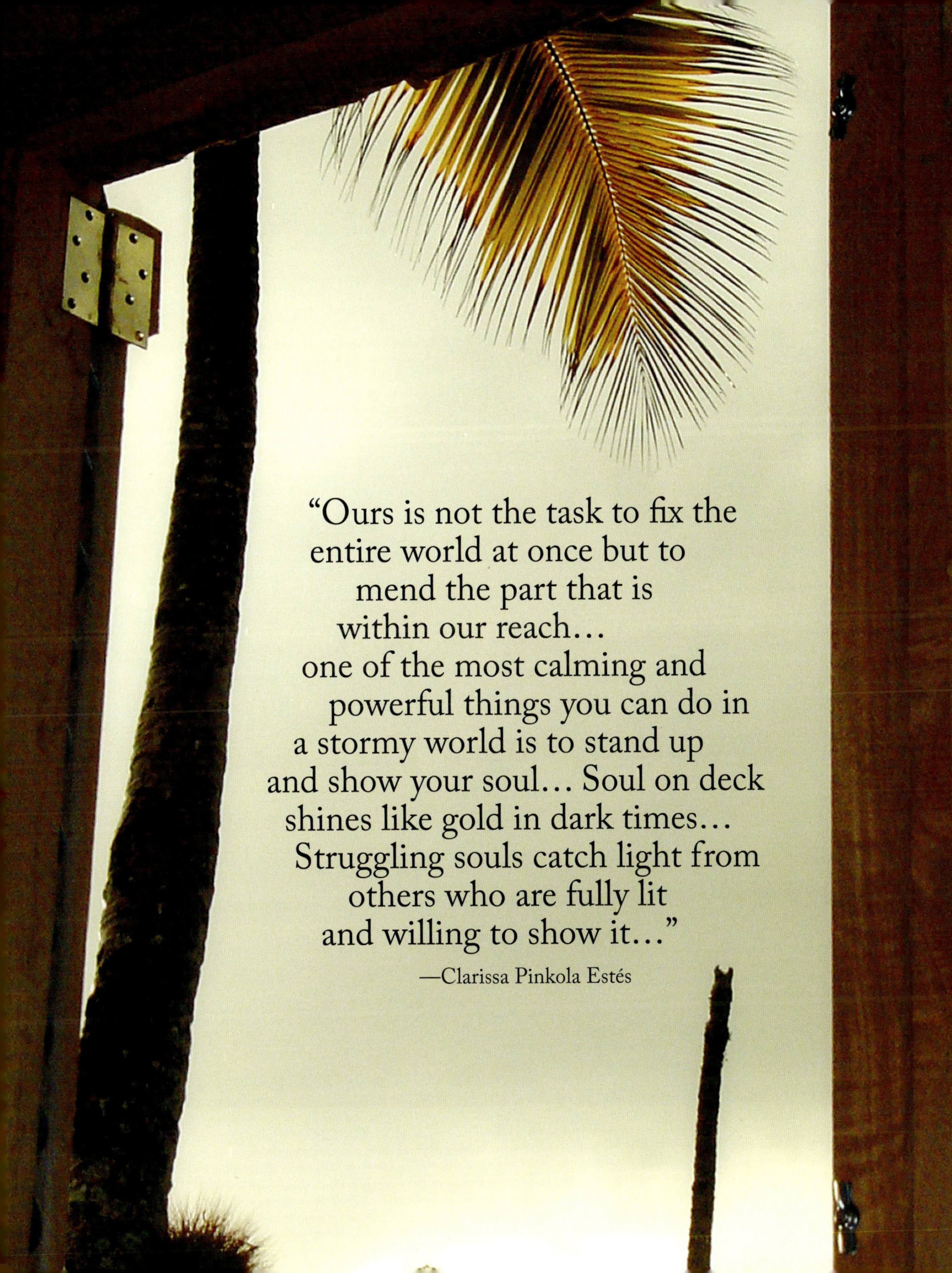
"Ours is not the task to fix the
entire world at once but to
mend the part that is
within our reach…
one of the most calming and
powerful things you can do in
a stormy world is to stand up
and show your soul… Soul on deck
shines like gold in dark times…
Struggling souls catch light from
others who are fully lit
and willing to show it…"
—Clarissa Pinkola Estés

Chapter 5:

Put the Pieces Back Together

*"Life survives through an accurate reading of its context.
It takes a deep, deep listening."*
—Janine Benyus

One day in Tai chi class, a world-renowned martial arts teacher was visiting and said something that stuck. He reminded us to always put the pieces back together in the end, to experience the completeness of the full form. Dig into the messy, complicated stuff of life in this time, but return to wholeness. With so much busyness, hurt, and disruption, it's easy to get overwhelmed, not sure how to be or act. Not to mention differentiating true need from the want of noisy, shiny crap, as companies spend billions of dollars to hack our biological urges and sell us more stuff.

Swimming in a consumer culture of disconnection, we may not even know we aren't "on path" or that there's a different way. We just know something isn't right. We stumble along in the dark until a different kind of shiny shows up, one with a deeper, truer resonance. We must follow those beacons that speak to us, finding our path and tuning into the cues to get back on track when we fall off. This is the ongoing practice of putting the pieces back together and returning to wholeness.

Given our planetary crisis, a heart-centered assessment of our situation and finding our part is vital to survival. We need to feel the urgency to inspire action. Though overwhelm inhibits our ability to focus on our place of power, our daily actions. Being present with what is, while tuning into your best next steps is freeing and empowering. It connects us to a larger purpose. Accepting *what is* doesn't mean apathy or inaction. Acceptance is a deeply engaged act of true freedom. By not judging or resisting, we can access the creativity and insight to choose our best response. Like in Tai chi, when relaxed, you can access and direct the most power. Regularly remembering to reverently recenter creates the space for wisdom and grace to enter and guide our lives.

With the turbulence of the times, there's a lot of pieces to put together and many are rethinking what matters and what contribution they are here to make. Waking to a deeper sense of aliveness can spur us to follow our passion and lead to encounters with transformed people and places, cracking open our perception of what's possible. Paying attention to who and what speaks to us can set us on a journey, an invisible path that gets clearer as we walk it.

For me, it was the air around a forest farmer, a businessman on a plane, and a tea maker in a hut. There was this progression from chance encounters with remarkable people to small gatherings, then bigger gatherings, on my way to glimpsing a culture of everyday nature connection. Then it all came together as I stepped through a backyard gate into an alternate universe. It was a practical example of living one's potential while regenerating nature and community, at home, in the garden.

It's often pain and suffering that spurs action. Waking up, breaking up, and losing loved ones or maybe yourself can set us on some unseen journey, to find the new references, relationships, knowledge, and skills that nourish our becoming, what we are here to contribute.

We can create the more beautiful world our hearts know is possible. We can regain our wholeness—our intimacy with each other and life—while meeting our needs and healing our planet. Though the grief, sadness, and frustration at the madness doesn't go away, there can be beauty with the hurt and inspiration with the urgency. We can affect profound transformation in ourselves, our gardens, communities, and world. But there's no going back to sleep. We gotta lean into the hurt, focus on what we can mend and shine, and share what lights us up.

What if everything to this point, the good and bad, has perfectly placed you in this moment to claim your power, heal your hurt, and to support this in others? What if the world was conspiring to wake us, to pull us forward on this path of transformation? The word *inspiration* comes from the Latin *inspirare*, meaning "to breathe in" or to be infused with divine influence. Why not find and live your inspiration in a way that regenerates nature and community? But how do we do this?

Just keep following the breadcrumbs of what speaks to you. Pay attention to the pain points and push through your fear to take that step. Once you do, keep an eye out for signs, mentors, and models that offer you a glimpse of the better self you are called to be, the gifts you are here to contribute. Deepening usually requires new practices, a community of support, and recognizing when to take another step and make another change. This is the pattern I repeatedly cycled through in the eight or so years leading to founding Daily Acts. And it has played out in the twenty years since.

But here's the spoiler alert for what's to come. Your heart will continue to break. You will lose loved ones and experience climate instability and devastation. We all will. A lot of us already have. But embracing the heartbreak can grow you more whole, alive, and in love with life. It can give you power, joy, and purpose beyond imagination. That's where this book begins and where it ends—taking heart and taking action. I want you to accomplish world-changing things beyond your wildest dreams, to transform yourself, your home, garden, neighborhood, organization, and community—all of it. This is what it will take to keep life as we know it alive. What you can most influence is you. Work on yourself to take care of the rest. Part of this process is becoming attuned to the subtle things that shape us, like the people, places, and influences we are surrounded by.

Here in this crisp, candlelit, predawn moment as I write these words, what's influencing me is the silently towering presence of a lone coastal redwood tree and the slowly growing glow of a new day. Reconnecting to the rhythms of nature as we find our way is critical. As you wake to the interplay of these planetary forces and your small but essential place in the unfolding cosmos, part of reverence as a path is right-sizing our presence in a much wider world. This means maintaining our inspiration and urgency without losing our sense of eternity, in a world beyond our imagining. Treasure and engage life's sensuous sentience, and regularly remember that you are made of stardust. Reverent pathfinding and cultivating a sense of wonder are potent aides for this big planetary moment.

Key Concepts

- Heart-Centered: Practicing heart qualities like love, compassion, forgiveness, and kindness
- Becoming Aware: Being present in ourselves and how we impact people and our planet

Key Points

- One aware, heart-centered, and engaged person can positively impact everything they touch.
- This power is amplified when aligned with others in collective intention, action, and practice.
- Follow your heart to find your passion, purpose, and the reference points to guide you.
- Embrace the tension between your current life and the greater possibilities that speak to you.
- Daily self-renewal practices are vital for health, awareness, and following your inspiration.
- Find a community of support for each phase of your life and significant area of interest.

Questions to Find Your Inspiration

- Personal
    - What are you most passionate about that makes you feel joyful and alive?
    - Where do you feel a sense of calling?
    - Who are the people who most inspire you and why?
    - Are you living your genius and being true to you? If not, what small steps can you take?
    - Do you need to reset your perspective to help life's aliveness guide you?

- Groups
  - o Who or what are the reference points that have informed your vision and path?
  - o Are there any points of view that are missing that could be important to integrate?
  - o What about these reference points is most important to your culture and work?
  - o Might your group benefit from a more heart-centered approach?
  - o How can you best face difficult facts that need to be addressed?
  - o Are people connected to and regularly acting from your deeper intention and purpose?

Steps to Take

- Personal
  - o Answer the previous questions in a journal or document. Make it easy to access.
  - o Review and refine your answers, identify patterns, and next steps to take.
  - o Regularly reflect on and listen to the urges, ideas, and experiences that speak to you.
  - o Take action, even if small, to surround yourself with more of who and what inspires you.
- Groups
  - o Set time to reflect and discuss these questions as a group.
  - o Integrate mindfulness practices, such as stretching, meditation, or practicing gratitude.
  - o Note what is important about your culture and where you may need to change.

"The stately
determination to
make something
worthy of the
materials and
the moment is
reverence."

—Deng Ming-Dao

Photo: Leslie Curchack

Nina making ripples. Photo: Gretchen Schubeck (a.k.a. mom, kickass leader and human)

Ripples

Live Your Inspiration

Because humor and fun are great strategies to move from personal to collective action.

Chapter 6:

Taking Action to Live Your Values

Where reverence is about becoming aware, initiating needed change in our lives, and finding what sets our heart on fire, ripples is about taking action day after day to be that change. Living your vision and values and the deeper purpose that animates your being not only changes you, it creates a ripple effect that changes the world around you. To best live this, three things are needed: 1) taking action; 2) finding and using your voice; and 3) developing your personal compass. While each of these elements applies at an organization scale, to affect wider change, we start with the most accessible whole system available to us: ourselves.

This matters because the survival imperative before us is to transform nearly every aspect of our lives and communities. While this can seem too big to deal with, it starts small, leveraging powerful neurobiology one act and one inspiration at a time. As we discovered in Reverence, turning our curiosities into passions on the way to finding our larger purpose taps into the deepest intrinsic drivers of human motivation. And it feels damn good. Taking action that helps you build skills and a sense of self-sufficiency adds two more important motivators: autonomy and mastery.

Tapping into nature's operating instructions through more locally self-reliant living is a critical next step to regenerating self, nature, and community. Connecting to the land while meeting even a portion of your needs with your own hands is healing and appealing. For many, waking to the pain of the world and feeling a pull to greater self-reliance comes with a desire for more time in nature.

Like the repeating pattern of waking to the state of our lives and world laid out in Reverence, for over two decades in life and leadership, I've seen a similar pattern play

out again and again while taking action. Honing one's voice and compass are critical, interconnected strategies for people and groups to be the change and stay sustained while inspiring others to greater, more meaningful action.

From Glimpses to Living It—Action at Home

There's something entrancing about the timeless truths of how life on Earth functions and how people have long lived well in place. Pondering the intrinsic forces that shaped our planet over billions of years—like the pulsing procession of ice ages—shatters one's perception of time. It opens a broader perspective that is expansive yet grounding. Feeling a part of this grander order can leave you with a sense of awe, connection, and an increased responsibility to act. After years of getting inoculated, I was ready to live the vision that infected me at regenerated farms, forests, and backyards.

Before, during, and after in author's Monte Rio garden.

When Mary and I moved to the small town of Monte Rio on the Russian River in 2000, I found a steep, degraded slope littered with debris. I feared the hill would collapse if I even stepped onto it. With nails, glass, and trash in the soil and limited sunshine, it wasn't a gardener's dream. But from the permaculture perspective of seeing problems as solutions, it was the perfect place to start. Rather than being a daunting mess, this was a juicy opportunity to apply nature's regenerative wisdom—or so I told myself.

Defined more precisely than an infectious transformative substance oozing out of certain people and places, the intent of permaculture is in the name: a synthesis of the words *permanent* and *culture*. While there is greater detail to come in Relationships, permaculture is a pathway to sustainable living that's rooted in the wisdom of nature and Indigenous people. It begins with the three ethics of Earth care, people care, and ensuring a fair share of resources. From here, ecological design principles guide implementation. Strategies may change with context and scale, whether you're designing an urban garden, a farm, or a 10,000-acre grassland.

I started creating walls to hold back the eroding hill while providing structure, a path, and places to grow. Since using onsite, organic, and recycled materials has a wide range of benefits and taps into the ecological design principle *produce no waste*, I used broken concrete or urbanite. Everywhere I went, I saw piles of opportunity. I knocked on doors and met folks happy to share their rubble. I built fifty or more terraces of all shapes and sizes out of recycled concrete, downed trees, and found materials. Slowly a meandering path with nooks, crannies, and catchments galore took form. One permaculture principle is that *each element performs multiple beneficial functions*. In this case, a recycled concrete wall on a hillside with limited light provides heat from thermal mass and reflects light off the surface, creating a more conducive microclimate for growing. Since the urbanite was recycled and dry stacked, it cost nothing, had good drainage, and took less expertise and emission-intensive new materials to make.

Using an undulating meander pattern to shape the paths created more edge to access and interact with the garden while tapping into the intrinsic forces of nature by mirroring the way rivers meander. This same pattern is how you fit twenty-five feet of intestines in your belly. All these twists and turns create more surface area and reduce the speed at which things move through you. This increases nutrient absorption. By wiggle-waggling pathways on the land, the same is true, with more fitting into a small space, while slowing your flow and aiding in absorption and engagement.

Meandering can also be a metaphor in our lives, increasing meaning and connection. Think about what you experience and how you feel when flying down the highway versus being on a gently winding country lane. Or how this applies to your daily choices when moving fast, consuming what's cheap and easy. When rushing straight from A to B, we experience and absorb less, lacking flow and connection. You already eat, drink, and breathe. Why not reap more from it, including the joy of sending forth more tiny positive ripples? Like our landscape, our food, clothing, and common details speak volumes about our relationship with the living world, each other, and the future generations we impact through each of our acts. By slowing down, we grow more aware, increasing our exposure to the beauty and the hurt, providing time to reflect on who and how we want to be.

LEAVES!

Experiencing fall in a forest with new eyes on nature's form and function is astonishing. This is especially true in a culture of seemingly endless "resources" and little relationship to them. Most of us don't consider soil and how it sustains us, that the real magic that makes life above ground flourish is below our feet. Where does this wondrous stuff get its most important secret powers from? Recycling. Nature produces no waste, recycling everything to renew itself.

I was feeling inspired by recycled garden walls and insights about working with nature while reclaiming the flow in my choices. But what had me jumping out of my skin was the chance to fill these new garden beds with another "unwanted

Photo: Leslie Curchack

waste"—leaves. Harvesting this free fertility that flutters down from the sky reconnects us to eons of seasons and billions of years of nature's renewing wisdom, slowly decomposing and turning into precious soil. There are more creatures in one teaspoon of fertile garden soil than people on Earth.[7] Soil is this precious thin skin that helps life flourish. Civilizations rise and fall by how they tend the soil.

Suddenly seeing free fertility everywhere is enough to send one into an inspired frenzy. The weight of the world melts away as we take action in alignment with the forces of planetary renewal. I was like a kid in a candy store, first filling buckets and then garbage cans with damp, decaying leaves to compost. Still being a neophyte gardener, I didn't know what to do with it, so I just buried it in the garden. Since then, I've learned a lot about composting leaves and other organic matter or using them as a mulch to build soil and conserve water. Consider how counter this is to conventional wisdom. Rake leaves. Put them in the compost or garbage bin to be taken away. Then buy mulches and fertilizers manufactured or harvested from who knows where and transported to you to feed and protect the soil that has been deprived of this precious leaf litter.

The Ephemeral Delight of Dappled Light

As I observed, listened, and worked with the land, I fell in love with this sun-flecked hillside, just watching the sun move through the sky each day and season, tuning into how plants would stretch into any sliver of warmth and light. While full sun is better for growing food, with less light you develop a deeper appreciation for the sun. The ephemeral delight of dappled light on a winding country lane drew me here. Such light gently pulls one's attention to the stillness and presence of a place, to the fleeting and subtle, bringing what it touches to life, like a spotlight capturing a beautiful solo performance. This can grow in us a sanctified sense of quiet connection.

By starting at home, connecting to and transforming a place, you begin to become more aware, to feel part of this living, breathing world in a practical way. This kind of action feels right on many levels. It starts to shift your perception of seeing problems as solutions and waste as a resource to treasure. As I built walls, harvested leaves, and followed patches of sunshine through the day, another shift was happening. I was slowly being shaped by the magic, and sentience of this place, moving from action to appreciation, further rewiring my awareness and sense of connection.

Sensing and Reconnecting to Life's Aliveness

Around this time, while the presence of falling leaves and dappled light were penetrating deeper into my consciousness, I read an interview with Eckhart Tolle, speaking to his experience of spiritual transformation.

> I opened my eyes. The first light of dawn was filtering through the curtains. Without any thought, I felt, I knew, that there is infinitely more to light than we realize. That soft luminosity filtering through the curtains was love itself. Tears came into my eyes. I got up and walked around the room. I recognized the room, and yet I knew that I had never truly seen it before. Everything was fresh and pristine, as if it had just come into existence. I picked up things, a pencil, an empty bottle, marveling at the beauty and aliveness of it all.

His words instantly wove together disparate moments of waking to nature and my body, to mountains of trash, cups of tea, vibrant gardens and gatherings. After years of painful and astonishing experiences, another something clicked into place. I felt a sudden coherence and ease wash through me. Awareness connected it all. It was that thing underlying my experience with the Japanese businessman, the look in Mark's eyes, Paul Strauss's presence, and Sark's words, this field of alert stillness that's always there, just below the surface.

Tolle wrote of how we separate ourselves from reality and in doing so lose our ability to sense the sacredness of nature and the aliveness in the world around us. He spoke to how when we connect to the presence in anything, be it plant, rock, or rusty bucket, that awareness grows in us, as with our relation to the life all around.

We are like fish in water, nourished by the invisible sentience in and between all things. Similarly, Thich Nhat Hahn has written,

"The miracle is not to walk on water. The miracle is to walk on the green earth in the present moment, to appreciate the peace and beauty that are available now."

The Sadness of Separation

One day, standing on our deck, looking out at the garden and valley, I felt myself becoming more still and entranced by the aliveness of the forest. I was so warmly engulfed in the moment that I disappeared into it, dropping into a different reality, where the vitality of everything exploded. I didn't just feel the valley; I merged with it in a timeless, mindless, brightly colored, peaceful euphoria that I had no reference for. Then as quick as it came, this warming embrace vanished, leaving me with a cold, dark, lonely sense of loss.

When my mom died, the heartbreak led to an immersion into the aliveness of the moment. This was immersion into loss, opening a new depth of our missing connection to the living world. At one point, before our ancestors became separated from nature, often violently ripped away, every human was part of a nature-connected culture, indigenous to place. This was inherent to survival.

Until we experience deep nature connection, we are unaware of the level of our loss, living in the sadness of separation. Consider the implications of a whole world of people oblivious to their birthright of a warm embrace and intimate connection.

More than just a debris-filled hillside when I started regenerating this place, after the 1906 San Francisco fire, these forests were denuded to rebuild the city. Some fifty-eight years before that, the discovery of gold had created a mass migration that built up San Francisco as it stripped landscapes, killed streams, and contributed to the genocide of native peoples. Given our history of harm to our people and planet, there is much listening, learning, and healing to do.

In *Sand County Almanac*, Aldo Leopold writes, "One of the penalties of ecological education is that one lives alone in a world of wounds." But this can be intertwined with growing more aware, alive, and connected, with more regenerative ways to be. How we hold and dance with our increasing awareness of the beauty and hurt matters.

As local Wappo Spiritual Leader, Clint McKay, shared with me, feeling deep ties with your people, the land, and animals provides a grounding and peace. For us all to again become indigenous to place, we must acknowledge our history and work to heal and make things right. This means taking action to regenerate the land and ourselves. Developing in ourselves this different way to relate to the beauty, majesty, and mystery of this precious planet is a gift in and of itself. But it also develops in us a spirit, a strength to do the deeper, bigger work of healing we are called to address.

From Class to Daily Practice—Make It Your Own

As we learn nature's lessons about revitalizing the land, having a movement practice can enhance another aspect of our awareness and sense of connection to life's aliveness. Tai chi, yoga, and the like aren't just for class or a specific time of day. They can be woven through everything, infusing mindfulness and intention into all you do.

A deepening connection to and healing the land coincided with evolving my movement practices. Soon, drinking tea and stretching became my morning ritual. Walking in the garden, I practiced focused breath and mindful steps. Drying off after the shower, I did Towel Chi Gung. Breakfast was Tai Chi Toast with a chance to connect body, breath, and intent.

As I further explored the theory and practice of movement arts and permaculture, it started to feel like they were connected; like Tai chi was permaculture for our bodies, and permaculture was Tai chi applied to the landscape and living in tune with nature. After all, they are both rooted in observation, understanding, and mimicking natural forms to regenerate and heal. A critical piece of deepening our connection to and healing the land and our bodies is becoming more aware of how they fit together. It's being fully present in ourselves as we restore the landscape, tuning into the subtle energies and patterns we are learning and applying.

When waking to new facets of our relationship to nature, self, and the alert stillness between things, sometimes we don't fully understand these new perceptions. Without a framework to hang these experiences on, they easily slip away. But once we see and name the pattern, we have a place to store and grow experiences. Together, these three pathways of connecting to the regenerative powers of the Earth, the aliveness in our bodies, and present moment awareness, form a more cohesive and potent whole.

Why just dry off, when one light, one wipe, and one shower at a time, you can grow more alive and values-aligned?

Towel Chi Gung - Chi gung is a traditional Chinese system of movement, breath and meditation used for health, spirituality and martial arts training. Applying this to your shower routine is great to shake off the morning grogginess and start your day in a good way.

1. Give a vigorous head rub to oxygenate your brain and open your mind.
2. Mindfully breathe in and gently rub circles around your eyes, affirming your vision.
3. From the base of your nose softly pull towards your ears to open nasal passages.
4. Massage your ears with the intent to hear more deeply and clearly.
5. Give an upward caress from the base of your neck to love up your thyroid and affirm your voice.
6. Tap or rub the center of your chest to stimulate your thymus gland and immune system.
7. Rub under your armpits to activate your lymph nodes.
8. Massage your lower back to give your hard-working kidneys some love!

After these steps, continue to invigorate your body and charge up your awareness and intention with more rejuvenating towel action around your hips, legs and feet.

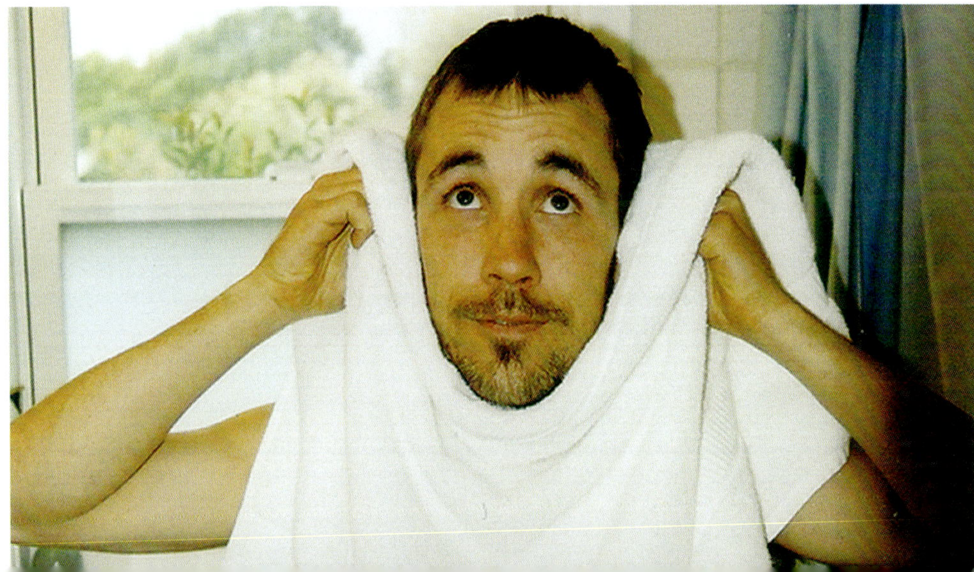

I THINK YOU ARE BEAUTIFUL ALREADY
I THINK YOU ARE BEAUTIFUL ALREADY
I THINK YOU ARE BEAUTIFUL ALREADY
I THINK YOU ARE BEAUTIFUL ALREADY
FOR THE LOVE
LOVE LOVE

Chapter 7:

Finding and Sharing Your Voice

"Whatever you can do or dream you can, begin it.
Boldness has genius, power, and magic in it!"
—Johann Wolfgang von Goethe

Once you start taking action to live your vision and values, sharing with others is important to further evolve your embodiment of what you care about. Moving from action to articulation requires developing a new level of understanding. Like with anything, finding and expressing your voice has an uncomfortable learning curve. It's awkward and vulnerable at first. It isn't just about the words that come out of your mouth. It's sourcing a clear connection to the higher purpose that speaks to you. It takes time and effort to hear the signal, more to live it, and an extra dollop to speak it. Applying this at an organization scale with blending voices and harmonizing together is even more complicated, which is why we start small, with ourselves to build awareness, skill, and momentum.

If your vision is the practical picture of what you want to create in the world, purpose is the divine wind of inspiration that moves through you, animating your being. Like many have said and Gandhi lived so well, we must be the change we wish to see. In writing about the habits of highly effective people, leadership author, Stephen Covey, similarly notes the importance of change beginning within. From here we build the clarity and commitment to have integrity in our actions and relationships. Building trust with others grows our positive influence, enabling us to move from living our vision and values to helping create a shared vision in organizations and communities. Finding and using your voice to inspire and support others to do the same is at the core of unleashing the transformative power of people and communities.

Making Ripples

In the aftermath of losing my mom and the silencing of dissent that followed 9/11, I thought we needed more, not fewer, diverse voices. We needed to become the media. I wanted to inspire people by sharing practical examples of the better world being born. As the first effort of starting a grassroots organization, I launched *ripples zine.*

The growing aliveness in me, full of inspiration and outrage, was begging to be shared, to call others to use their joyous, agonizing waking to be and do different. The combination of personal and national tragedy acted as a catalyst for what had been years of buildup. I started *ripples* because things like social media didn't exist yet, and it wasn't easy to get one's voice and ideas out in the world. It signified the powerful ripple effect of one's every action. Since much of the writing I had read seemed to be void of passion, purpose, and values, I wanted to focus on sharing ideas, images, and any damn thing that might help shake the dust off of life's luster and inspire positive action. I wanted to convey the life-nurturing verve that had infected me because powerful emotions stir action. It meant saying YES, there are awful things happening, but we need to do more than bury our heads in the sand of apathy and inaction or just seek a bigger, tastier slice of the pie.

So I started gathering quotes, images, and scraps of inspiration, as well as writing poems and short articles and piecing together a list of simple, daily actions people could take to channel their inspiration and outrage. What was magic about *ripples* was that with just enough vision, a sense of urgency, and a willingness to act, the right people and parts came together. This happened a lot once *ripples* got going, but it all started with running into an old college friend, Andrew Bisbee, who was a graphic designer. He offered to help design *ripples,* creating a coherent and compelling look and feel for the zine and twenty years later this book.

It's as true today as it was twenty years ago: the ripples from each of our choices matter. I'm talking about every interaction and purchase, what we drive, what our investments are nurturing or destroying—twenty-four hours a day. Collective action starts with each of us reclaiming our power to more fully live our values. Once you start asking bigger questions and living the answers, writing helps clarify your vision and intent and helps you make sense of the batshit craziness out there. Writing is an important avenue to develop your voice and find what brings you alive. Sharing with others adds power and motivation to live into those high ideals. Together, finding your voice and taking a stand for your vision helps build a foundation for change.

Raindrop Fairies

As I pieced together the first *ripples*, the pages came to life. Then one morning, all hopped up on inspiration, I felt a voice surge through me. It spoke with strength and clarity about *stretching past what we believe we can be because we are limitless when we choose to own this*. The instant I felt this, fear doused my enthusiasm over the thought of these words being in print, for the world to judge. I felt insecure about sounding too blissful or airy-fairy. On top of that, what lit me up and came out on the page was this flowy, poetic, grammatically impaired style that I hadn't seen before. So there was this extra fear of being rejected as outlandish or ridiculous. Being social creatures who have survived as part of a collective, our security in the group is closely tied to survival. With psychological survival being right next to physical survival, exposing our true self can be frightening.

But within seconds of this surge of inspiration and the fearful voice that followed, outside my window through the dim, wet redwoods, some unseen ray of light hit a solitary raindrop on the tip of a redwood needle, causing it to glisten like mad. As I was mesmerized by the shimmering light, a strong, clear voice came through, saying, "Honor, don't deny, what gives you shine."

As I snapped back to reality, I was trying to wrap my heart and brain around whatever in the hell just happened. It's like I was taken over by the forces of good and evil with the raindrop fairy of conscious delight and the dark lord of doubt battling it out on my insides. This wasn't some *look at the pretty raindrop* thing. A crystal-clear voice moved through me, overriding any conscious or unconscious disbelief I had about such stuff.

Once the seal was cracked, in the coming months a dozen such experiences enveloped me with a presence that felt powerful, purposeful, and a part of me but beyond me. It was a different voice than the usual banter in my head, arriving with a heightened presence and focus, feeling more connected to the air, trees, and falling leaves. These experiences came in moments of fear, insight, or delight. They egged me on, affirming that we are a part of something larger, that it's our responsibility to own our connection and bring our gifts into the world. How many other encouraging little sprites might be flashing through our days with us oblivious or constructing barriers to such things?

Author Marianne Williamson said:

> Our deepest fear is not that we are inadequate. Our deepest fear is that we are powerful beyond measure. It is our light, not our darkness that most frightens us. We ask ourselves, 'Who am I to be brilliant, gorgeous, talented, fabulous?' Actually, who are you not to be? You are a child of God. Your playing small does not serve the world. There is nothing enlightened about shrinking so that other people won't feel insecure around you. We are all meant to shine, as children do. We were born to make manifest the glory of God that is within us. It's not just in some of us; it's in everyone. And as we let our own light shine, we unconsciously give other people permission to do the same. As we are liberated from our own fear, our presence automatically liberates others.[8]

Soon, with the support of friends, family, and otherworldly sprites, *ripples* was born. It was a small, black and white zine, DIY, but clean, spacious, and high quality. But would 2,000 copies of this spunky little recycled paper publication actually ripple?

Then one afternoon, Bob from down the street appeared through my window with a beaming smile and a donation check in his hand. He said everything I could have hoped for about *ripples*—how deeply inspiring and invigorating it was, and that it motivated him to take action. Having been bound up with so much excitement, fear, and insecurity, I was fed beyond belief. Soon more emails and calls came in. *ripples* had struck a chord. People were ready to reclaim the power of their choices, to turn hurt and outrage into positive action and meaningful living. As we pieced together more issues of *ripples*, each time we coalesced what felt most inspired and authentic.

The combined powers of inspiration and urgency, with the boldness to push past one's fears, is a potent recipe for something powerful to emerge. As we get better at finding and living our inspiration, this lays the groundwork to do so with others, amplifying the passion, purpose, and joy by working together for a higher good.

As more folks got involved, every issue of *ripples* was full of synergy, coming together out of shared effort and inspired fervor. Often, we'd get to a point where we didn't know if we had the energy to go on, and magically, a supportive message would arrive to power us through. There was the guy who wrote about losing his job and crashing his car, but how he found *ripples* in just the right moment. Or the eighty-nine-year-old grandmother who sent a typewritten note about getting re-invigorated by *ripples*; or the gal in Canada who wrote, "Now I know what it's like to be in love."

Then one cold day in San Francisco at an anti-war march, feeling chilled, I stepped into a warm patch of sunshine. Standing there, eyes peacefully closed in a sea of protesters, suddenly I hear, "Are you *ripples*?" As I open my eyes, a bright-smiling woman named Jen slaps a big hug on me. With thousands of protesters, how did someone recognize me from this itsy-bitsy zine with only a few thousand copies?

It's astonishing how this little zine found its way to the right hands and hearts at the right moment, and how folks responded to us at the right moment. Somehow *ripples* was inspiring and drawing in others through all sorts of synchronistic, mysterious ways. This is the power of finding that deep, true resonance and how it can move through us into the world. Once you feel a spark that begs to be shared, listen closely to nurture and spread it.

Taking a Tour—the Smell, Touch, and Taste of the World Being Born

I knew this zest for life could be transmitted through words on a page and when exposed to it in person. Exposure to Sark and other writers showed me this. As did touring reverently regenerated forests and lush backyard ecosystems with crazily inspiring people.

Want to effect change? Infect people with the beauteous world being born. Inoculate their mind, body, and emotions with courageous, contagious, and vibrantly alive people and places. Do it in a way that speaks to you, while connecting like hearts and minds and nourishing networks of engaged people and leaders. Part of finding our voices is making real in the world more of what lights us up. When you build off what deeply impacts you, there is less risk because you know the approach works from personal experience.

What better way to discover and support solutions than to share with others? And what better way to make friends and make change than to say, "Hey, can I bring a bunch of people by your place to oohhh and ahhhh at your good works and wise words?" Come on, who wouldn't love that?

Shortly before I launched *ripples*, I started thinking about sustainability tours. If you search online for that kind of tour now, you'll get millions of hits; but at the time, I couldn't find anything. I knew I had to change that, so I reached out to some of the mind-blowing sustainability enthusiasts I had been meeting to organize sites for a tour. Knowing the importance of consuming food that cares for the Earth and supporting farmers and my community, my first stop was Laguna Farm. Farmer Scotty is a bright beacon of a being who wasn't just farming; he was an eco-Inspector Gadget, innovating equipment, establishing a biofuel depot at his farm, hosting events, and more. Laguna was an oasis of community connection and the perfect place to kick off the kind of tour that could crack open hearts, minds, and paradigms.

My next stop was with permaculture activist, Erik Ohlsen, who had transformed his small backyard rental into an edible paradise. Inspiration effortlessly effervesced from Erik as he talked of delectable edibles, DIY recycled greenhouses, and how the invisible interplay of a hot west-facing sun reflecting off his small pond's surface would perfectly nurture nearby peaches into optimum tastiness. What? Who does backyard microclimate Tai chi with peach trees and ponds?

Finally, I visited Janine Bjornson, a natural builder, earthen plasters expert, and artist. Janine and friends had modeled a wide range of beautiful earthen finishes at Ocean Song Farm. She was teaching natural building and transforming places with cob and natural plasters and paints. When putting nature's native colors and textures on display, even a plain wall comes to life.

These three sites and stewards were perfect for a tour, with my family's own newly terraced garden planned as the fourth stop. When people started calling to register for the tour, I was in inspired disbelief. By the fiftieth person, excitement became fear. Fortunately, when my nerves started to fray, I stepped onto the hillside, took some breaths and mindful steps, picked some tea, and nibbled nerve-soothing herbs to regain my ease. Our tour was bursting at the seams with seventy-plus engaged do-gooders. I split people into two groups, and we crisscrossed the county to tour sites in a bunch of newly released Prius hybrids that the local dealership had loaned

Because people need to see what's possible and connect with the like hearts and minds to make it so. Daily Acts Sustainability Tour, San Francisco, CA.

me. It was an incredible coming together to celebrate what's working and connect concerned and engaged people and leaders. The speakers and eco-efficacious solutions blew folks away. Being with like hearts and minds rejuvenated everyone.

For all the lonely struggles, isolation, and frustration at people who don't "get it" or are lost in their own small problems, such kindred spirits nourish and give hope. Not hope as in a blind faith that our problems will solve themselves. This is a hope you can touch and taste, one that clings to your insides and begs to be shared. It's hope as an embodied, engaged optimism that says screw *the gloomy facts*.

The folks from that first tour are still in my life today. Like a dented old pot of mountain tea, I am steeped in them again and again. For two decades I've ambled into the high sierras with Farmer Scotty. As I scratch these late-night words, I'm leaning against a handcrafted clay plaster on our wall from a workshop with Janine. Across the street is a cob bench built in a workshop she led. It sits in front of Daily Acts' first public food forest, installed with 150 volunteers and Erik's expertise.

Boldly stepping forward with your dreams requires a leap of faith. But it draws in those who resonate with your voice, values, and vision. Then they add their skills and connections, and your shared dreams and ability to achieve grow. As we find and befriend the bright lights we are drawn to, their friends become our friends, further weaving a vibrant quilt of community, one with greater joy, connection, and capacity for good. Through time, this reshapes us in the best of ways.

Even more, the goals of that day twenty years ago are as true now as they were then:

- Highlight inspiring models and leaders

- Educate, engage, and connect concerned folks

- Become the media to amplify solutions and stories

- Strengthen and grow networks of sustainability-minded people and places

- Create a replicable model that others can use and improve

Each goal reinforces the others. Showing folks how to live sustainably by sharing mind-blowing yet practical examples inspires them to create and share their own. This strengthens and connects networks of changemakers.

As you encounter and create experiences that blow your mind and connect you to a bunch of great folks, you may think, as I did, what in the hell was that, and how do I do it again? In the book *SWITCH,* the authors Chip and Dan Heath write, "In tough times, we'll see problems everywhere, and 'analysis paralysis' will often kick in…To make progress on a change, we need to provide crystal-clear direction— show people where to go, how to act, what destination to pursue. And that's why bright spots are so essential: They provide the road map." We must highlight and copy success to grow more of it.

In dark times, being exposed to people living the vision they speak is intoxicating. Share your inspiration and concerns in a way that empowers others to act. Provide real examples, with the smell, touch, and taste of the better world being born. When we reconnect people to place, to their inspiration and power, they can live their best and ripple this infectious energy to others. Exposing people to problems in the context of inspiring leaders and practical solutions and models can infuse them with the agency to act, and to inspire others. Growing organizations and networks built around such strategies further amplifies and spreads this force for good.

Stage and Plane

A thing about finding your voice is that the inspiration doesn't always flow effortlessly and eloquently, especially at first. It takes strength, vulnerability, and resolve to keep showing up. After all it took to push through my fears and put my voice to page with *ripples*, I assumed the hard work of finding my voice in writing would translate to speaking. Not so much.

One day, I got an email from a fellow named Pride who was lit on *ripples*. My sister had dropped a stack at the coffee shop in the small town where she lived, and they rippled. Someone picked up a copy and knew it would resonate with Pride, who was focused on effecting cultural change by making it enticing. We hit it off. Pride expressed interest in publishing my writing and putting me on the stage. The next thing I knew, I was on tour in Oklahoma with veteran singer-songwriter Patrice Pike, playing college town cafés, clubs, and churches. I was amazed at Patrice's presence and ability to connect with an audience. While some humbling stumbles showed me I wasn't ready to hold a stage the way she did, I kept showing up and pushing through fear to speak from the heart.

It felt good. Not good as in when things are comfortable or easy, but the good of digging deep and finding something I didn't know I had. This didn't make the experience any easier, but fear began to lose its grip. The trouble with listening to those inspired, righteous voices in us is that they get more emboldened and keep pushing. So there I was on the flight home reflecting on this emotional rollercoaster of a trip. I was reading some fiery words about patriotism by Terry Tempest Williams and reflecting on the courage of Rachel Carson in publishing *Silent Spring*. I looked around, dumbfounded and outraged that we can fly across the planet, but we can't figure out how to recycle soda cans and coffee cups on planes? I thought, *Are you kidding me?*

Then in an increasingly familiar flash, a voice in my head said, *You need to make a public service announcement.* As soon as I thought this, fear rushed in with another voice saying, *Holy crap! You can't do that.* Not only was I terrified about speaking up to a plane full of strangers, but after 9/11, I had concerns that I may get arrested or never be allowed to fly again.

I went for it anyway. Half-standing in my seat, I shouted, "Excuse me! Could I have your attention, please?" As a plane full of surprised folks turned to look at the odd fellow spouting his mouth from 33B, I went on, "Excuse the interruption, but I'd like to mention something that could enrich all of our lives. Each day, countless thousands of plastic cups and bottles are thrown away on planes, like the ones just discarded on this flight. While I love the surge in patriotism after 9/11, expressed through waving American flags, what about care of the earth, air, water, and lives that those stars and stripes stand for? Imagine if each person on this plane filled out the comment card on page 121 in the *Delta Magazine*, asking them to reuse or at least recycle these containers. Imagine if we each did this on every flight, inspiring others to do the same. In the words of Margaret Mead, 'Never doubt that a small group of thoughtful, committed, citizens can change the world. Indeed, it's the only thing that ever has.' Oh, and thanks for your time."

As everyone in the entire plane stared blankly at me for an eternity, I smiled through the awkward silence. But then I could hear a quiet but growing cascade of ripping pages, as comment cards were torn from magazines. Amazing as it was, the momentary result wasn't the most important thing. Each person on that flight had one more pebble of awareness rippling through their minds. Engaging and encouraging people by raising awareness and pairing it with practical action offers a chance to wake and embrace the morals absent from mindless actions. In doing so, we reclaim the power of our choices and voices, connecting to something larger.

As I stepped off the plane, I felt more alive. It had been a year and a half since that first *ripples* and sustainability tour. I had continued to find and share my voice, pushing through fear and doubt to speak at events, host tours, and create more *ripples*. When we claim our work in the world, we are fueled less by fear and more by the growing fire inside us and by an emboldened voice that speaks and acts from our higher self.

Find Your Voice and Shine Your Light

In stepping up to find and shine your light, you must cross a minefield of fear and self-judgment. Luckily, there are a number of practices and reminders that help address these challenges. First is awareness. When we recognize these patterns, we can practice self-compassion, honoring that we did our best without the self-judging that can inhibit our growth.

After awareness comes practice. As you develop your voice, be it through speaking, writing, or whatever, reflecting on what worked and what didn't is a helpful habit. Then practice getting comfortable with being uncomfortable and acting without all the answers. Regardless of the discomfort, listen to the voice inside you. A secret weapon in this regard is knowing that your voice isn't really about you. As dancer and choreographer, Martha Graham, reminds us:

> There is a vitality, a life force, an energy, a quickening that is translated through you into action, and because there is only one of you in all of time, this expression is unique. And if you block it, it will never exist through any other medium, and it will be lost. The world will not have it. It is not your business to determine how good it is nor how valuable nor how it compares with other expressions. It is your business to keep it yours clearly and directly, to keep the channel open…keep yourself open and aware to the urges that motivate you.

Just keep finding yourself and honing your gifts day after day.

Another practice is continuing to watch for what sets you on fire, be it a page on a wall, a sparkling raindrop, a book, talk, or whatever. Going back to your core references and places like conferences in your field is a great place to start. Once you find your reference points and bright spots, ask yourself or others a few questions. What's their secret formula? What revelations, difficulties, and practices shaped them? Part of finding our path and best self is understanding how others have done the same. This is part of why I've written this book.

One day when I was about to do a talk, I asked a friend and legendary activist, Kevin Danaher, if he ever got nervous before talks. To my surprise, he said he still gets butterflies, but they just learn to fly together. Part of the butterflies learning to fly together is developing the habit of leaning into your growth edge, which is uncomfortable. That's why getting comfortable with being uncomfortable is important. This requires faith and practice.

By finding and sharing your voice, others can experience your difficulties, insights, and breakthroughs. The same is true for you and me. By surrounding ourselves with inspiring people who speak to something deep in us, we reshape how we are. By finding our voices and speaking with emotion, clarity, and conviction, our ability to live our vision and infect this in others is amplified. When stepping into our power to contribute something of worth, we find who and what we need to encourage and support us. Given the challenges our world faces and the emotional minefield we need to go through to do this work, it is all the more important to double down on what sets our hearts and souls on fire.

A less obvious pitfall comes when things seem to be going great. Even when we achieve some portion of our goals, there can be a tendency to feel afraid, unprepared, or to kick ourselves for some misstep, focusing on the negative versus celebrating our success. Concentrating on small victories in our daily actions helps us practice attaining our goals and provides sustenance for the longer journey. When we pause to breathe, reflect, and give thanks, there is often much to celebrate.

Keep finding what lights you up and putting yourself out there, tending the higher cause that seeks to speak through you. Slowly your faith will grow; your butterflies will fly together; and if you listen and believe, you may even get some surprising sources of support from the living world. Practice helps.

"**There is a vitality**, a life force, an energy, a quickening that is translated through you into action, and because there is only one of you in all of time, this expression is unique. And if you block it, it will never exist through any other medium, and it will be lost. The world will not have it. It is not your business to determine how good it is nor how valuable nor how it compares with other expressions. It is your business to keep it yours clearly and directly, to keep the channel open… keep yourself open and aware to the urges that motivate you."

—Martha Graham

Chapter 8

Honing Your Compass Part 1—Why It Matters

Even after you've tasted a bit of vision and empowered action and started claiming your voice, living this each day is difficult. The big question is: "How do we regularly be the change we wish to see in the world?" Most of the time, we are operating way below our potential. How much time do you spend triggered, off-center, or just not putting your attention to what matters most? It's easy to get burnt out or overwhelmed trying to live well and make a difference with so much going wrong. Keeping a clear picture of our best selves to guide our way really helps. From here, it's relentlessly returning our attention to what matters, day after day, as we build the life of our dreams and make our best contribution.

"Find your highest light, schedule, and live it."
—Peace Pilgrim

This simple directive sums up so much. The first time I read these words from legendary peace activist, the Peace Pilgrim, I had that increasingly familiar *aha!* The words were so clear, specific, and simple, a practical directive to live one's potential, in eight words no less.

What a Compass Is

A compass is used to find direction, with its needle always pointing to true north. For the hard work of finding and following your true north in a topsy-turvy world, a compass creates a structure to discover your purpose, your important roles and goals, and natural strengths and passions. It helps clarify what you value, learn from those who inspire you, and focus on what's needed to stay on path. Ultimately, it's about developing a clear guide to navigate life's twists and turns, from planning your day to making major decisions.

Composting Limiting Beliefs

Developing and frequently refreshing your compass is important because, without it, we are not equipped to navigate the overwhelming array of issues we face. When we do ask the big questions in life or get a glimpse of our light, we often sabotage ourselves or lower our sights. In *The 5th Discipline*, author Dr. Peter Senge speaks to the damaging belief that feeds this self-sabotage—that people don't have the ability or resources to meet their needs or don't deserve to do so. How often have you thought or heard, "*I don't have enough*" time, money, skill, or whatever? While many people are dealing with structural, systemic disadvantages and racism, which adds a whole other layer of difficulty, how often do we simply give our power away?

Limiting beliefs are part of the invisible structures and forces that keep us from living our potential. It's not an issue of resources; it's about resourcefulness and relationships. It's having the passion and perseverance to always do the best with our situation. A more beneficial belief is that we can meet our needs AND deserve to do so. Addressing limiting beliefs like feeling we don't have what we need to succeed or deserve to do so, brings us face to face with cracks in the foundation of our self-value. **Your intrinsic worth as a creature of this Earth has nothing to do with what you do and whether you succeed or fail.** It's not determined by the color of your skin, your race, class, or gender. **Pause and soak this in.** Think about when you've felt hurt or judged because you took a criticism, mistake, or failure personally. We wrongly take these things as an assault on our worth. Believing in ourselves and the value of our contributions addresses a lot of issues from the story in our hearts and heads about our value.

A positive response in any situation begins with our breath and practices to get present like the ones highlighted in the first chapter. Starting here provides the space to untangle issues and transform our wounded, less helpful ways of being. Consistently cultivating the awareness to pause, reflect, and choose our response grows our ability to respond with the full potency of our best self. Like Martha Graham said, "There is only one of you…keep yourself open to the urges that motivate you." Ultimately, it's about reclaiming our sense of sufficiency.

The three main elements of building your compass are:

1. Determining your North Star
(purpose, passion, values, strengths, etc.)

2. Developing the habits and practices that help you follow your star

3. Assembling the tools and systems that keep your compass calibrated

A compass will look different for each of us. It's really just whatever helps plant your priorities deep in your heart and supports you to live them.

Compass Part 1 - Clarify Your North Star

To begin, clarify your passion, purpose, values, and strengths. Who and what inspires you? What are you passionate about? What are you good at that you love to do? What are you willing to sacrifice for? What difference do you long to make?

Focus on who and what you most value because as do-gooder extraordinaire, Lynn Twist, reminds us, what we appreciate appreciates. Your subconscious mind is many times more powerful than your conscious mind. Just asking these questions and marinating in the answers that come is fuel for your subconscious to help you live them. Gathering the quotes, phrases, and images that inspire and guide you is more fuel. Who are the people that most remind you of who you want to be? Ask yourself, "How do I turn these glimpses of inspiration into my daily living? What's my version of that?" This is how we make it our own and help others do the same. We can start to see how the incredible people, teachings, and experiences that speak to us fit into a larger, more coherent path for our own transformation. The same applies at an organizational scale, just with more people and moving parts, which is why we start small, with ourselves, and build.

Once you've identified your guiding principles and passions, you'll be ready to lay out the habits and practices that help you follow them. The next chapter offers guidance on how to achieve such a feat.

"We are what
we repeatedly do.
Excellence, then,
is not an act
but a habit."

—Aristotle

Chapter 9

Compass Part 2
—Developing Your Habits and Practices

Key to creating and calibrating your compass is developing the habits, practices, routines, and rituals that help you answer the big questions in life and live up to those answers. Of course, the real Jedi moves are in figuring how to do this not just when you have ample time but through whatever curves life throws you. It helps to land them when not in a crunch or emotional low so that when things get difficult, you have your supports in place. Doing this is a discipline, as in being a disciple to what grows you whole.

Aristotle wrote, "We are what we repeatedly do. Excellence, then, is not an act but a habit." Whether you call it ritual, routine, habit, or practice, *we are what we repeatedly do* gets to the essence. Our daily acts determine who we become. Find and be what speaks to you.

The 7 Habits of Highly Effective People and *The Power of Habit* are two bestselling books that approach dealing with habit in different ways. According to the author, Stephen Covey, the 7 Habits represent a set of universal, timeless principles of character and human effectiveness. They are an actionable, sequential framework of thinking that shapes who you are. The first three habits add up to "make and keep promises." Then from a place of empowerment and integrity, the second three habits focus on how you interact with others with respect, valuing difference and seeking understanding. The seventh habit is about self-renewal and honing your compass. It's what makes all the others work. High ideals are of little worth until by practice they become part of who you are, day after day turning principles into universal habits and situation-specific practices.

In The Power of Habit, author Charles Duhigg breaks down the science, showing the consistent pattern any habit follows. He writes about how to hack a habit, how to stack new habits into existing ones, and simple keystone habits, which can transform one's life or even a Fortune 500 business. Habits emerge because the brain is constantly looking for ways to save energy by converting a sequence of actions into an automatic routine. Duhigg cites a study that found over 40 percent of actions taken by people are actually habits.

While Covey focuses on a specific set of habits, through which you act upon your ethics and values, Duhigg looks at the structure of any habit, conscious or not. He writes about the three-step process of a habit: cue, routine, and reward. A cue tells your brain to go into auto mode. It can be something on TV making you want a snack or a time of day, like how waking up in the morning makes you want to brush your teeth. The routine that follows can be physical, mental, or emotional. It's the physical act of getting the snack, the mental routine of saying a mantra to yourself when cued to, or the emotional response of getting angry when triggered by something that causes stress. The reward is what helps your brain figure out if something is worth remembering. It's the satiation from a snack, the grounding from a mantra, or the gratification of accomplishment. An undesirable habit might involve a cue that causes stress, an emotional routine of getting angry, and a reward of the momentary feeling of release.

A surprising example that Duhigg writes about is how Pepsodent toothpaste changed the habits of a nation. Prior to Pepsodent's success, only 7 percent of people had toothpaste in their bathroom. They created a simple cue, awareness of the film that develops on everyone's teeth. The routine was brushing your teeth. The reward was having clean teeth. The craving that drove it was the cool, minty feeling of brushing, which indicated a feeling of freshness. Something most of us take for granted, though beneficial, was literally created by a savvy campaign to sell a product.

Habit energy is powerful and tough to transform. Once a new pattern is created, whether it's going to the gym or getting a beer after work, it can become automatic. One way to change a habit is to keep the old cue and reward but create a new routine. For example, if you want to change your diet, when cued for a snack or beverage (lunch, end of the day, etc.), switch to something healthy like carrots and hummus instead of chips, or tea instead of a glass of wine. Creating a plan to handle specific trigger situations that are likely to happen helps you respond in a way that affirms who and how you want to be. It's important to consciously acknowledge and celebrate this. It also helps when you make the good option easy and the thing you are trying to do less of more difficult. Choosing a positive response in a moment of weakness or frustration is easier if in advance you came up with a clear alternative. It's even better if you've practiced it.

While changing bad habits is great, lessening their impact also helps. I used to get triggered when rushed or late and even more so when kicking myself for doing it "again." While I've created more space in my schedule, I've taken most of the stress out of the situation when it occurs. By simply habituating a breath, I reset, anchor in my body, and reclaim the story in my head. This acts as a positive trigger, bringing more presence and spaciousness into busy days. It starts with becoming aware that yet again I'm in a rush to get somewhere. Through practice, this cue kicks off the routine of taking a slow deep breath in through my nose, followed by a long, slow exhale. This brings me more fully into my body. Rather than feeling the "oh shit" stress trigger of I did it again, as I breathe and ground myself, I accept the situation and use it to recenter. I see it as another gift that brought me into the moment.

Habit Stacking

Another way to create new habits is to tie them to an existing habit. This can be adding to a routine like going to the gym or hacking an unconscious activity like turning on the faucet. If you are trying to get healthy, instead of saying *I want to eat better,* be clear and specific: *at lunch, I will eat salad with my meal.* If you're trying to bring more happiness into your life, research shows the power of gratitude and making it a habit through practices like keeping a gratitude journal.[9] What about inserting gratitude into any of those easy-to-overlook, mundane details of life? Like turning on the faucet to get a drink. Clean water is rare, precious, and worthy of continual appreciation.

Some years ago, I came upon one of my most treasured meditations, the dry sauna. After just fifteen to twenty minutes of sweating, stretching, and resetting my intent, I'm a new person. It releases stress and fatigue and provides a refreshing ease, so I can better engage in life's details. Even initiating something that's good for us and aligned with our values like grabbing your gym bag and walking out the door sends a dose of feel-good neurochemicals into our bodies. With my sauna practice solidly habituated, I started layering in other practices like a walking meditation to and from the gym, practicing gratitude in the shower, and doing Towel Chi Gung when drying off. Then with a few slow breaths before getting dressed, I let the words of poet Mary Oliver reverberate through me: "Never in my life [have] I felt so plush/ or so slippery/or so resplendently empty." Thus, a twenty-minute good habit with forty minutes of previously mindless activity becomes an extra potent hour.

Each aspect of our lives, from existing good habits to unconscious actions, is a chance to grow more aware and to feel and live our best. There's an untapped world of possibility to explore in bringing a more spacious, grateful, alive sense of being into our actions, thereby building our power, joy, and positive impact.

Keystone Habits—Starting a Process That over Time Transforms Everything

Once you change one habit, a world of opportunity opens up to change others. Getting a win builds confidence, momentum, and motivation. A keystone habit is a habit that leads to multiple positive behaviors and effects in your life. As Charles Duhigg noted in *The Power of Habit*, the simple act of making one's bed was correlated with greater productivity, well-being, and stronger skills at sticking to a budget. Another example is exercise. Once people start, they often change other patterns like eating better. Having a morning routine is a keystone habit that many successful people utilize. Duhigg writes, **"Small wins fuel transformative changes by leveraging tiny advantages into patterns that convince people that bigger achievements are within reach."**

Routine and Ritual

A routine is a sequence of actions that can reinforce habits and practices. In a world of rapid change, there's something soothing and grounding about routine. When the Dalai Lama was once asked, "What is the single most important thing that I could give attention to?" without a thought, he answered, "Routine."[10]

Ritual is a series of specific actions that have a habitual or routine quality and are done with intent and a sense of sacredness. With so many distractions in our lives fueling our fragmented, disconnected sense of being, many people crave meaning and connection. Good habits and routines can bring increased mindfulness, heartfulness, and presence into our lives, organizations, and communities.

Practices for Self-Renewal

Whether through habit, ritual, routine, or whatever, investing in yourself is the key to success in all areas of life. Four widely cited dimensions of renewal are physical, social/emotional, mental, and spiritual. For physical renewal, it's exercise, good nutrition, and managing our stress. Social or emotional renewal comes through service, developing empathy, and our intrinsic sense of security. Mental renewal happens through activities like reading, writing, planning, and visualization. Spiritual renewal is through the ongoing work of clarifying our values and commitment to them.

Activities to address these four dimensions include journaling, study, meditation, and developing a morning practice to refresh one's compass daily. When it comes to practices, it's about being consistent but not static. Practices should change and grow with your needs and life. **Be deliberate. Believe in yourself. Act with conviction.**

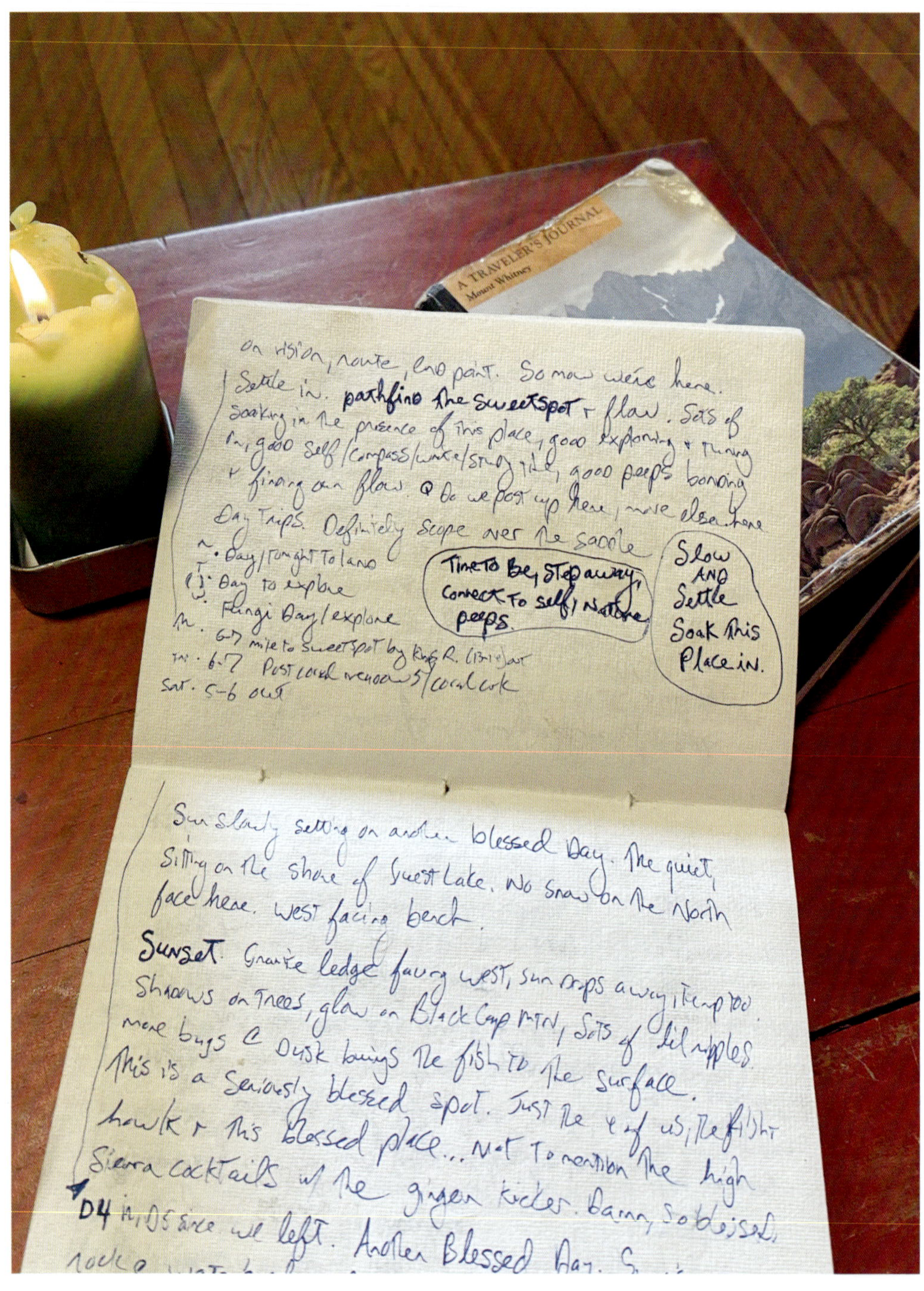

A TRAVELER'S JOURNAL
Mount Whitney

Journaling

Putting words to page helps make sense of the world. It can provide immeasurable joy, solace, and insight. It can also provide the safety of sanctuary or a wise, trusted advisor. Writing one's questions, concerns, and experiences has great gads of benefits, from catching your dreams to processing painful emotions and releasing tension. A journal is a sacred vessel of alchemy to align spirit, body, and mind, affirming what matters most to you. The path to a better understanding of self and world and how they relate in richer ways is long and challenging. Journaling is bread for the journey, a warm shelter in a storm. It's a chance to pause, rest, and catch your breath, to appreciate the beautiful views, or reset when you've lost your way.

Over the years my practice has evolved from utilitarian notepads and efficient computer input to reclaiming some aesthetic and time from technology with line-free recycled paper journals. I often review journals, tracing key words, mantras, and insights, practicing the power of diligence to transform what unsettles me and draw in what brings me into my power. When my mind and emotions start spinning, it's grounding to thumb through pages and drink in the insights, mantras, and probing questions I need to spend time with. For years, the first three words I would etch each morning were, "Another blessed day." "Pause, breathe, listen" and "it's all such a gift" are other phrases that have been woven and blessed into my spirit and flesh again and again.

There's a case to be made for having a range of journals, such as a daily all-purpose journal and specialty ones for gardening, travel, etc. A pocket notebook helps to catch fleeting insights or to recenter. If you are a gardener, seeking to change health habits, or whatever, a place to note key activities and ideas to review later is helpful. For many folks, travel is a time where you relax and reflect. It's great to generally catch these thoughts and experiences, but for honing one's compass, being able to look back on a decade's worth of trips in one place refreshes you in the magic of those moments. Don't be afraid to go deep into the geekery of finding and walking your path, and do not assume this will happen on its own.

To start and end the day, I journal, beginning with peace and closing with gratitude. When I get triggered, have an insight, or need help navigating the day's to-do list, journaling grounds me and clears distractions. It feeds my spirit and body, transforming challenging emotions and highlighting positive ones. Journaling helps develop a clear connection to your voice and path, bringing you back to the big questions in life and how to live up to the answers.

Study

Another source of sustenance is when we read or hear things that inspire us. Give notice to what tickles your insides. Even better, highlight it. Then take it up a notch by turning highlights into notes. Or be a personal compass jedi-in-training by organizing and reviewing your notes.

Any step you take to more frequently be with what grows you whole does just that.

There's only so much you can read. Why not spend an extra few hours to catch and organize inspiring ideas and to marinate in them until you are well-seasoned with the flavor of insight that's just right?

Make the words, thoughts, and experiences that resonate your own. What if rather than just whipping through this book, you went deeper with some line or section that spoke to you? Bust out your highlighter, make stars, exclamations, or smiley faces. As author Dr. Bruce Lipton notes, we are literally shaped by our perception and environment. Why not spend more time focused on what you want to be shaped by?

Consider how much life energy goes into a book. For a few hours of your time, you get to soak in what can be decades and thousands of hours of work. I've spent over fifteen years on this book, and it highlights lessons and tools from close to thirty years of living and leadership. That's a chunk of time. A few more hours inputting notes, and these hard-won insights are yours for life. There's a small piece of newspaper taped to the inside of my study folder with these words from Ralph Waldo Emerson: "Make your own Bible. Collect all the words and sentences that in your reading have been like a blast of triumph." I have a range of notes from countless books I've read. In minutes, I can revel in Covey's timeless truths, Malcolm Gladwell's tipping point archetypes, or Peace Pilgrim's insights on living your light. I do Tai chi moves with the sweet grooves and mindful mantras of Thich Nhat Hanh, stare at the horizon with David Whyte, and get riled up by Naomi Klein. Creating such a bundle of notes becomes a treasure trove of the words and ideas that feed some deeper part of you, and they're there for review at anytime, be it a quick scan to start the day or week, on a mountaintop, by a stream, or on vacation. It's another keystone habit that creates multiple, positive effects and benefits in one's life.

Whether you prefer a tidy online file or a pile of insightful scraps scribbled on the backs of napkins, it's not one-size-fits-all. The medium is the message, and it's no less than your essence in action. What sets you ablaze and rekindles your flame? Why not train in the craft of finding and walking your path? Any small effort that helps you pay attention to *what is* makes a difference. Take the time to internalize what you need. Prune what no longer serves you. By choosing what shapes us, we develop a lived wisdom of where our truth meets the world.

Meditation

Meditation consists of two elements: stopping and calming our mind and looking deeply to gain insight. Even simpler, meditation is paying attention, which you can do in any situation. Then life becomes a meditation as you work to calm and center your mind. Being mindful in any activity or interaction can bring a spacious sense of presence to the moment. When you feel bored, anxious, or upset, a long, slow inhale to fill your body with air and awareness brings you back and connects you to the quiet that lives just below your surface; that's always there.

A meditative intent that brings awareness to body and breath can help you recenter in most any situation. It's the spaciousness that can be infused into a busy schedule with even *just a few slow breaths and mindful steps between here and what's next*. This little phrase has become a mantra that helps me reclaim the quiet that exists even in that brief, often hurried space between things. With practice, you can bring mindfulness to all manner of situations, from eating and driving, to walking and rocking your baby in your arms.

Gratitude is a mindfulness practice. Consider your daily meals a chance to thank the earth, rain, and people who grew them; the generations of farmers who selected seeds; and the many generations of organisms that turned rock, bark, and decaying body into living soil. There are countless times where you could infuse presence and appreciation, like the simple act of turning on the tap. Even just feeling blessed and the act of blessing has big benefit. This is self as service. It's about elevating the range at which you participate in the unabashed opulence of your one precious life.

Bringing It All Together—Creating a Compass Practice

Morning is the birth of a new day, a fresh start, with infinite potential. It's the perfect time to realign with what matters. Stephen Covey writes that spending one hour a day on physical, social/emotional, mental, and spiritual development will "affect every decision, every relationship, improving the quality, effectiveness of every hour of your day including depth of sleep and restfulness." After two decades of practice, I know this to be true.

Landing on a daily practice has been one of the richest, most influential forces in my life. It has shaped and reshaped who I am, what I dream, believe, and bring into being day after day. A good morning practice lays the foundation for everything else to work better. Getting started is one of the biggest hurdles, but don't be intimidated. Just start where you are and build from there. Begin with your inspiration and what positive actions make sense. Even a few minutes to pause, breathe, and recenter on bringing your best makes a difference.

The next chapter has a walkthrough of my practice as an example. The core elements are a set of stretches, words, and phrases that affirm my purpose, priorities, roles, and goals. It includes a series of visualizations that connect me to past experiences and embody key values. At the end of the chapter is a set of questions to help build your compass. Additional resources are available at the **Daily Acts** website.

AS IS
THE GARDENER

SUCH IS THE
GARDEN

-HEBREW PROVERB

Chapter 10

Compass Part 3—Creating a Keystone Practice

At its simplest, I wake each morning, pour some tea, and sit on a little wooden stool in the garden to breathe, stretch, and reconnect to what grows me whole. I release what I'm vexed with and call in what I'm blessed with, beginning each day freshly connected to self and place. I scan my body and mind to see what has my attention, ease any stress, refresh in my purpose, say a few mantras that recenter me, recalibrate on my priorities, and move into the day.

With a bit more time, I move through a set of stretches that go head to toe. I affirm my vision, mission, values, strengths, and core reference points. But more than just affirming, I dip myself in the full color and flavor of the people, places, and experiences that are my beacons. I call in the resonant ideas from my favorite articles, books, and trainings. I journey from healing hot springs to 11,000 feet in the Eastern Sierras, from the Big Sur coast to the milky green waters of Belize. Each place connects me to something powerful beyond words. Each experience is tied to a word or phrase that reminds me of what I want to be and do.

Over many years, my practice elements have arranged themselves in a natural sequence. First comes centering my body, breath, and intent with a set of stretches, phrases, and mantras. This leads to affirming three organizing principles in my life—spirit, leadership, and nature. Looking back at my most influential references, they were embodied in one or more of these elements, whether it was a reverence-centered farmer, an author who tapped into her *joie de vivre*, or a peaceful stranger offering fresh flower tea. Through time I began to organize my self-development into these three categories, and they naturally landed in my practice.

Next comes a sequence of core values—speaking a word or phrase while visualizing past experiences tied to each. I move from the inner values of forgiveness, peace, and nurturing silence to outer values of peak experiences and community stewardship.

After core values, I affirm and center my primary roles and relationships. This again begins with self and then moves into tending to family and life before moving out to work in the world. Once this initial set of stretches, affirmations, and visualizations is complete, I open my eyes and move through the rest of my stretches with additional meaningful phrases.

While there is more to releasing stored trauma and living your potential each day than briefly marinating in forgiveness and your mountaintop highs, anytime you take is important. When the pathway in your mind, body, and emotions becomes well-worn from practice, even quick visits can reach deep and stay longer. Many days I take an hour or more to go through my practice. After two decades of leaning into the light by weaving experiences and insights into my morning routine, this daily ritual is a rich tapestry of life's treasured moments and mantras. It has shaped who I am.

> At its core, my practice is about three things: **breathe, stretch, and connect.**

Here's why:

Breathe—Our ability to act from our values and vision begins with our breath. If we catch things here, much difficulty is avoided. Many of the 23,000 breaths you take each day offer you a chance to not lose yourself in life's details. From waking to kissing another day goodbye, simply follow your breath. It's always there for nourishment, insight, and companionship.

Stretch—Movement helps further infuse awareness into one's body. It's about feeling the aliveness seep into your pores and noticing what needs attention and where you may be stuck. In a fast-paced, high-stress world, a good stretch helps us prepare for the gifts of any given moment.

Connect—Once in your body, turn your attention to the living world. Feel the air, the earth, the sky. Connect to nature where you are, be it backyard or balcony. Listen for what's chirping and buzzing. Notice the sun, seasons, weather, even weeds in a crack.

It's about being in a constant conversation—a call and response with life. Because what we seek to notice and address responds in subtle and sometimes jarring ways, be it the still presence of a falling leaf or something that tests your belief, like a hawk swooping by to answer your thoughts. Even after years of such experiences, it's astonishing when the world responds to me. Like English poet, Ralph Hodgson, reminds us, "Some things have to be believed to be seen." Watch closely and remember: with your dreams, your fears come too. These words are here for you, to help what speaks to you stick to you, to find and shine your truth.

Gift boxes made out of recycled calendar pages. RIP Thich Nhat Hanh.

A More Detailed Version of Practice

Here's a more detailed walk through my practice with values and ideas I believe to be widely applicable, including a few notes and stories for how and why they landed in my practice. I start each day sitting on my stool in the garden with a gourd of hot tea, my journal, and my planner. I take my shoes off to feel the earth, take a breath, close my eyes, and cycle through a series of phrases and mantras. I begin with my purpose, which is *to be whole, healthy, and peacefully present, to fully love myself and this life with all I've got, through each breath, step and bite, by living in a reverent reciprocity, which expresses itself through a balanced, loving, easeful service to self, family, home, Daily Acts, my people, and planet.* The short version that takes me there quick is *through each breath, step and bite.*

Next, I affirm—being spiritually awake, leadership-skilled, and nature-inspired. After saying each aspect, I say the names of key reference points, many who are quoted and cited in these pages. Then I speak qualities associated with them.

Spiritually Awake

As I affirm the intent of being spiritually awake and cycle through reference points that embody this for me, I say the words **reverence, peace**, and **equanimity**, feeling the qualities of each. Then come the words **non-judgment, non-attachment**, and **non-resistance** as I reflect on my current challenges. I speak the intent to *wear this civilization without being lost or caught in it.*

Soon, Thich Nhat Hanh's voice enters my heart and head: "The foundation of real happiness is faith, diligence, mindfulness, concentration, and insight." **Faith** is leaning into a path of freedom, liberation, and the only success that matters: transforming oneself. **Diligence** uproots negative seeds in one's mind and replaces them with good seeds, remembering that the longer they stay, the stronger they grow. **Mindfulness** is the miracle that allows us to become fully alive in each moment. Sourced in the power of a clear mind and calm heart, mindfulness finds the insights to transform challenges. **Concentration** encourages us to see deeply the nature of things. **Insight** from a Buddhist lens centers on two truths, impermanence and non-self, reminding us that nothing lasts and that there truly is no "other." Everything is connected. We are the air we breathe, water we drink, and the sun and soil our bodies are made from.

Leadership-Skilled

After affirming that I am leadership-skilled and cycling through my leader references, I say to myself *model, pathfind, align, and unleash.* **Modeling** reminds me to lead with how I live by doing what I say, being proactive, and taking initiative. Acting with integrity and values increases our positive influence, helping build trust and harmony with others. **Pathfinding** is coming to a shared vision, values, and a clear strategy for how to achieve what matters in a way that strengthens people and organizations. Once clear, **aligning** is making sure people and groups are pointed in the same direction. By consistently working at personal modeling, shared pathfinding, and aligning, we can unleash the collective power of our people and groups.[11]

Five years into Daily Acts, I was in desperate need of leadership skills when I took a Rockwood Leadership Institute training, later integrating their core practices of purpose, vision, partnerships, personal resilience, and performance into my practice and life. Some mornings I just say these words. Others I affirm their intent. **Purpose** gives access to inner power, connecting to what infuses our lives with meaning. For me, **vision** is being so damn entranced with the world being born and my part in it that I can't help but live and speak this in a way that inspires and helps others connect to their power. **Partnership** is about the power of relationships, appreciating differences and finding common ground. **Resilience** is about centering in our power and managing ourselves and our reactions. **Performance** is achieving results that further one's vision.

What helps you live your values? Who stretches you into your potential? What is it to align with your purpose and vision? Might doing so regularly help you affect greater change? What leadership skills or strategies would you benefit from regularly affirming?

Nature-Inspired

After grounding in spirit and my ability to live and lead well, I return my attention to being in right relationship with this precious planet. As I write this (on my stool in the garden), a gentle breeze moves through the landscape, a wren chirps, and the rustle of spring's supple green leaves washes over me. Every day I give thanks for the elements of life's flourishing wonderment. As I say each word, earth, air, water, fire, I sense that element and feel gratitude.

I feel the moisture-conserving, soil-protecting mulch under my feet, moderating temperature and storing nutrients below, where earthworms and roots do their daily commute. I feel the air we share, knowing that at any given moment, in my body is the breath of Gandhi, the blood of dinosaurs, and the tears of children fallen to sweatshop floors.[12] What better example of life's reciprocity than when we exhale a waste stream of CO_2 that feeds the plants and trees, which grow the fruits and leaves and produce the oxygen we need?

As with the air, water, too, cycles through life in a closed system. Your next cup of tea could literally have Cleopatra's bathwater in it.[13] I nurture interdependent connection to past and present with each mindful breath and sip. As we enter the flurry of any given day, how do we stay connected to our breath and return when we forget? Part of our work is to regularly refresh our connection to the larger whole, to reclaim our wonder and astonishment at a world of such richness.

Being spiritually awake, leadership-skilled, and nature-inspired provides a framework for deepening my core connections to self, nature, and community. Such practices can remake the paradigm and beliefs that shape us. Being a whole person in healthy relation to an Earth of interdependent connections is quite different from being a disconnected consumer on a disposable planet. In a world that affirms disconnection at every turn, we must consciously immerse ourselves in the different beliefs, values, and visions we seek to be influenced by.

Values

After cycling through the intentions for how I want to be in the world, I refresh in my core values and the experience of living them. Sometimes it's simply saying the words. I begin with forgiveness, peace, and a sense of nurturing silence. Then I affirm "From this forgiving, peaceful, self-nurturing place, I can rise up to my mountaintop highs." This subtly names the sequence of priorities. From here I commit with conviction, feel a sense of completion, and close with community stewardship and celebration.

Elvis said, "Values are like fingerprints; we can't see them, but they are on everything we touch." Our beliefs come from our worldview and shape the values that drive our behavior, be they disconnected and disposable or affirming wholeness. It's important to align our values with how life functions. Too often, there are the

values we speak, how we'd like to see ourselves, and then there's the values our actions show, with often a gap between. But what if you could consistently feel and be influenced by the experience of living your values? What if these experiences wove together in a way that helped uncover your path and potential? What if that invisible fingerprint you left on everything you touched was true to the best you? **Integrating one's values into a regular practice is a significant step to living them**.

Life's vital insights and peak experiences can show up in a range of places from an exalted flash atop a mountain to jotting down thoughts at a café. Maybe a phrase pops into your mind and moves you, leaving the lingering sense that you need to rub up against the fragrant scent of this reminder. Why not gather together the bits of life that shock you with delight and provide a sense of power, peace, or whatever you most need? This is pretty much how I've built and evolved my practice.

As we clarify our values and put them in our practices to be summoned through a word or phrase, we re-experience their emotion and power. Here's a run-through of the values and experiences that have made their way into my daily practice.

> *"Be kind, for everyone you meet is fighting a great battle."*
> —Ian McLaren

Forgiveness

We no longer start fresh. With too much accrued hurt in our lives and world, suffering begets more suffering until we break the cycle and quit accumulating more. This is no easy task. We must gently unearth old wounds and process new ones while they are fresh. Even with good practices, the residue of turbulent days and weeks needs processing. Be it contentious politics, tragedy, or so many people living stressed and disconnected from their power and ability to meet their needs; this can seep into us. With greater awareness and responsibility comes more noise, trouble, and hurt to navigate.

And holy shit hell is there a lot of difficulty to process and forgive. Even after decades of a reverent intent, mindful mantras, and all the rest, most days I'm actively forgiving something in myself and others. From the reality of leadership struggles to the lost temper that makes me feel like a bad dad to self-judgments about this book and all sorts else. It was years before forgiveness made its way into my practice and then to the front of the values section. That's how important it is. After naming forgiveness, I say a phrase that affirms my intent for self-compassion, that *I'm living, loving, and doing the best I can and truly that's enough.* Then I reflect on people who are challenging me, and practice compassion for myself and them to release any stuck emotions.

Getting from insight to action to living one's potential is no easy thing. It sets us up for repeated exposure to all the ways we feel altogether not very together. Weaving forgiveness, patience, and compassion into your practice is important. Being too hard on ourselves creates more suffering and sometimes finger-pointing. With forgiveness comes compassion and the ability to take responsibility for our actions while not taking the actions of others so personally.

Peace—Imbued with Sanctity

From forgiveness, I move into peace, to further release my judgments and enter a more serene state. To be calm in one's heart requires acceptance, which means letting go of our suffering and forgiving. A surprisingly effective practice is bringing acceptance into our non-acceptance. It's astonishing how many times I've been stuck in judgment, attachment, or resistance, and by simply saying to myself, "I accept that I can't accept this situation," it has created an emotional release.

When caught in our small problems, we have no space for the big stuff. A peaceful presence provides the space to notice bigger problems and do what we can to help. It affords us the compassion to work better with others to untangle our challenges together.

I return to past peaceful moments by naming them with a word or phrase that conjures rich emotional imagery. One afternoon as I walked a dirt path in southern

Belize, I suddenly felt this deep reverence wash through me as the ground, breeze, my body, mind, and emotions all fused together. Right then the words *imbued with sanctity* came to me. As strong experiences do, this stuck. I kept it alive by writing this phrase as a mantra, conjuring that euphoric feeling again and again.

Later I began to relive that moment in my practice, visualizing where I stood, the sticky tropical air, and exotic bird chirps. Having a regular practice makes it easier to revisit experiences. Consistently and vividly recalling one's magic moments creates new neural pathways, making it easier to call upon these energies. This roots us in the power of diligence by planting and nurturing the seeds of our good feeling and giving us another tool to lessen and replace negative emotions.

We need silence to hear
the wisdom of nature
and each other and
to find our voice and path.

Nurturing Silence and Connection to Source

From forgiveness and peace, I slip away to another favored sacred space—a natural spring with a hot pool in a small room. Physically I'm here a few times a year, but my emotions pulse with this place most every day. Here it's life's rhythms and not humanity's static that clings to me, sings to me, and speaks with truth. Even with an ever-expanding set of demands for meaningful lives and a livable future, we need to stay slow and sane, to rest, renew, and nurture silence. Our problems are too big for thinking alone. We need silence to hear the wisdom of nature and each other and to find our voice and path. A peaceful presence is not immune to noise, trouble, or hard work; it just knows what's primary, and through practice, it can source from there. Then we begin to share with each other a spacious sense of sufficiency instead of a frenzied insufficiency.

From *nurturing silence* in my favorite hot spring, the words *ever and effortlessly renewed as my connection to source flows through* seep into my mind. Suddenly I'm crouched on the bank of a milky green river, mesmerized as my favorite swimming hole seamlessly fills and flows by. Regularly connecting to places that make us feel alive and aligned with life's rhythms is vital.

There is much urgency in our world, but in our rush to respond to unending crisis, without silence, forgiveness, and peace, are we skilled enough to act in accord with the times? Regularly returning to stillness provides renewed clarity and insight to choose wisely.

Refreshing in Peak Moments

Freshly dipped in peace, forgiveness, and the warmth of ancient hot waters, I climb to 11,000 feet at Kearsarge Pass in the Eastern Sierras. With views of forever, I can nearly touch the electric blue sky. Standing with friends in the granite grandeur of nature's most inspiring cathedrals, my sense of vitality, wonder, and connection is off the charts. Just as I'm about to burst with aliveness, I have an aha moment. "Why not live and feel this way all the time?" How much more of a joyful, effective Earth steward and leader might I be with this verve pulsing through my veins daily?

View from Kearsarge Pass

Of course, living this day after day is no small thing. But if an infinite procession of itsy-bitsy snowflake crystals could form glaciers that shape mountains, surely a more modest accumulation of spirited moments could sculpt a life of significant richness and contribution. Peak experiences infuse us with vision, vitality, and a sense of being in sync with what grows us whole. They imprint deeply and, with proper tending, can keep us living our highs more of the time.

Commit with Conviction

After discovering our peak highs, commitment, conviction, and support are needed. Too often we lessen our dreams for fear we can't achieve them. How do we muster the courage and commitment to push through fear, to access our innate wisdom and to develop the upgraded mindset, skillset, and support to live our potential? Refreshing our minds and emotions in actual examples of doing so significantly helps.

Shortly after that transcendent Kearsarge experience, I pulled something in my knee. By the next day, going cross-country off trail, I couldn't carry my pack, so my friends distributed my gear among themselves. I remember being both mesmerized

by soft, spongy high mountain meadows and in pain, terrified by visions of a heli-copter rescue swirling through my head. Looking up at a steep cliff face with a tiny tight chute at the top that we intended to pass through, I couldn't imagine what was down the other side. One slow, careful step at a time, we made it down the steep chute at dusk to land in camp just in time for a beautiful sunset. The rest of the trip out over the next two days brought me more into my body, breath, and each step than I had ever been, offering an enduring lesson in presence.

For our next backpacking trip, I was excited but concerned. I couldn't charge uphill the way I used to, but I didn't know how else to do things. Once we discover our peak highs, we may need to develop a new approach to operate at that level physically, mentally, and emotionally. We also need to get more present, listen closely, and man-age the internal dialogue of fear, doubt, and all the rest. A key awareness and intent to develop is learning how to stay just on the right side of a healthy stretch, rather than hitting our peak in no shape to sustain or make it back down. This is also important for working with teams in difficult terrain, when people are at their edge with a lot of fears and unknowns. Remembering times where you successfully persevered with grit,

commitment, and conviction helps you relive such experiences, building confidence in your ability to do so again.

Completion

Walking the path of living one's vision personally and organizationally is a long journey. As has been written, finding our North Star doesn't excuse us from the hard work of following it. As much as there is a disciplined tenacity and perseverance required to regularly embody our highs, pausing to celebrate our successes instead of just moving the goal post is as vital. Value and honor milestones both big and small. Practice a sense of arrival, achievement, and satisfaction.

Picture yourself as an artisan lovingly honing the creation of your life. Yes, you want something of beauty in the end, but it's what goes into the making that matters most. It's habituating an appreciation for the art of finding yourself, working out the rough spots and trimming away what's unnecessary. Just keep polishing and crafting your conscious daily actions, turning the fear, lack, and ego crap that happens into the mantras and magic to see past life's distractions and just let your peace happen. What quotes, mantras, or reminders bring you into joyful acceptance of who and where you are on your journey?

Community Stewardship and Celebration

After meeting one's needs through focusing on internal values, we can more easily turn outward to steward and celebrate our people and place. If we tend only to everyone else without sufficient self-care, we risk burnout, resentment, or just not bringing our best. As we get better at living our light, we are more equipped to create conditions for others to live their potential and to bring this to our organizations and movements. Along with increasing our capacity to steward others, celebration is an essential ingredient for feeling good, spreading joy and connection, and healing the sense of *less than* infecting our lives and world.

The celebrations that I remind myself of in my practice are officiating friends' weddings and getting married myself. At weddings we experience the community version of peak moments, coming together to bask in love, life, and our relations. Consider your most memorable celebrations, the joy, love, and nourishing sense of connection. Who couldn't use more of that?

Once those rarified moments pass, why not relive them again and again by affirming this as a value and intent? Think of the infinite array of opportunities to do so from birthdays and holidays to first rains, flower blooms, full moons, and meals from the garden. Reliving such celebrations bathes us in their richness and can help infuse this spirit into our everyday mundane. Life is rarely the big flashy bits, but we can use them to enhance the small, more common bright spots.

Hanna, Chez, Ella, Jim, and Ryan being neighborly

Stewardship as a value is about tending the larger whole, listening for what seeks to emerge, and rising to it. It's also remembering which relationships need more time and attention. Every morning I picture my wife Mary on our wedding day because, before our daughter was born, it's the happiest I've seen her. Amidst life's demands and the work of world change, we must find and design ways to stay present with the joys and needs of those we cherish.

Creating Mission Statements for Your Priority Roles in Life

Once we've marinated in the felt experience of our values, they get expressed in life through our primary roles, such as self, family, work, and community. Like with a personal purpose or mission, having short phrases that capture the essence of who and what matters most can conjure a deep resonance that helps us root our priority roles and relations into our mind/body system.

After silently speaking my values and visualizing experiences that represent them, I affirm my intent for each of my primary roles. For self, I begin as *stillness in motion*, affirming how I want to move through life in a state of peace even amidst the noise, trouble, and hard work. This reinforces the belief that to be of best service, self-care comes first. From here, I silently speak *tending my rose and sprout*, feeling warmth in my heart for my wife and daughter. I affirm the vision of our home as a *warm, clean sanctuary of elegant simplicity* and our garden as a *lush, productive, resilient ecosystem*. For my peeps, it's about *accepting and enriching them with compassion and encourage-ment*. As I speak each phrase, I feel the emotion and affirm the commitment behind them. For work, I call in a strong sense of *thriving where we're at* because, when we do the best with who and what we have, more becomes possible.

Returning to Your Body

After moving through this meditative labyrinth of vision, values, and experiences that calibrate my compass, I ground back into body and place. Even as I stretch, I integrate affirmations—gently rubbing my eyes while affirming my vision; rubbing my ears with the intent to hear inner silence; and motioning my hands across my throat to use my voice more clearly; tapping my thymus gland (under chest plate), and rubbing my armpits to activate the lymph glands that stimulate my immune system.

Act and Unfold and Have Faith in Your Unfolding

Does all this compass geekery mean that you won't get ruffled or that there won't be piles in the sink or yard? Not so much. But visualizing, repeating, and recommitting to your intentions, values, and higher truths moves you towards living them more of the time. What we pay attention to brings a higher level of connectivity between our conscious and subconscious minds, putting a powerful resource to work for us.

Bruce Lipton, PhD neurobiologist, said, "The switch that controls life is perception; perception controls behavior…You can drink poison and walk across fire with your belief system." The environment we perceive and are shaped by ranges from the core of our being to the edges of the Earth and beyond. By doing such practices and visualizing and affirming key references, we literally reexperience them. Whether things are physically felt or richly imagined, the same neuropeptides pulse through us. Neuropeptides are tiny molecules that send messages to our body when we experience emotions. While there is a lot of complicated science behind understanding neurochemistry, starting to leverage the molecules of emotion and motivation is powerful, fun stuff.

Antoine de Saint-Exupéry wrote, "If you want to build a ship, don't drum up people to collect wood and don't assign them tasks and work, but rather teach them to long for the endless immensity of the sea." If you want to build an inspired life, don't get lost in the details, but rather learn to long for the life of your dreams. Then craft the compass to guide you there.

Adopting the Tools and Systems to Live Your Vision

As powerful as a morning practice is, we are dealing with complex intertwined personal and planetary challenges. Thus, to reclaim our wholeness, we need more than a practice; we need some seriously rocking systems. In the case of your compass, systems are what help you find and stay on track with what matters day to day, week to week, year to year.

As David Allen, author of *Getting Things Done*, puts it, it's about paying attention to what has your attention, be it finding your purpose or getting groceries. A primary issue people face is having thoughts in a way that doesn't resolve, advance, or manage the content in their minds and emotions. If our commitments are not funneled into a system that helps us act on them, they end up in our psyche, making it easier to get confused and thrown off. Allen addresses the gap between understanding what's important and translating this into action.

When you get thrown by life, good systems, habits, and practices help you recenter. The same roles, goals, and tools can work across everything from our daily meditation to weekly schedule, yearly goals, and life path. Doing periodic reviews of your areas of focus helps you stay clear and grounded. The frequency can vary, but given the times, realigning more frequently makes sense.

A personal planning system helps you act on balanced priorities, which is the essence of effective time and life management. It's about accomplishing important stuff while nurturing our relationships, preparing for the future, and developing ourselves. This starts with clarity of purpose and values. Next comes identifying your important roles, that is, self, family, friends, home, work, etc. From here it's setting goals, scheduling, and whatever daily adapting is needed. At the end of each day, it's practicing gratitude, noting what went undone, and setting the next day's priorities. A great Covey mantra for this is: "Schedule your priorities; don't prioritize your schedule."

As I developed and evolved my morning routine over the years, I tested and refined a quiver of practices and habits, such as journaling, meditation, and using mantras. At the same time, creating and refining my personal systems has been essential to get the habits and practices to stick amidst life's competing priorities. At the core is a weekly planning system in which I set goals for each important part of my life. Then I schedule those priorities each day and reflect at the end of the week on what worked and what didn't. In addition to a weekly and daily planning tool/system, through time I have evolved a rocking set of trackers, with the two most important ones for tracking my time and priority activities that I want to do more or less of. I first started tracking my time as a two-week exercise from my first leadership training, integrating those concepts into my morning practice. I found the time tracking so helpful that I never stopped! An example of the activities I track relative to life priorities include how much I exercise, read, hike, and sauna as well as things I want to manage like my intake of alcohol and sugar. In the last few years of COVID crazy, I started using a Fitbit and then a Whoop fitness tracker to dial in my sleep, level up my exercise, and track heart rate variability and the like, kicking up the geekery to a whole different level. This has led to improvements in my health, body awareness, rest, and how I handle stress.

The Freedom and Joy of Measuring

A well-known saying is *measure it to manage it*. Measuring helps us get clear and specific. When I consider this saying, I think it's less about a goal and more about the systems we create and work within. Systems help achieve goals. These systems can range from spreadsheets to calendars, journals, and other creative tools.

After a talk I gave on developing one's compass and systems, a woman reached out to share how she adapted the tool. More artist than spreadsheet geek, she created a page with seven flowers, one for each day of the week. Each had petals for the daily practices that were important to her. When she did the practice she would color in a petal, practicing mindfulness and diligence while reinforcing the positive. Get creative at tracking in a way that's true to you. What are the values you want to live more fully? Is it taking back your time, being more sustainable, managing emotional triggers? Measure it to manage it.

Our Relationship with Time

Maya Angelou, author and activist, said, "Life is measured not by the number of breaths we take but by the moments which take our breath away." These words are an island of solace in the turbulent sea of busy days and weeks. People often say that they don't have enough time. With so much stress and busyness, we've lost our sense of timelessness, our freedom, and spaciousness. Ironically, taking time to measure your time can result in more of it. Not more hours but more presence and appreciation in them, increasing the moments that take your breath away. It's the simple, disciplined day-to-day reclaiming of your precious minutes and hours. Could you benefit from consciously choosing how you greet and close each day and how you live the moments in between?

One night after I tossed and turned in bed for hours, I finally got up in the cold dark. Since tracking time was becoming a gratifying habit, I decided to wrap November and reflect on how the year was going. As I combed the spreadsheet that documented each hour from the previous eleven months, I couldn't believe what I saw. I was on track with it all—meditating, exercising, studying, writing, and spending more time with Mary and friends. I even increased my productivity and impact with Daily Acts and Green Sangha, the two organizations I was working for at the time. And I did all this in fewer hours than in the previous three years. It was shocking. Even after years of tracking, I had this nagging voice in my head about

"Life is measured
not by the number
of breaths we take
but by the moments
which take our
breath away."
—Maya Angelou

how I wasn't doing "enough." But there I sat curled up atop a heater vent, looking at clear proof I was on track with what mattered.

Once you've established a system and habit, tracking takes a few minutes a day and a deeply satisfying ten to fifteen minutes at the end of the week and month. That's really almost nothing considering the gift of knowing how one spends this vital resource. It's also an incredible mindfulness practice. As we are becoming more present, there are often significant gaps in time where we can't remember what just happened. Pausing to breathe and noting how you spent half an hour or one full hour brings you more fully into the moment. Then there's that satisfaction of looking back over a week, month, or years even to gain clarity on how we are living what's important to us and where we need to either accept things as they are or change. AND time actually expands. For example, if I'm in the garden having fun, getting stuff done, and chatting with a Daily Acts supporter or partner, that's triple time with work, play, and exercise. Or if I'm snowboarding with a business partner, I'm in nature, exercising, having fun with a friend, and moving the good works forward. That's like a five-for-one deal!

Calibrating Your Compass—Tracking Cycles

The daily and weekly setting of priorities is another practice. In the book *When*, author Daniel Pink writes about the potent impact of being in harmony with our natural biorhythms and the negative impacts of when we are out of sync with them. Setting productivity goals for focused periods throughout the day is one way to use tracking in alignment with our natural rhythms. In addition to daily and weekly planning, the month and season are great recalibration points, as is a yearly personal retreat for assessing and celebrating another cycle around the sun.

Putting the Pieces Back Together

Creating our compass is about asking the big questions in life and doing our best to live up to the answers. While that little voice in our heads always wants to rub our noses in it when we are off path, in truth, falling off is fine. It's about noticing and accepting what is and then deciding the right action. Life is a constant process of correcting course, of learning to live in that space between vision and reality. Being "off" isn't bad; it's full of opportunities for getting back on the path to rock your most inspiring truth. The right mindset, tools, and systems make a huge difference.

This isn't one-size-fits-all. Just find what's right for you and keep it close by. To live our inspiration and make our greatest contribution to the better world being born, we have to take action to express and improve ourselves again and again. Having a good compass and a set of practices, tools, and systems helps us stay true to what matters.

Key Concepts
• Compass: A structure and set of tools that helps you be your best self. It can include anything that supports you to live your gifts and contribute to a greater cause.

Key Points
• Taking action to live your inspiration brings new insights, connections, and reference points.
• Finding and sharing your voice helps draw in whom and what you need.
• Once you take action and find your voice, a compass helps clarify your purpose and path.
• Good habits, practices, and systems help you stay true to your compass and refine it.

Questions to Inspire Action and Develop Your Voice and Compass

• Personal
    o Where are you called to take action to live your vision and values and use your voice?
    o What mantras and ideas speak to your heart and soul?
    o How can you regularly refresh in past experiences that embody your values and ideals?
    o Who are the references that you would like to consistently remember or call in?
    o What are your important roles in life, such as self, family, community, and work?
    o How might you use a compass practice to affirm being your best self in each important role?
    o What one small change could make the biggest, positive difference in your life?
• Groups
    o How might you use these practices and tools to help your people live and give their best?

Steps to Take

• Personal
    o Develop a short phrase that expresses your personal mission, purpose, or intention.
    o Make a list of the habits and practices you currently have and ones you'd like to add.
    o Reflect on the above questions—use creative processes such as drawing, art, or movement.
    o Create a new compass practice or adapt an existing one. For example, add mantras, affirmations, and your values into your yoga practice or morning walk.
    o Develop systems and tools that help you act on your priorities. For example, using a planner to set goals and track progress weekly, monthly, seasonally, and annually.
• Groups
    o Use the previous questions and steps to create a community of support and practice.
    o Identify good group habits and practices you currently have and ones you'd like to add.
    o Discuss what systems and tools can help you clarify priorities, track progress, and reset.

If you want to build an inspired life,
don't get lost in the details, but rather
learn to long for the life of your dreams.
Then craft the compass to guide you there.

Planting civic transformation. Sebastopol City Hall. Photo: Jay Swetech

Relationships

Life Is Relationships—Nurture Community

Photo: Leslie Curchack

Chapter 11

Following Nature's Guidebook

From our beliefs and attitudes to the operating instructions for ecologies and economies, life is in how we relate with the Earth and each other.

> # "Ecology is the science of relationships, and nature sustains the web of life by creating and nurturing community."

These words by scientist and author, Fritjof Capra, cut through the noise and get to the essence of what matters. Nurture community is a core operating principle and simple guide to transformative change. Through all manner of difficulty, starting with our hearts and then reclaiming the power of our actions in a way that cares for life's relations is a pretty infallible approach.

Being heart-centered provides increased mental clarity, strengthened immunity, better emotional management, and greater overall resilience.[14] It grows our self-awareness and the emotional intelligence skills needed to play well with others. This is the foundation of good relations whether in everyday life or in leading larger change. While we start with our daily actions, how things really shift is in community. Ecosystem restoration is the easy part. The ego-system restoration of dealing with humans is difficult.

We live in a star-making galaxy that spirals the same as your blood and bones. You are made of stardust. While crafting your path and stepping into your power, remember your relation to the mystery and wonder of a world that is much wider than the peaks and valleys of the Earth and your mind.

In a sense, reverence and a love of life is the why; the ripple of our daily actions is the what; and building strong relationships is the how. From the ecologies of our bodies and towns to the natural systems sustaining us, every action is in relationship, influenced by and impacting people and planet. All human endeavors are an inseparable subset of nature. So we start here.

Tapping the Wisdom of Nature

Tapping the wisdom of nature is like putting on a pair of X-ray glasses. You start to see, hear, and understand things differently. You ask better questions, like why trees are denser on north-facing slopes vs. south-facing ones, or you notice that point on a hillside that stays green longer and has more life. With eco-X-ray vision, everywhere you look things seem more alive and make better sense. This richer sense of connectedness naturally imbues you with vitality and joy. Part of what's so amazing about these new superpowers is that this vast planetary wisdom can be applied at home in your life. But beware. Encounters with transformed people and places is contagious.

Through powerful experiences and exposures, something sticks to you in a way you can't shake. You feel this growing longing to connect with others who are similarly infected. It's the aliveness of beautiful natural places, land that has been devastated and renewed, and people who are happier and healthier, despite what they know.

While I had inspiring new references and was taking action to live more sustainably and encourage positive action through *ripples journal* and the sustainability tours, I needed to deepen my eco-design skills with new knowledge, experience, and ref-

Josh Beniston and tourees soaking in the magic of a regenerated backyard ecosystem.
Permaculture Institute of Northern California

erences. Though there are many pathways to richer lives and a better world, permaculture is a vibrant locus of focus for applying nature's operating instructions to your everyday life. This stands in opposition to our disposable culture, in which we operate as if we have unlimited "resources" to consume, pollute, and throw away. Of course, there is no "away" on Earth, and life is about relationships—not resources.

Though there's no magic planet-fixing pill, permaculture has a lot of answers. It's a moral response to a world in crisis, a global grassroots movement, and just the smart way to do things for one-planet living. Permaculture is a living, evolving community and body of knowledge and practice, and it provides a relational foundation for how different sustainability elements fit together. It has acted as a placeholder for Indigenous folks to remember and revive their traditional ecological knowledge, which permaculture has been informed by. It's an ancient knowledge that reconnects us to nature in a deeper way while meeting our needs.

Start in the Garden

Permaculture is instantly practical in your life. It's most commonly applied to landscapes designed to mimic natural patterns and relationships. The lessons you learn in the garden about nature's operating instructions can be applied to your neighborhood, community, and beyond. Given the profound degradation and loss we are experiencing, taking action that's intrinsically aligned with the regenerative powers of the Earth kicks ass on enough fronts to melt most hearts and minds. And for organizations, it's a great strategy to inspire, educate, and mobilize.

"It depends" is a phrase you often hear from permaculturalists. It's not a cookie-cutter solution. Like a personal compass, it's a set of design tools and practices for how to think and solve problems with your ethics intact. Permaculture is applied differently, depending on the issues of each generation and region. Are you rural or urban? Are you focused on local self-reliance, food, or climate justice? You may also frame things differently whether discussing recycling nutrients in the garden or making the case to legalize sustainability with greywater policies. In both cases, the ecological principle and directive is the same—produce no waste.

This taps into an essential pattern at the heart of how nature creates conditions conducive for life to thrive through cycles and recycling—hydrologic cycles, nutrient cycles, seasonal cycles, and even human life cycles. It's the salmon that go out to the sea to feed and grow, returning upstream to lay eggs and die; their flesh refreshing entire watersheds.

We Don't Grow Vegetables, We Grow Soil
—How Place and Relations Shape Us

Permaculture is full of sticky sayings that help you remember what's important, like "we don't grow vegetables, we grow soil." Healthy soil grows nutritious food while providing other benefits as opposed to using artificial fertilizers to grow food devoid of minerals, nutrients, and vitality. Artificial fertilizers also destroy the precious thin skin of soil that helps life flourish. We can't just take without respecting and renewing the places that sustain us.

The San Francisco Bay area has long been rich with life in many forms—from salmon to grizzlies to an incredible array of Earth stewards and regenerated landscapes. Local author and Tribal Chair of the Federated Indians of Graton, Rancheria Greg Sarris, recounts a memory from his great, great, great grandmother, Tsupu, said to be the last Miwok tribe member in the Coast Miwok village that became my home city of Petaluma. She said:[15]

"Ducks and geese flew up from the Petaluma River and its tributaries so thick as to obliterate the sun for an hour at a time, and seasonal swarms of monarch butterflies passing through the Petaluma Valley a mile wide, several miles long, forced the Lekatuit there to take refuge for sometimes a full day."

Can you imagine the majesty of a mile-wide swath of butterflies blanketing the sky? Or clouds of geese blotting out the sun for hours? Though it's painful to know that the biological and cultural richness of this place and ones like it everywhere have been and are being decimated, the intrinsic pulse of this planet is to help life flourish. When we listen to nature's wisdom and Indigenous stewards, the rapid regeneration of self, community, and the Earth is possible.

The Wizards of Oz

Since permaculture started in Australia, Aussies are some of its most advanced practitioners. The insights beautifully compiled and synthesized by two white guys (David Holmgren and Bill Mollison) comes significantly from Indigenous people across the Earth who figured out how to live well without degrading their people or place. Again, showing the power of a workshop, within the first few years of launching Daily Acts, influential permaculturists who taught courses in Northern California significantly impacted our organizational development, and the boldness of our vision. From these courses, I grew hopeful and emboldened that we can effect large-scale change and was left with a profound sense of the power and preciousness of every scrap of carbon, drop of water, and act of living.

As highlighted in his book, *Permaculture: Principles and Pathways Beyond Sustainability*, David Holmgren grounds timeless truths about how life on Earth functions into simple phrases that act as a checklist for applying nature's wisdom. Holmgren spoke about the foundation of all understanding as a continuous process of observation, recognizing patterns, and reconnecting to the mystery of life through practical interaction. He emphasized focusing on where we have influence to rebuild natural stores of landscape wealth at home and locally.

Geoff Lawton exudes a confident charisma, busting out pithy one-liners like, "You can save the world in a garden." He's trained thousands of students while seeding demonstration centers across the planet and applying permaculture from backyards to a 43,000-person refugee camp. Lawton's expansive vision and experience seeded the up-leveling of the organizational side of permaculture for Daily Acts.

Holmgren gave me the framework and an operating principles lens to apply to Daily Acts. Lawton inspired the hell out of me and got me dreaming bigger for how to apply permaculture to organizational development to help cover the world in food forests and rehydrate the Earth.

"Ducks and geese flew up
from the Petaluma River
and its tributaries so thick
as to obliterate the sun
for an hour at a time,
and seasonal swarms of
monarch butterflies
passing through the
Petaluma Valley a mile wide,
several miles long, forced the
Lekatuit there to take refuge for
sometimes a full day."

—Tsupu

Roots of Color

While permaculture has been heavily rooted in white-led environmental efforts in the US, with some very inspiring Black, brown, and Indigenous-led shifts around the world, it's practiced more widely by communities of color. As this ancient knowledge of living well while caring for people and planet is brought back to life, we have some uncomfortable truths to address. We were all once native to place. To become Indigenous again to the lands we inhabit, we must acknowledge and heal past wounds of the people whose lands were stolen and lives enslaved to build the United States. To readopt an Indigenous lens of "relationships, not resources" means to reconcile that we have not been good to our relations. We still aren't. But change begins with awareness, humility, and repairing harm done.

Honoring and learning about the stewards on whose land we live. Kule Loklo ceremonial round house in a recreated Coast Miwok village.

Start with Something That Inspires You

There are a lot of pathways into regenerative living. Start with what inspires and better connects you with this precious planet and all our relations. Find the folks who crack open your perception of what's possible and infuse you with the spirit to make it so. Stay surrounded by these people and places to stay awake, engaged, and sustained. As we do these things, a larger rewiring occurs in how we relate to life and our ability to radically regenerate the world around us.

Marty Falkenstein sharing the tools and handcrafts of local Indigenous stewards.

Before and after in the author's garden.

Chapter 12:

Level Up Your Homegrown Solutions

In *Radical Homemakers*, Shannon Hayes notes that we must understand how our homes went from being productive social units to isolated consumption units. She speaks to the impact this deterioration has had on our culture, leading us down the path of wasteful, destructive disconnection. We've lost the knowledge and skills for daily living and survival, which has led to a loss of meaningful relations and interdependence with our neighbors, communities, and the living world. At the time of the Declaration of Independence, Hayes writes, the home was the vanguard for producing patriotic, virtuous citizens. Industrialization led to a shift from people being owners and self-reliant homesteaders to employees, placing value on the "real world" of work. Industrializing our food system made families consumers rather than producers. Hayes makes the case for homesteads and homemakers as a core aspect of revitalizing our food systems and moving us from a destructive and extractive economy toward a life-serving economy.

It's no wonder there has been a huge split between income and life satisfaction over the last five-plus decades. We work more than medieval peasants[16] while fewer people know and connect with their neighbors. Studies show a significant association between fewer work hours and increased happiness and eco well-being.[17] The less time we exchange for money, the less resources we need, waste we create, and stress we feel. This makes it easier to eat and live healthier, exercise more, and enjoy connection to family, friends, and the living world.

Essence—The Good Life

With the devastating effects of living so disconnected, what's deeply inspiring is that there has never been a time when our daily actions have mattered more. In *Radical Homemakers*, Shannon Hayes writes, "When people center their lives on their homes, creating strong family units and living in a way that honors our natural resources and local communities, they are doing more than dismantling the extractive economy; they are rebuilding the life-serving economy." She goes on to say, "The major work of society needs to happen inside our homes, putting the homemaker at the vanguard of social change." This is home as hope, as an inspired state of living with your sleeves rolled up, taking action that matters, is fulfilling, and meets one's needs while tapping into the regenerative juju of life. Doing what's right for self, family, and community feels damn nice and even carries a bit of that world-saving superhero vibe.

Our natural response to the alive, interconnected wholeness of nature is a profound reverence and respect. Once we reconnect to and begin mimicking natural systems, we heal our sense of separation rather than projecting our disconnectedness onto the world. With each need met in our homes and communities, we strengthen our independence from the extractive economy and find ways to simplify and rebuild local culture. Having nature as a mentor and model teaches us how to be in a healthy relationship with the living world.

As Dale Dougherty of the Makers Movement has said, "If there is something I could wish for America, it's that we would restore resourcefulness as a middle-class virtue. In the old sense of DIY, there was the understanding that if we worked on our home or made our own clothes, we had a better life as a result. We had something that money couldn't buy—the rewards of our efforts, satisfaction, and engagement with others. Those things are at the heart of how and why we live."[18]

Part of the infectious power of regenerative homesteads is who we become along the way. Words can't convey the richness of inhabiting one of these edible oases or what this brings to one's life and relations. Research shows the benefits of even small doses of exposure to nature and the therapeutic effects of gardening.[19] The garden is a great place to chew on life's big questions and get recharged while healing the hurt of waking. It could be at a home garden, a community garden, or even on a balcony.

Renter's Mind

A critical part of moving from an ego-system to an ecosystem paradigm is getting over our renter's mind: the lack of care or connection to what's perceived as not "mine." We recover our wholeness through reinventing how we are connected and by contributing to something larger. For me, moving to Petaluma was a chance to save my young marriage and make a big leap in mindset and relations, but it wasn't easy. Instead of gazing up a forested valley with a gently meandering creek below as I had in our previous home, our place in Petaluma looked at a fence out back and a stream of cars out front. Knowing the peace, aliveness, and connection that the redwood hillside gave me, I was sad and fearful to leave and wasn't sure I could recreate that feeling elsewhere.

About the time we moved to Petaluma, I met this wonderfully crazed farmer named Bob Canard on a farm tour. With that familiar sparkle in his eyes, he reminded tour attendees that you don't just grow vegetables; you need to produce a yield that nourishes soil and humans alike. He frothed with vigor about how food grown in healthy soil and from the heart can overcome deficiencies with such an etheric sweetness that it accumulated the kind of completeness that can leave one in the grip of carrot dreams. As he adamantly spoke about not growing with an adversarial attitude of problems and pests, almost on cue, a gopher popped out of a hole and astonishingly just wandered through the crowd.

This encounter was perfectly timed, with the tour once again providing a dose of inspiration just when I needed to look at life through new eyes. While I had some grumbles and figured we probably wouldn't live in this apartment for long, I thought, "Who in the hell gives a damn cheese doodle? When we move out of here, the little scraps of land around this place are gonna be so damn loved, the next renters will know the grip of our carrot dreams." Along the way I'd build skills, save seeds, meet neighbors, and grow food, medicine, and wonder. This was a chance to internalize those forest highs and find them in less obvious spaces, again turning perceived problems into eco-savvy solutions.

Recycling

One of the core patterns to grow healthy soil and food while healing our disconnection is by recycling the way nature does, reconnecting to the regenerative cycles of our planet. Recycling isn't chucking stuff in a green bin. That is downcycling, which results in a lower quality material than what we started with and can be done only a limited number of times. Rather than having the stuff that feeds, clothes, warms, and entertains us trucked, transmitted, and flown in from far away, we can start to close loops through creative reuse, buying recycled, and adopting regenerative growing practices.

Instead of only being a passive consumer of packaged entertainment, we can make music, play games, and get crafty with art and the art of mending and fixing. Compost your green waste and recycle your greywater to grow food, fuel, and fodder while catching the rain. Pruned scraps become medicine, animal feed, habitat piles, firewood, garden stakes, and fencing.

While it can seem a daunting extra set of details in life's busyness, there's a beauty in the simplicity of working with the truth of what we consume. To get a real account of what your life costs and contributes, try measuring your ins and outs—the trash and recycling you produce, the electricity and water you use, and the waste streams you transform. This is meant to better understand, use, and build the power we have. It can be tracked in a notebook, on a piece of paper or in a spreadsheet. Individual action is not the end point or the main problem, but we start with ourselves.

Why not enlist compost worms who are happy to munch and poop as they close the sacred loop in how your lunch scraps are renewed, as you harvest microbial-rich worm tea to nourish the soil that feeds you. While dreams of a sweet automatic greywater system are great, a simple pot in the sink collecting water and some meditative trips to the garden can turn waste water into lunch, reconnecting another nutrient cycle. Speaking of waste, urine is nature's perfect nitrogen-rich liquid fertilizer. Then there's all the soil-building fodder available from the carbon cycle, like recycled cardboard, street leaves, and wood chips from local trees, as well as recycled concrete to build garden beds. Once you start tapping into this planetary superpower, you may be inspired to vision further. How about bees behind the shed? Fruit trees in barrels? Un-pave some sidewalk? Rain tanks? When looking through inspired eyes with *the problem is the solution* mindset, the opportunities are near limitless. Fear and constraints become fuel for creative action.

An example of the problem is the solution in action is when a friend had a snail depot (aka a bucket with a lid) on her porch where folks would make deposits so someone else's pest became her chickens' free-range, chard-fattened escargot dinner.

Part of the beauty and challenge of creating a living, breathing, regenerating eco-system is that stuff grows everywhere. When spring greens pop up in the path, why not transplant them or give them away? The same for prunings. Sometimes they go to the coop, compost, or green bin. Or each of those grape cuttings can be a new plant producing shade, food, or wine in someone's garden. There is a near infinite diversity of potential yields and connections.

Taking neighborhood-scale recycling to a different level, Mark Lakeman from The City Repair Project in Portland and his neighbors recycle all the organic matter from their sixteen-house block. They've established a neighborhood garlic patch in one yard and have taken down fences and made paths and rain gardens that reconnect yards, regenerate the watershed, and re-enchant village life.

Street Peas for Peace in Politics?

One afternoon I was out in the garden when a fellow passing by paused, lured in by the sugar snap peas growing up the telephone pole at eye level. He was from a family of longtime Petaluma farmers and taught agriculture at the high school. We bonded over peas, snacking, and talking for a nice long while. More than a neighborly nod or courtesy chat, it felt like a connection that bridged a bigger cultural divide. All because my wife Mary and I were growing food out front.

Sidewalk kale, peas, beets, calendula, and more. What easy-to-overlook nooks and crannies in your world are ready to be reclaimed and filled with life?

Playing in the Rain

Along the vein of interesting curbside encounters, late one rainy night coming home from a long day of meetings, my attention was drawn to a series of puddles. I had turned our median strip into a rain garden to harvest runoff from our neighbors' downspout as it flowed across our landscape. Soon I was lost in the moment, playing in the rain and mud and adjusting how water flowed through the gardens. That season we sank over a thousand gallons of rainwater into the earth, removing it from our stormwater system just by digging a few simple rain gardens. That's nearly four tons of water, a drop in the bucket compared to what falls from the sky. One inch of rain on a 1,000 square foot roof is 600 gallons of water. That same inch on the city of Petaluma is about 240 million gallons of water. Small adds up, be it small problems or small solutions.

I don't know how much joy, awareness, and nature connection I harvested alongside that rain, but it was a lot. What if every home and garden installed rainwater catchment and directed their downspouts to recharge groundwater with the rain? What if after a long day more folks played in the rain, rebuilding the wealth of our world one yard at a time? What if this was the start to something bigger?

Community

Once you start to take action, you meet all kinds of inspiring new friends and references. It's amazing how people artfully apply ecological design based on their passions, skills, and constraints. Permaculture is a type of eco-design, which is basically understanding how nature functions and using this wisdom to create and grow things that are more beneficial and less harmful. Whether urban, suburban, or rural, rented or owned, folks are creating deeply inspiring solutions that fit their lives and places. Some bring business or building skills, some a passion for teaching kids, writing books, making music, iron-smithing, community organizing, and more.

All across the land people are having enchanting Cinderella pumpkin parties and honey harvest solstice parties with feasts of homemade food and beverages. They are creatively turning constraints and problems into delectable solutions from gardening and beekeeping on chicken coop roofs to sharecropping unused backyards. By taking action and engaging their inspiration at home and in the community, people are changing their lives and the world around them.

As we begin to act and live in this way and connect with others doing the same, our lives, like our gardens, begin to fill in with a rich array of scents, flavors, critters, and characters. As folks serve up their inspiration and skills, saving and swapping seeds, sharing plants, and lending a hand or a wheelbarrow, the community ecosystem grows and spreads.

The Chickweed Patch, aka Paul and Suzanne Mackey's Urban Homestead

The Mackey's urban homestead is so many things bundled up in one fragrant, colorful bouquet of homegrown goodness. Stepping into their kitchen is like walking into a wonderland of homemade treats, with seasonal fruits and veggies on the counter and things being dried, fermented, canned, jammed, frozen, and woven. You can't help but feel the fervor of their carrot dreams.

On a recent visit, I encountered some beautiful just-made soaps and a bowl of fresh picked plums and apricots. We had a scrumptious breakfast on their back porch—a potato, zucchini, and carrot hash scramble with eggs from their hens and homemade nettle pesto along with fresh jam made with apricots gleaned from the neighborhood and homemade yogurt. We did some birding while eating, as Suzanne inspired me with stories of the backyard kids' bird camp she had just finished. Tucked in a suburban backyard, their place is a cornucopia of replenishing connections that reweaves nature, neighbor, and need. Throughout Paul and Suzanne's home and garden are handcrafted touches aplenty from timber-framed gates to a

Before and after at Paul and Suzanne Mackey's homestead. After years of unsuccessful attempts at healing their land, Suzanne credits a shift in her inner landscape with being able to create such transformation in the outer landscape.

fun and funky greenhouse made of scrap wood and recycled windows. Even the fibershed arts are present as bright orange coreopsis flowers dry on the counter, ready to infuse some patch of fabric with colors.[20]

As joyous as the many homegrown touches are, like life, the Mackey's place is a work in progress. Piles and projects are anywhere the eye wanders, showing the signs of a home that pulses with life. But I only see all they have accomplished and how beautifully they have built their lives out of the fertile ground, the found, and the artfully refurbished. It's too easy to forget that a life that is homegrown, hand-built, and artfully repurposed is sometimes messy and rough around the edges, often incomplete. But it's a life that's incredibly rich, laden with loving relations, learning, and bounties galore. It has removed its power from the extractive economy and feeds a life-serving economy imbued with the stuff of the better world being born.

Walking away with a full belly, a reinspired vision, and a refreshed sense in my cells, I reflect on the countless times I've left their place crazy lit and with a quiver of treats. Today it's a bundle of chard, sunflower starts, fresh plums, dried nettles, and some recycled tomato cages. Putting plant starts or other homegrown goodies in folks' hands as they leave a visit is a distinguishing feature of people like Paul and Suzanne, whose homes, gardens, and lives pulse with life and are begging to be shared. How different is this from the fear, scarcity, and sense of insufficiency gripping our lives and world? Which dream do you wish to feed and belong to?

Forces of Conscious Ferment

It's cold and dark out as I sit by candlelight, staring at the slowly growing glow of a new day. There's something rich and right about waking with the day, how a place is transformed in the gentle transition from dark to light. Soon my to-do list will grip my mind and emotions with rapid-fire emails, calls, and urgent matters to attend to. My body tenses at the thought. But in this moment, the earth, sky, and silently towering presence of a lone coastal redwood just to my north still hold sway. With the pressures of our quickening lives, it's vital to renew ourselves every day. We must recenter on what matters and reconnect to the sensuous living, breathing world just outside our walls and the confines of our busy minds.

Lately, in the early morning light, I've been meditating on the invisible forces that transform a substance, be it flesh, food, or community. While some frontline communities have long been awake to the challenges, there is still much to make sense of as we work to wake more of our communities to the urgency of now. This has me pondering: what creates conditions conducive for wild organisms to thrive and proliferate? How can we grow a culture that cultivates these unseen forces of conscious ferment?

One of many homegrown rhythms is concocting fermented food and beverages with family and friends. The evolution of human culture and fermenting food and drink have long been entwined. As author Sally Fallon writes, "Fermenting foods is as old as humanity and at the basis of human culture." Fermentation preserves and creates nutrients. It can remove toxins and make plant nutrients more accessible. It also has medicinal benefits, supplying essential living cultures.[21] Through time there has been great ritual and lore around these microscopic agents of transformation. Fermentation by its nature is artisanal, conducive to homes, small farms, and local economies.

Recycle, Reuse

With all the energy it takes to create a bottle and get it in your hands, using glass or plastic once and "recycling" it to be trucked away, sorted, melted, remade, trucked, filled, trucked, and all the rest is insane. I'm not saying to quit recycling. But as the most consuming generation ever, it's very short of what's needed. Doesn't it make more sense just to refill that beauteous bottle? Would you use your favorite wine glass once and chuck it in the green bin?

While we need larger civic change to promote large-scale reuse, you can significantly cut your recycling by reusing bottles. It's enriching to enjoy a local, organic drink for taste and to align your values. Putting a homemade beverage in a reusable bottle taps the cyclic wisdom of our planet. Even more amazing is making it with friends. The richness spreads as your heart sings with the freeing ease of knowing there really is no "away" on this little blue planet.

The depth of our living grows as we add such layers of relation, meaning, and fruitfulness, reclaiming another easy-to-overlook nook in our lives. Quality time with friends, tasty home-brewed beverages in reusable receptacles, and needs met with our own hearts, hands, and community. Just another small act of transforming a big problem by tapping into nature's wisdom and our need for meaning and connection.

Sitting in my pantry, I'm surrounded by stories as I bottle a batch of last summer's ferment, a honey wine made with mead mentor, Sam Ruark, as well as honey, lavender, and chamomile from the garden. Each reused bottle is a story or more, from whence they came and the good people they were shared with. Some bottles are four generations in, with the one in my hand from some friends' backyard wedding. Tonight, we'll brew a batch, sample Sohrob's Prickly Pear cider, and hear of late-night fermentation fetish fiestas after the kids have gone to bed.

Like our homes and gardens, our bodies are ecosystems that benefit from a diversity of relations. When we ferment with the wild organisms present in our lives, we become more interconnected with the life forces around us, just as we do with each act of creative reuse, growing, composting, or catching the rain. The power of this level of integration and connection to place transforms a substance, be it flesh, food, or community. In an increasingly unstable world, tuning into the wisdom of nature while meeting our needs and strengthening community creates conditions conducive for life to thrive and proliferate. And so we go, one home and neighborhood at a time all across the land, growing a handcrafted culture of creative reuse, tasty libation, and healthy relations.

Homegrown at Scale

Can we really live this rich and solve the crises we face by taking a homegrown mindset and solutions to scale? In the last talk Daily Acts hosted by the late Toby Hemenway, a cherished friend, partner, and the author of the bestselling permaculture book *Gaia's Garden*, Toby spoke about the critical importance of making a societal shift from agriculture to horticulture. He laid out human history in three primary cultures beginning with a forager/hunter-gatherer culture and culminating in our agriculture-based society that is closely tied to a mindset of disconnection and domination. Between the two were horticultural societies focused on small-scale self-reliance and mixed crops in still-functioning ecosystems as opposed to large-scale agriculture that wipes out natural systems. Similarly, leading agroforestry scientist, PK Nair, has called home gardens "the epitome of sustainability," noting that in regards to drawing down climate emissions, such gardens have some of the highest levels of carbon sequestration in agriculture.[22]

Toby believed that if you can create a regenerative garden, you can create a regenerative neighborhood, community, and culture. While we can't do it all on this scale, shifting to decentralized, localized solutions that are tastier and more fulfilling while building resilience and local self-reliance is a hell of a value proposition. Unless people see a more rewarding vision, they aren't likely to get behind the kind of big change needed.

In a toxic, consumptive culture of big—big business, big centralized solutions, big agriculture, and equally big problems—we need a paradigm-level change in our beliefs about the power of small—small acts, small gardens, small groups, and just how rich we can live on less. It comes down to changing our relationship with each other and the wisdom, beauty, and mystery of the living world.

Why not get reskilled and recharged by using less and growing, sharing, and connecting more? Grow and share to meet your needs and those of your neighbors, to build awareness and skills, and to reconnect self, community, and this big planetary moment. Building local self-reliance is a critical strategy for increasing quality of life for more people and creating a livable future. We need practical, accessible, and low-cost solutions that are low tech, nature-sourced, people-powered, and place-based but also scalable. Why not homes and neighborhoods that use 80 percent less resources while increasing quality of life and enriching neighborly connections? Why not nutritious, culturally relevant, homegrown food and medicine? Why not habitat that regenerates our ecosystems? Why not apply these land stewardship skills and lessons to building the true wealth and security of healthy, regenerated landscapes, lives, and communities? The lessons we learn and actions we take in a garden start to remove us from a death economy while growing a living economy through a mosaic of locally self-reliant, richly connected homes, neighborhoods, and communities.

We can change the world in a garden with the power of our actions, our relations, and our communities. But to do so, we need more inspired change agents and places that pulse with the regenerative stuff of life. And we need more civic engagement. So how do we get from one garden to lots of gardens? From neighborhoods to communities, cultures, and the world? For this, we need another type of garden.

Petaluma
Health Center
350 home & garden challenge

Chapter 13:

Invest in the Power of Small Groups

"Institutions should be like temples, enduring, timeless,
and built for the benefit of humanity."
—G. Venkatswamy, known as Dr. V

Cultural anthropologist, Margaret Mead, wrote, "Never doubt that a small group of thoughtful, committed citizens can change the world. Indeed, it is the only thing that ever has." These words speak to the power of small, of persevering for a higher purpose and overcoming the insurmountable. They are a rally cry that strengthens resolve and were some of the first words I spoke on Daily Acts' inaugural sustainability tour. Though many are inspired by this idea about the power of small groups, what does it look like in action? How do you do it?

While it's easy to be frustrated with the institutions destroying our world, organizations can achieve a higher purpose and be potent vehicles to unleash the power of community. That is, if they are run in ways that help people tap into their power, and if they can enlist other co-conspirators for wider change.

We are drawn to leaders, organizations, and movements that clearly communicate what they believe and embody those values in what they do and how they do it. As an organization, it's critical to know what brings you alive and why you exist. Then it's about finding the folks who resonate with why you're doing what you're doing. Two keys for this are communicating to people their worth and potential and helping them discover how, by working to solve their personal issues, they can increase their influence and that of your group. This creates a synergy and momentum that can amplify your positive impact.

As we move from inspiring references to deeper nature connection and taking action to heal the land and our bodies, we build skills, relationships, and a perspective that looks at life through the lens of relationships. With more time following your inspiration and finding your voice and path, you start to develop a sixth sense, an ability to read the landscape and what the materials and moment are calling for. This entails developing a faith in your unfolding and confidence in your pathfinding. With the lessons we learn in a garden about relationships and developing our compassion, we can foster the patience and encouragement to nurture the many different types of relations required for bigger change.

A more recent understanding of how small groups change the world is that they don't do it alone. They act as ecosystem catalysts in larger communities of change-makers. In *Forces for Good*, Leslie Crutchfield and Heather McLeod Grant write, **"As field-wide thinking evolves and more emphasis is placed on fostering networks, understanding ecosystems, and galvanizing collective impact, local NGOs must be at the forefront of adopting these changes…They are the vanguard of social change. It is imperative that they maximize impact."** As noted in their book, of the 300 billion dollars given to nonprofits each year in the US, the majority of this goes to small organizations that net under a million dollars, with most netting under $500,000. Why this matters is because in a world of big problems, and storylines dominated by big institutions, maximizing the impact and resources of small organizations is a big opportunity. This doesn't even include countless volunteer-run groups in grassroots movements.

Forces for Good highlights six evidence-based practices for affecting wide-scale change. Many a group with small resources and big goals can apply them. They are:

- **Share Leadership**—internally and with volunteers and partner networks
- **Inspire Evangelists**—aka strong supporters
- **Nurture Nonprofit Networks**—this ranges from social ties to more formal networks
- **Advocate and Serve**—this is about both running programs and working on policy
- **Make Markets Work**—work with or change businesses, start a social enterprise, etc.
- **Master the Art of Adaptation**—be prepared to adapt and innovate

When I discovered this book a decade into Daily Acts, the insights felt validating. While we were much smaller than the organizations in the study and had organically found our way into implementing these practices, seeing a research-backed framework that illuminated a new way of thinking about how to drive transformative change felt invaluable.

Distributing leadership throughout organizations and networks is important for resilience, and because driving change at multiple scales can't be done alone. Having deeply engaged volunteers, donors, partners, and other supporters who are connected to your group's mission and values greatly amplifies your impact. High-impact organizations don't just succeed on their own; they build networks and advance whole fields or communities of actors. Often groups either work on advocacy or delivering programs, but by doing both you can address immediate needs in your community while advocating for larger systems change, which often happens through networks. Influencing businesses and leveraging market forces is also important for social change. And in this rapidly changing world, being adaptive by cultivating organization-wide learning is critical. We must constantly listen, learn, and know when to tweak our approach based on external cues.

Daily Acts 1.0 – Finding Our Voice, Vision, and Tribe

Daily Acts was founded on the belief that through the power of our daily actions, each of us can transform our lives, homes, gardens, and communities. The plan was simple: lift up and connect sustainability leaders and models while inoculating others with this vision. Anywhere solutions to problems exist, highlighting what's working to grow more of it is a strategy that's timeless and true.

Reclaiming the power of one's actions is the core act of transformation that makes bigger change possible. Leadership isn't about having all the answers or skills but about taking initiative through one act and one challenge at a time and finding your vision, voice, and people along the way. Daily Acts grew to become a bright beacon that attracted those who were looking for an antidote to apathy and overwhelm. It was saying, *yes, there is much suffering, AND there are amazing people and solutions all around.* Sharing the inspiration that infects you in a way that connects you to like hearts and minds is a powerful combination.

As a cluster of volunteers emerged, it became clear that people had different passions and strengths. The key was to find where folks shined and give them something to run with. While there are always difficulties with humans, focusing on purposeful positive action goes a long way. As Daily Acts grew from a stool and a stack of *ripples* to a storage shed and then an office, everything evolved. We moved from a small core of volunteers to staff and from a startup board of directors helping with whatever was needed to a governance-focused board helping mature the organization.

Programmatically, the three legs of our stool were *ripples*, sustainability tours, and events. We were finding and expressing our organizational voice (*ripples*), sharing practical examples of our vision (sustainability tours), and participating in community events. Each of these strategies worked to draw others in and to build our network of relationships and partners. This was the foundation that would lead to bigger things.

Daily Acts Leadership Institute cohort and presenters. Photo: Kerry Fugett

Gatherings and Events

Events are temporary oases where we replenish ourselves, our relations, and our connection to what grows us whole. They are great to practice embodying one's values and vision and to find like hearts and minds. True in most any field, events are where we connect to the larger whole we seek to be a part of.

Many organizations are familiar with "tabling" to share a message, programs, or products. As early Daily Actor Chas Moore used to joke, for Daily Acts, "it was really 'stooling' because we didn't even have a table. It was just Trathen sitting on a little stool with a big smile and a stack of *ripples*." Then one day a woman named Julie, who was inspired by *ripples*, showed up to help. Before long she was leading our events. Her work ranged from creating spaces for hundreds of people to paint inspiration flags, to helping create our twenty-foot-long cultural composting puppet, Wormla, which would poop copies of *ripples* out of a back flap as the giant, smiling worm meandered through crowds of puzzled onlookers.

If there was a place where it all came together, it was the Green Festival. As Daily Acts was launching, the largest sustainability festival in the US was also getting on its feet. When we were asked to help anchor the community engagement part of the festival, everyone stepped up. The event really fed our team with volunteers noting how encouraged they felt by the positivity Daily Acts brought, how often they were thanked, and the connections made. Green Festival coproducer Karri Winn noted:

> Daily Acts is one of few groups who has not only seen our vision, but whose tireless contribution has made this an indelible part of the event… This group of people is unlike most that I know in an organizational capacity because they all embody a shared vision that empowers each individual to be fully present and equipped to participate in the direction and stewardship of the organization.

Finding Our Shared Values

Things were so new that we didn't exactly know what we were doing or how. We just followed our inspiration, encouraged each other, and gave 110 percent when an opportunity arose like organizing at the Green Festival. Each time we participated in an event or hosted a tour, people felt nourished, inspired, and part of something larger. It was the connections made, the sense of achieving something together and how inspired and appreciative people were for what Daily Acts' crew had done. We were often in disbelief by what a small group could accomplish together. Those first references in forests, gardens, and at Bioneers became key coordinates on our compass. Now new bright spots and the daily actors creating them were starting to guide us in further finding our voice and vision as well as our core tribe and offerings.

The legendary Wormla in action.

What really brought us together as a group was when we did an exercise to identify our core values. People wrote all sorts of inspiring ideals on sticky notes as we lumped, tweaked, and combined words. Then all of a sudden, our shared values were on the wall. The excitement in the air was palpable as we found who we were together in a deeper way.

Figuring out who we were as a group allowed us to better articulate and share that message with newcomers like Kevin Bayuk. Before I met him, Kevin was a successful serial entrepreneur in the tech industry, yet he felt frustrated and disempowered by conflict, poverty, and planetary destruction. He had ideas about what policy makers and businesses could do but didn't realize how he was contributing to this mess. Just when he was in need of a different perspective, one of his coworkers said, "You gotta check this out," and handed him a copy of *ripples*. Kevin shrugged it off, but within days, another coworker left a copy of *ripples* on his desk.

Kevin was inspired by what he found in *ripples* that he could implement, realizing his everyday actions were *moving the world*. He started buying organic, fair trade, and bringing his own travel mug. Soon he went on a Daily Acts tour, later saying, "What I heard, saw, touched, smelled, and tasted, changed my life. Immediately, I recognized ways I could redesign my life."

After that tour, he left a lucrative job and potentially millions of dollars' worth of equity in the startup he had founded. He learned to teach gardening and composting; he completed a permaculture design course, simplifying his life. He also started speaking, teaching, and leading in bigger ways to share his inspiration with others, noting how Daily Acts inspired, empowered, and supported this life change.

I introduced Kevin to my friend and permaculture teacher, Kat Steele. Soon Kevin was co-teaching with Kat, and he has since taught over forty courses and 1,400 students. He has also helped launch the San Francisco Permaculture Guild, created public food forests, and co-founded Lift Economy, an impact consulting firm. He is now a senior fellow at Project Draw Down, where he helped develop the analytical backbone for assessing the one hundred most substantive climate-change solutions.

Kevin was one of our first major donors. He ran tours for us in San Francisco and aided in thinking about how to further grow our inspired upstart. Most importantly, he is a lifelong friend, mentor, and deeply inspiring ally.

Finding your path personally or organizationally is not something you figure out once and check off the list. It's an ongoing process of choosing who and what becomes part of your North Star. It's finding the people who resonate with what you're doing and are excited to get involved. Trust your intuition and what signs the world gives you as you take the next step.

Lessons From a Dancing Fool

Years ago, a funny video on leadership lessons from a dancing fool went viral. It's a narrated clip of a guy at a concert busting out crazy dance moves. Before long, a huge crowd joins him. The core insight is that leadership isn't about the dancing fool who starts things off. It's about the first followers who translate what the fool is doing so that others can engage. The first followers are who transform a lone nut into a leader. If you're that lone nut, nurture those who seek to get involved. If you're that first, second, or third follower, embrace your urge to join the fool. For everyone else, keep an eye out for fools and followers, and be ready to rush in.

Julie Young was our first follower in the truest sense. From the beginning, she was a joyful, natural nurturer and a tireless worker. Critical to success in any cause is finding people who "get it" and know how to make things happen. I couldn't say how many times Julie stayed up all night to hand draw farm maps for a donor party or wash 600 rocks to be given out at an event, finding just the right word of inspiration to write on each one. For the difficulties of showing up day after day, year after year, this kind of unconditional support makes all the difference.

If I could wish one thing, it'd be that everyone trying to grow something could find their Julie, Andy, Gavio, Mike, Marty, Loi, Sarah, and Cynthia. Those first folks who feel the groove and step up to help shape the voice and vision are why groups like Daily Acts exist, grow, and thrive. Fledgling groups need their Jen, who was there with an unexpected warm embrace. And countless others who lend a hand or send a kind word or donation at just the right time. Notice and nurture those small acts of kindness and support. Soak them in. Save and pass along quotes, love notes, and stories of appreciation with your team. And don't forget the reciprocity of frequent hugs and words, and acts of gratitude. They are bread for the journey that keeps your peeps going.

Above/After: Cavanagh Center Food Forest.

At left/Before: Kelli and Tiffany digging rainwater-harvesting swale trails on a sweltering day.

Chapter 14

Daily Acts 2.0—Leveling Up Our Impact and Operating Model

As with people finding their path, organizations need to pay close attention to the signals saying it's time for a change. While a lot was going well, as Daily Acts grew into its fifth year, our challenges and stresses were growing. I needed to pay the bills, and Daily Acts wasn't cutting it. So I took a part-time job as executive director at Green Sangha, a small nonprofit working on spiritually engaged environmental action. If growing one small nonprofit is difficult, certainly it makes sense to take on another. But I had a thing for these small groups of scrappy world changers, and like in past transitions, I knew change would lead me to new lessons, relationships, and opportunities.

The next core of daily actors showed up, as did opportunities to evolve our approach. A strong foundation of passion and purpose with an inspired community is a great start, but ultimately, Daily Acts needed a more sustainable financial model that also increased our impact.

Beyond paying the bills, Green Sangha's work resonated with and informed Daily Acts' spirit of reverence and mindful action to care for people and the planet. It became a small, nonprofit lab where I could test and implement different systems and see how they worked in similar organizations. Like many small groups, both Daily Acts and Green Sangha had passion and purpose but limited resources, underpaid staff, and a difficulty creating and maintaining organizational systems. When understaffed or dependent on volunteers, effective planning and execution looks different than when you can pay a proper wage. It affirmed the importance of having three legs to a small nonprofit stool with leads for programs, administration, and someone who wove it all together by focusing on fundraising and executing a plan that helps inspire and align the team and supporters.

Working with Green Sangha further confirmed the value of honing one's compass and systems. I saw its impact in two organizations. That deepened my understanding of the power that one aware, engaged person has to impact everything they touch. It clarified the importance of mindfulness practices when working with others in high-pressure situations.

Civic Partners—Can Government Be Fun, Effective Eco-Warriors?

As Daily Acts started to work with local government, increasing our reach and impact while improving our finances, we started to see that partnering with government could be a pathway to building capacity and bigger change. This didn't happen overnight, and as a mostly volunteer organization running programs that were heavily subsidized by us, it was a real hurdle to ask for the resources to actually pay the true cost of the programs. Cities were starting to see that groups like Daily Acts had strong community relationships and could offer cost-effective engagement and valuable sustainability expertise.

For cities and government agencies, there are significant benefits to partnering with grassroots groups who bring passion, purpose, expertise, and an ability to connect with the community. As partners, they can help heal the distrust many people have in government and politicians. They can bring a vision of the world being born with passionate guides who connect people to real solutions and this bigger moment. And not in agency speak or engineer jargon. The same way these programs support speakers, sites, and teachers to live their best, they support change agents in government to do the same. These are people who can be frustrated by trying to move big, slow bureaucratic systems and not having the support to achieve their goals.

Daily Acts' first small lawn transformation with Mayor Litwin, Erik Ohlsen, Marty Falkenstein and friends. Sebastopol Police Station. Start small with friends and fun. Build from there.

On the nonprofit or grassroots side, there are equally many benefits to working with local government. In addition to increasing your reach, impact, and financial sustainability, this can lend credibility to groups. It also helps NGOs better understand government to best impact it while finding allies on the inside to work together for bigger change.

Taking a *change the world in a garden* approach, what follows is a series of examples of moving from inspiration and education to application, transformation, and mobilization. This is a pathway that, through time, hits on all six evidence-based practices from *Forces for Good*, as well as a bunch of other important insights. In short, start small and build. Start with your inspiration, with good partners, and with nature's operating instructions (which are mostly about relationships). More detailed case studies and resources can be found at https://www.dailyacts.org/.

There's Something about Greywater

I'm not sure what it is, but there's something about greywater that captivates folks. It's sort of a gateway drug into understanding natural systems, since part of re-connecting to the cycles of life is using our water more than once. In what is now semi-permanent drought, it's crazy to do laundry, shower, or wash your hands and just let the water drain away. There is no away.

In the California drought in the '70s, lots of folks reused their dish and laundry water. But somehow it became taboo, seemingly dangerous. Really, laundry water? Beyond putting a bucket in the sink, installing a greywater system had become mired in fear and regulation. This was an opportunity for Daily Acts to remove some barriers by installing the first permitted, household greywater system in Sonoma County. This led to a bigger step of installing a public garden, then a bigger public garden, and then LOTS of them. Over several years, one greywater system led to joining a coalition that worked with other groups around California to change state policy. With better policy in place, one greywater system became five in our neighborhood in a day, thirteen in two cities in a weekend, and a one hundred-greywater system challenge.

Reinforcing the positive impacts of educational events, at a permaculture workshop, I reconnected with a friend who was a civil engineer and had installed permitted greywater systems. Once Daily Acts started to partner with our city on educational programs, it was easier to make a case to the building inspector when we had an engineer who could design the systems and provide a proven example from another city. With a more risk-averse culture, agencies often dislike being first on something. With beneficial relationships, an example in hand, and the support of friends and local businesses, we installed a constructed wetland greywater system that mimicked what a wetland does in nature to clean water. Doing this as a workshop enabled us to teach people and agency leaders from around the county. It also got us on the cover of the local newspaper and ultimately in an award-winning video seen by hundreds of thousands of people, amplifying our reach.

Let's Plant a Food Forest! What's a Food Forest?

One day sometime after the greywater installation, I was standing on my porch with Dave, Petaluma's Water Conservation Coordinator, looking across the street at a water-wasting, emission and pesticide-intensive city lawn. I excitedly said to Dave that we should plant a food forest there, to which he responded, "What's a food forest?"

Dave gave me my first taste of what lurked inside many an agency: REALLY cool, inspired people committed to positive change. Once he heard we could save water by planting an edible ecosystem that provided a tasty array of other benefits, bundled up in a beautiful garden, he loved it. He also knew his boss would question the other stuff because their mandate was just to "save water." But he got the project through. The Cavanagh Center landscape transformation was on.

At some point I looked up, wiping the dirt and sweat off of my face, and saw the director of Petaluma's Water Department walking towards us with his young kids in tow. I'll never forget the intrigued look on his face as he strolled up on a sweltering Saturday afternoon. Surely it was the buzz of fifty people covered in dirt, sweat, and smiles as they dug, mulched, and laughed. While new state mandates required cities to cut summer water use, we were creating a ton of extra benefits. This was big, new, and different for the city on a bunch of levels.

At the end of a long, hot weekend, over 150 volunteers had transformed 3,000 square feet of turf, saving about 86,000 gallons of water a year. We dug bioswales and rain gardens to keep stormwater on site, built soil instead of taking it away, used the green waste, and planted over one hundred food, medicinal, and habitat plants. People were

Above/After: Permaculture Design Course students taking a break on the cob bench at the Cavanagh Center.

At left/Before: Erik Ohlsen and Patrick Picard planning the Cavanagh Center Food Forest.

inspired to learn, connect, and transform. Landscape professionals were enthused to collaborate on a community project, and the city saved a bunch of water and money while engaging residents.

The beauty of a permaculture garden, like in nature, is that things like water conservation, stormwater mitigation, food production, soil-building, carbon sequestration, and habitat creation are naturally integrated. Unfortunately, this isn't how cities operate. The water conservation department was focused on saving water and not on the impacts of stormwater runoff, pesticides, or lawn mower emissions, let alone growing healthy food and engaging the community. But we are working to change this!

Then there's turf removal. Cities tasked with new conservation mandates created incentives that paid people to "remove" their turf. The problem is this means removing between a half inch and an inch of soil that took nature 500 to 1,000 years to produce. In many cases, this turf would go to the landfill where it became methane gas, which has fifty to one hundred times the emissions of carbon dioxide. They were saving water but creating other big problems.

The Cavanagh Center cracked the seal on something. Within months we were installing another public food forest in Cotati and helping to create a civic incentive program to spread these landscapes. Then came the chance to rapidly mobilize partners and volunteers for an even bigger transformation. It was 350.org's first Global Day of Climate Action, said to be the largest mobilization in human history. With hundreds of volunteers, partner organizations, businesses, and the city, we transformed the Petaluma City Hall landscape in a day. We had mountains of mulch and compost delivered by semi-trucks. Over 250 volunteers saved the city a million gallons of water per year and $60,000 in installation costs with a day's work (and a fair bit of prep). We mulched turf, dug swales, and installed rain tanks, community garden beds, fruit trees, and kiwi vines.

Like in a garden, which is a system of nested wholes, working in one city can influence others or even instigate countywide change. Before the city hall mobilization, I had met with an ally at the City of Santa Rosa who longed to do a big transformation of their city hall. But it was politically unfeasible until the Petaluma City Hall landscape transformation graced the front page of the local paper. Within days, we had a meeting with the mayor, who was inspired to make something happen. It still took years of work by folks in the city, but eventually the Santa Rosa City Hall landscape transformation happened. Learning the knobs and levers of how to move things forward in a city and supporting the change agents in that system is important. And there's nothing like a little positive competition to keep upping our collective game.

From Collaborative Programs to Mobilizing Collective Action

On the heels of the city hall transformation, with the growing climate crisis and building bigger and bigger successes, I came to an important compass question: "How can we reach ten or even one hundred times our impact and do it without a big growth in resources or burning out?" We needed a big, inspiring goal, and it had to be holistic and community powered. Seeing other examples of next-level organizing like the 350.org mobilization and the Village Building Convergence in Portland inspired me to dream bigger. Then it all coalesced when I came across the Santa Monica 100 Garden Challenge. It was ambitious and inspiring yet clear and simple: plant one hundred gardens.

With all of this inspired action, locally and beyond, I wondered, what could we do that's similar to a one hundred garden challenge, big but simple? I started talking to other organizers and partners about this idea. At some point, local organizer Sarah McCamant called me on my inspira-speak and said, "Okay, when are we getting started?" The nudge came at the right time, having recently connected with the Santa Monica Garden Challenge folks about how they ran their campaign. Then at a party for the Leadership Institute, a nonprofit partner, I shared the idea with Geof Syphers (future CEO of Sonoma Clean Power), who offered to help put together a proposal to the Sonoma County Water Agency. Agency involvement felt important for wider reach, buy in, and funding to make it happen.

This led to a handful of organizers getting together to start planning a big action. As I walked out of the meeting, I was inspired and terrified, which is usually a sign that it's the right path. Tying into 350.org's work to call attention to getting climate emissions back to 350 parts per million, we had just set an outlandish goal to plant and revitalize 350 gardens in a single weekend three months from then. The goal was so big, it was scary to even mention at first, blowing up our perception of what we thought possible by planting hundreds of gardens at once.

In parallel, Daily Acts was part of a newly formed coalition working through the Sonoma County Health Department to launch iGROW, a home food-growing initiative. Always looking to use lessons learned in a garden, we thought *how can we plant 350 gardens and also get agency players to act in a more integrated way with the water people thinking about food, the health people thinking about water, and all of us more aware of climate and the power of small actions?* So we tied the launch of iG-ROW to the 350 Garden Challenge.

When the dust settled fourteen weeks after our first meeting, the community rose to the challenge, nearly doubling our ambitious goal by registering 628 gardens. Hundreds of people and over forty schools, churches, cities, county agencies, and businesses planted fruit trees and rows for the hungry, mulched thirsty lawns, and revitalized community gardens. We gave out one hundred culturally relevant "salsa gardens" at apartments, providing wine barrels, soil, pepper, tomato, and basil plants. Having heard about the challenge, Victory Lee of the Victory Garden Foundation immediately rallied, and in weeks had over one hundred more gardens registered around the country. Government partners expressed astonishment that anything could happen that quickly. The challenge transformed people's perceptions about what was possible, especially in a short time.

From there we kept doubling our goals and spreading the challenge to other communities, as it morphed from the 350 Garden Challenge to the Community Resilience Challenge, eventually resulting in nearly 100,000 actions and projects to grow food, save resources, and build community over the next nine years. One day I

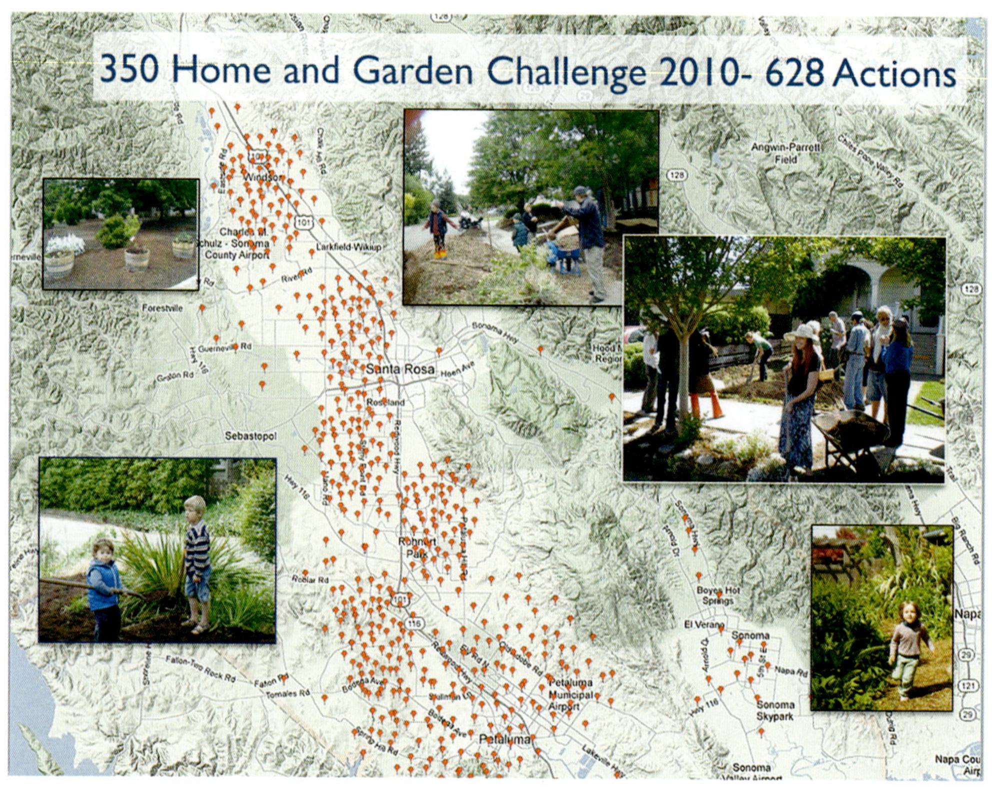

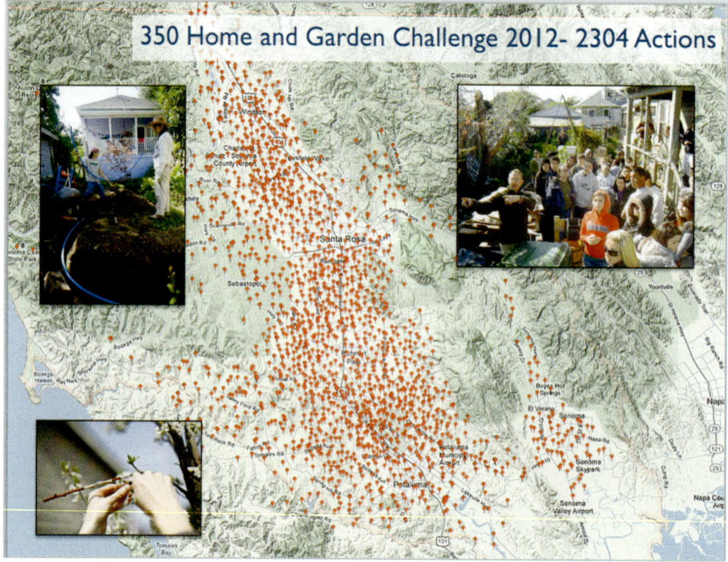

Action maps for the 350 Home and Garden Challenge.

got a call from Tina, who was starting a sustainability group in her community. She came up for a chat in the garden. After laying out our approach, I encouraged her to give it a try. Within months, her group, Sustainable Contra Costa, had registered over 900 actions, establishing dozens of new community partnerships and helping to launch the sustainability movement in their community. Near a decade later, they have registered over 53,000 sustainability and climate actions and projects, and this has led to government contracts, grants, and new partners.

In addition to saving resources, growing food, and building community, people get inspired and filled with hope through these programs. These gardens educate and empower many more people. Creativity is unleashed as kids get inspired to roll down the street handing out strawberry plants and light bulbs in their wagons. Will Bakx, an incredible friend, ally, and business partner from Sonoma Compost, whom we lost recently, shared the story of a father picking up a free load of compost as an incentive to register his action. With tears of joy in his eyes, he told Will what it meant to do his own project with his kids for the first time.

You can feel the power of community when small groups think and act like a garden, engaging a range of stakeholders toward bigger change. It's a case of dreaming big, working together, and encouraging others. It's giving a helping hand with an idea or, if you are in a position of influence, taking a chance on a wild idea. All these things lead to new relationships, innovative approaches, and the felt experience of the power of small.

Like a holistic garden, such campaigns
are infectious, reweaving
the fabric of resilience in a people and place
and acting as a beacon of hope.

Rise
AND
Shine
MOTHER CLUCKERS

It had been a decade since I stepped through the gate at the Permaculture Institute Garden. It all seemed to lead up to that Cavanagh Center transformation. After that, things quickened. From our first tour, it was always about building relationships, highlighting inspiring models and people, and connecting our network of leaders to grow more of them. A natural step was to teach workshops and engage on the policy front to support sustainable change through city programs. Then came landscape transformations and bigger, more complex mobilizations with more people and partners and linking up with larger initiatives. When the dust settled on that first 350 Garden Challenge, Daily Acts was still mostly volunteer driven with just three underpaid staff. **This is the power of community.** As our programs evolved, the same was happening in regards to finding new mission-focused ways to raise funds.

Ripple the World!

It was 8:40 a.m., and over 350 people flooded into the Petaluma Community Center, more than we had seats for and apparently more than the fire code allowed. It never occurred to us to set a cutoff point for guests. But that was not our biggest problem. After months of work culminating in an all-nighter to prep a perfectly orchestrated ecosystem of seat assignments, a small mix-up meant that was out the window. As team members Susan, Ellen, and I stood there in a sea of people streaming by, for an instant everything got quiet and slow as I took in the exhausted dread in their eyes.

Months before, I had heard from a fellow nonprofit leader about the Benevon fundraising model, which helps build long-term relationships and embody a mission while raising money. Our budget was still well under $100,000, and we needed ways to strengthen our impact and capacity.

In that slow-moving moment amidst a sea of people, as our hopes and dreams were caving in on us, there was nothing to do but rapidly accept the situation and make the best of it. Six years of scrappy grassroots organizing and working with who and what was at hand was apparently good cross-training for such moments. I quickly said, "Don't worry, we got this. I need to make an announcement." I turned and walked to the stage with my heart pounding, waiting for the words to come. When I got there, I said something like, "Good morning, amazing daily actors! In a world with countless crises, adaptability is key to building resilience. So we are mixing things up this morning. Your seat assignments are out the window. Grab a spot anywhere and meet someone new." This meant that our emcee, Sebastopol Mayor Craig Litwin, and his family ended up against a side wall with breakfast on their laps. In the end, despite our first-time party-planning gaffes, the event was a success, bringing our community together, raising money, and invigorating spirits.

Late the night before, I'd felt a mix of serenity and anticipation. Standing in a packed room that day, I felt the strength of our community in a new way and a surprising sense of humility and vulnerability. Our biggest event wasn't about us. It was something working through us to meet a larger need, holding space for changemakers from all sectors. It brought this movement together in a powerful new way, reminding people of their part in something larger.

Leading up to that first event, one of the unknowns was how we were going to come up with the expensive video that the model we were following called for. Then magically, a retired filmmaker named Eve reached out to volunteer. We didn't know Eve was facing a life-threatening illness. As often happens, just when she needed hope the most, someone handed her a copy of *ripples* and told her to check out Daily Acts. It was eye-opening to work with someone who expressed the real possibility that she might not make it to the breakfast or finish the video. In the end, Eve recovered, and we got a great video and an amazing friend and volunteer. As Eve noted, Daily Acts was literally lifesaving; it was critical to her healing journey. Once involved, she transformed her garden, putting in greywater, rainwater, and enough eco-goodies to receive an award from her city.

Another benefit of such gatherings is changing organizational and movement culture from one of competition to cooperation. After one breakfast, in reference to the collaborative spirit of the event, a leader from out of town said, "You could never get this to happen in our community." But you can. It's building trust and relationships and knowing that, while each of us has to meet our needs, we need each other and have to invest in the larger ecosystem.

Many a daily actor likens it less to a fundraiser and more to a revival, a celebration of community, life, and creating a better world. We couldn't have imagined that starting this event to raise money would have so many transformative impacts on our organization, our community, and our relationship to this larger field of changemakers. We've gained volunteers, partners, government contracts, staff, and board members, and have had a hell of a good time throwing a great party.

As organizations grow, a critical need is evolving one's programs and operating model in a way that increases impact and capacity. Government contracts and evolving our individual fundraising, spurred by this annual event and the Benevon model, became two critical revenue streams that reshaped Daily Acts in a number of ways. One thing it quickened was the growing shift in how we work and relate with a larger ecosystem of community members and partners.

Ripple the World annual gathering.

Chapter 15:

Nurturing and Connecting Networks

The next evolution that was emerging after planting lots of eco-savvy gardens was formalizing networks to drive bigger change. This was while trying to raise money, manage a growing organization, and working with the tensions of engaging at a range of scales. This brought the additional complexity of new relations and needing to understand larger systems. In a rapidly changing world, top-down, siloed approaches that deal with one cluster of problems at a time no longer work. We have societal systems that are designed not to learn, lack transparency, and are set up to benefit the few. Enter networks.

Over billions of years, nature has done a lot of testing to find the best way of doing things. Life in an ecosystem is interconnected through networks. But what is a network, and why are they so ubiquitous? Network as a noun means a group or system of interconnected people or things. As a verb it means interacting with others to exchange information. From the systems in your body to the exchange between pollinators and plants, the internet, and social groups, networks are key to life's function.

The biological network that first captivated me at Bioneers, a network itself, was the mycelial network—the underground part of mushrooms. Mycologist Paul Stamets estimates that in the underground space occupied by a single footstep there are as many as 300 miles of mycelial networks, providing an incredible array of services to help life flourish. This is the Wood Wide Web of interspecies communication. In nature, each system is a whole connected to and nested within other wholes. Getting one's paradigm cracked open in a permaculture garden or at an inspiring gathering helps rewire your mind, senses, and sense of possibility. This change in awareness and identity lends itself to seeing organizations as living organisms interacting within larger ecosystems.

The book *Leading from the Emerging Future* frames up key issues and needs in regard to changing from an ego-system awareness focused only on self to an ecosystem awareness that cares about the well-being of all. Authors Otto Scharmer and Katrin Kaufer cite bridging this gap between ego and eco as the greatest leadership challenge today. It involves a shift in mindset or paradigm, which is the highest leverage place to work from, because it influences societal rules, policies, and culture.

Solving urgent, complex problems requires moving from a reactive business-as-usual approach to a new type of collective action, engaging the wisdom of all parts of our communities. This means shifting the awareness of people and groups in a system to understanding and valuing different perspectives and needs. It also means creating new seats at the table for missing voices. Part of the awareness shift is being clear on your part but open, adaptive, and tuned into the needs of the whole. It's effecting change by being the change together and aligning many stakeholders for increased impact.

Since life is about the relationship between things, learning to observe the patterns and principles that underlie a garden ecosystem can help us develop the ability to sense more complex social ecosystems, and how the parts form a larger whole. Because Daily Acts was born out of exposure to ecological oases that were holistic by nature, this shaped our relationship-based approach. Things evolved from simple cross-connections at events to collaborative programs, civic partnerships, and bigger transformations and mobilizations. Each time, we followed our inspiration, leaned into the materials and the moment, and embraced our shared potential.

From simply taking action yourself to doing so in a group is a big step. Then adding lots of partners who work with your group is another step up in complexity. Working across multiple scales is dipping your toes into a whole other level. But like in a garden, you start small, taking action where you can. This builds the awareness, skills, and relationships to manage increasing levels of complexity. Beyond an initial inspiring exposure to a permaculture garden or network of changemakers with consistent engagement, you start to understand what's going on and can sense a pattern

"The quality of results produced by any system depends on the quality of awareness from which people in the system operate... All sectors and systems deal fundamentally with the same challenge – to develop the capacity to act from the whole."

—Otto Scharmer, Katrin Kaufer

at play. It's the collective planetary immune response environmentalist and author Paul Hawken highlights in *Blessed Unrest*, a movement of movements emerging across the Earth. This powerful force has a deep, intrinsic pull. Like the wonder of being in nature's grandeur, you feel infinitely small yet connected to it all.

For those craving bigger change and a richer, more joyful experience, the work of moving from ego to eco has a powerful draw. The following stories and insights are a few glimpses into how we can consciously grow this part of our larger selves, our eco-identities.

Three Keys: Working at a Range of Scales; Gatherings; Bridging Difference

1. Working at a Range of Scales: From Local to Regional and Beyond

As this next level of organizing was emerging, local alliances, networks, and collaborations started connecting people, groups, and agencies with a common cause. While a number of issue-specific networks that Daily Acts was a part of emerged, we worked closely with the Sonoma County Greywater Working Group to influence greywater legislation, the iGrow coalition to support backyard food growing, and the Sonoma County Food System Alliance to vision and help create an equitable, regenerative, and economically viable food system.

A key barrier in moving from ego to eco is that it's easy to get so focused on your issue, that you don't see or value other parts of the community and how we fit together. A critical gap is between people facing the immediate emergency of meeting basic needs to survive and the long-term emergency that is rapidly transforming our communities through devastating climate crises. Fear of scarcity and competition for resources can also result in too strong an emphasis on one's organization or sector. Then there's just busyness and the unseen, hard-to-pinpoint impacts of growing up in a segregated, disconnected culture that shows up in everything we do. Another barrier is understanding differences in approach and culture, the many different issue areas and sectors like government, business, or nonprofit, as well as size and phase of development (small vs. big organizations, new vs. established, etc.). As if centering on your own purpose, vision, and goals isn't enough, there are all these other complexities to become literate in to play well with others. Just start with your heart and with action aimed toward building relationships. Reflect, refine, repeat.

All of this emphasizes the need to hone one's emotional intelligence when acting and leading in difficult terrain. This entails developing three things: self-awareness, self-management, and an understanding of how we are interacting with and impacting others. Increased emotional intelligence lends itself to evolving our identities and values as people, organizations, and coalitions. It also requires deep internal work and a constant balancing between self-interest and shared interest in life, work, coalitions, and the rest. Luckily, it's the same stuff we've been learning along the way by following our inspiration and taking action to regenerate our connections to self, nature, and community.

Connecting to a larger whole while building relationships, finding shared values, and valuing differences furthers our identity shift. We start to understand our role within the community ecosystem in new ways, like how a small, nimble, holistic organization differs from a large, slow-moving, siloed government agency. We see the different strengths and challenges of a person working on the ground vs. in mid-management or as an elected official. Each can do and say different things because of their unique position in the ecosystem. For example, because most community systems are top down and siloed, a manager in a government agency may not be able to say what's needed to a high-level elected official that a nonprofit or community member can say. Such structures limit feedback and engagement to problem solving, innovation, adaptation, and change. As more people and leaders understand how these societal systems work, we can pull our levers together to change for the better.

The Transition Town Movement

In a time of larger-than-life crises, beyond the local, it's empowering to be part of bigger movements. Author Rob Hopkins had a vision of applying permaculture not just to gardening but to social change in something he called Transition Towns. He wrote the *Transition Handbook* to offer solutions and a path to more healthy, resilient communities.

With permaculture providing the eco-design glue and ethical foundation to Transition, the idea rapidly spread. It was holistic rather than issue-focused, using hope and proactivity as drivers for action instead of fear, and it was intent on acting as a catalyst rather than being prescriptive. What helped it spread was encouraging self-organizing with steps people could take to create a compelling vision, raise awareness, form working groups, develop practical examples, and help people re-skill in local self-reliance. Transition US (TUS) formed as an early national hub organization to connect and grow this movement in the United States.

Since Transition shared a similar strategy and values to Daily Acts, I was excited to connect with this bigger movement and joined TUS's board of directors. With an urgency to rapidly spread a movement capable of addressing massive issues, an emerging eco-ethos of decentralized, networked collaboration made sense. It was about inspiring a network leadership approach that encourages people to initiate, innovate, and experiment. Joining this national effort while supporting local, self-organizing pulled Daily Acts into a bigger scale of collaboration and co-creation, getting us involved in the international Transition and permaculture movements.

While local groups are great at place-based relationships and programs, a national network can provide connection, ideas, and training to help local initiatives. The US is big, and important elements were missing. This spurred the next scale of emergence and self-organizing regionally.

2. Gatherings

A key way networks and movements evolve and flourish is by coming together. It's getting cracked open by amazing changemakers and the inspiration, education, and new relations that entails. Once exposed, you want more of the engagement, skill-building, and relationships that come with gatherings. Such events help us recharge, level up our vision, and get deeper into the culture and values of the better world being born. The best gatherings bring people into a state of flow. Having mind-blowing inspiration and learning, music, fun, nature connection, and tasty food and beverages all creates conditions conducive to heightened joy, connection, and social bonding. This can foster openness to new ideas and cultures, seeding the evolution of one's identity and values through time.

Some of the beauty of movement spaces and gatherings is that there are always

ways to get involved, from volunteering to teaching, collaborating, and co-creating. It was through gatherings that a number of us involved in seeding change in these movements recognized a need for regional hubs to distribute knowledge and resources and to connect local groups. The regional scale is perfect to leverage and strengthen the power of local while connecting it to larger scales. As the Transition and permaculture movements evolved and intermingled regionally, the same was happening through international gatherings of the two movements.

Where Bioneers offers the power and joy of being with thousands of changemakers and the Norcal Convergence provided a smaller regionalized version, at Localizing California's Waters (LCW), you can saddle up at an old timey bar and land in an easy chat with world-renowned eco do-gooders or a high-level Jedi from the governor's office. It's small, intimate, surrounded by beauty, and has a rich blend of characters. Not to mention a great tavern, good music, silly skits, and late-night strategy sessions by the fire.

LCW began as the first California state greywater conference before morphing into a vision of localizing California's waters. The gathering draws diverse leaders interested in bridging the worlds of small, localized solutions with the *big picture, big solution* thinking from high up in government. It's for unlikely allies interested in transforming water management and use by advancing local policy and best practices in an intimate setting. Change happens better when it comes both from the edges and from those inside a system. It's about breaking down barriers in understanding, from cultural or organizational differences. There's a special breed of people and leaders drawn to these spaces of innovation and emergence, many of whom bring diverse network connections. Then these leaders connect and cross-pollinate sectors and movements.

In permaculture, *using edges and valuing the marginal* is an important design principle. Edges are often the most productive elements of a system, like the estuary where forest meets river. For leadership and cultural change, this can mean including and listening to voices and perspectives that aren't part of the mainstream.

Nurturing our relations at the Summer Soiree Garden Party.

Gatherings that bring a diversity of cultures and ideas together are valuable and productive.

Gatherings of the right sort create conditions conducive for the change we need. Being in natural, intimate settings with interesting folks while having impassioned, purposeful conversations sends a neurochemical cocktail pulsing through your system, your conversation, or a whole convening that has a transformative effect. It puts us in a state of flow of heightened joy and connection that enhances social bonding, improves performance, and unleashes our potential. It's bread for the journey to nourish the body and spirit of hardworking, heartful do-gooders be they activists, policy wonks, or business leaders trying to address urgent, complex problems. Given the confluence of crises, it's no wonder there's a profusion of gatherings popping up in most fields. It's awe-inspiring to see the infinite array of organizations, coalitions, and movements rising to the moment.

3. Bridging Difference

As would-be world changers gather and connect to build collective power, a key part of moving from ego to eco is bridging difference. Who do we see as *self* and *other* in our lives, organizations, movements, and communities? Who is essential to the transformation we seek? Who don't we see or include? Two important areas to bridge are between grassroots and government and, within grassroots, between predominantly white efforts and communities of color.

Building Bridges—Communities of Color and White Fragility

If we are talking relationships, nothing I say could fully recognize the pain and harm caused by the systemic oppression and injustice imposed by the dominant White culture. A culture that I grew up in, have been shaped by, and have benefited from. Finally, the world has woken to the injustice this mindset has consciously and unconsciously inflicted on and within communities of color. If we really care about transformative change, how can we not address the connected oppression of our people and planet? As if the climate crisis isn't overwhelming enough, dismantling the racism the US was founded on is no small work. It is important for those of us working on the climate crisis to publicly recognize that these two issues are intricately intertwined. As Hop Hopkins shared in an article for the Sierra Club, "You can't have climate change without sacrifice zones, and you can't have sacrifice zones without disposable people, and you can't have disposable people without racism."[23]

Like with most things, we start with ourselves, unpacking our own internal unconscious biases, assumptions, and stereotypes that often default to favoring, trusting, and choosing White folks over people of color. As we do this internal work, it's also critical to educate ourselves about systemic racism, and find ways to change the policies and practices that create and support unfair advantage to some and harmful effects to others based on their race. And it helps to celebrate progress along the way. Daily Acts was founded on a vision of creating a more healthy, just, and reverent human culture. Though originally my awareness was mainly around far-off injustices like with sweatshop labor and children who didn't have running water or couldn't go to school because the coffee their families grew wasn't fairly traded. For most of us who try to be good, kind people, it's not easy to think that we likely have racist beliefs because of the culture we were raised in. I realized that my own resulting guilt and defensiveness at such ideas perpetuate this system, and this is why I do my own internal anti-racist work as an important foundation for larger change. As Daily Acts awareness grew, our efforts evolved from starting and participating in coalitions that prioritized justice to anti-racism training for our team and working on creating a safer, more aware, and welcoming culture, with plenty of missteps along the way.

Bridging cultures and healing hurt with such a deep history of injustice is no small thing, even in more aware, values-based movements. There are difficulties people of color deal with in being in White spaces, from micro-aggressions to the awkward-ness of White people waking up. The important thing for White-identifying folks is to build cultural humility and awareness and not to look for Black, Indigenous, Latinx, Asian, and other people of color people to educate White people on White supremacy, White fragility, or the ways we unknowingly perpetuate systemic racism. In *White Fragility*, Professor Robin DiAngelo describes White supremacy as a sys-tem of structural power that privileges, centralizes, and elevates White people as a group. This isn't about good vs. bad, but who has power and control, whose views and interests are protected and promoted. Looking at the racial breakdown of those who controlled US institutions in 2016–2017, she noted that 90–100 percent of people in congress, state governors, top military advisors, those who decide which TV shows we see, books we read, and which music is produced are all White. There were sim-ilarly high numbers across several other categories, such as teachers and professors. A component of this system of structural power is White fragility, which DiAngelo describes as the discomfort and defensiveness White people can feel when discussing racism. When we are not able to examine and talk about racist systems, the systems and policies default to staying in place. Because most of us feel we are good people with good values, our defensiveness can keep us from acknowledging where we may be making, or unconsciously supporting, cultural assumptions, stereotypes, or behav-iors that are racist and thus cause harm to others.

A number of times I've heard Latinx and Black allies express that they'd rather be in their own spaces and want White folks to work on waking White folks to anti-racism work. That's fair. As is aiming to be more inclusive and diverse in our organizations and movements while being aware of not pulling power, focus, or skilled leaders from people of color organizations and efforts. White folks have to first do our work of getting educated, compassionately educating other White folks, and figuring out how to be good allies, and importantly, work towards becoming accomplices.

The term **ally** is defined as someone who advocates for groups or individuals who do not come from the same place of privilege as the ally. This is considered a first step in race and social justice work. **Accomplice** encompasses allyship but goes beyond it to advocacy, using one's privilege to challenge existing conditions at the risk of their own comfort and well-being. [24]

Building Bridges—Government and Grassroots

As Daily Acts built bridges across different movements over the years, we began doing the same between grassroots and government with both sides recognizing the value in working together. There are often spaces dominated by a particular mindset or culture, like grassroots activists vs. government agencies. Then there are shared spaces like the Localizing California's Waters network, which has government and grassroots working to bridge the gap between local and state-level efforts. Edge spaces are often messier and under-resourced. But when you can get people together from different parts of a system, there's a higher potential for seeding evolution.

At both grassroots gatherings and agency-dominated ones, what started with sharing successful stories of collaboration evolved into organizing speakers and facilitating panels. We were bringing in government leaders excited to help community groups understand how to get resources and influence government. On the government side, agencies were inspired by the results of such collaborations and wanted to know how to build partnerships with local organizations. Listening to players from different parts of a system riff on how best to engage and drive change is incredibly informative. Another important area of awareness and action is understanding the spectrum of equity work from frontline activists working to dismantle systems of injustice to reverence-centered Black farmers and Latinx leaders working to center equity from within government.

There are all sorts of ways things can evolve, be it through local collaborations and campaigns or at gatherings. Building connections by partnering and bringing allies into different spaces can lead to opportunities to volunteer, collaborate further, and even serve in leadership roles. Our team members have served on a wide range of boards of directors in organizations focused on government, grassroots, the Latinx community, and more. For us, this started with collaborations and events.

Once I began serving on the board of directors for a statewide organization that was more municipal agency-driven, I saw the potential of spreading community-based solutions by inoculating a government network system with some grassroots network vision. In these agency spaces, I shared successes and made the case for supporting and growing a network of community-based organizations in order to take a systemic approach rather than finding partners in a one-off fashion. Sure, it would be great to have a Daily Acts–type group in every community, but with a network of groups in regions across the state, so much more is possible. With the urgency and scale of the challenges, we need to think in terms of growing and connecting whole fields of groups who are creating collaborative solutions and sharing the best practices with each other. Such collaborations build understanding, relationships, and the skills to effect wider change in communities and the agencies that serve them.

Partnering with a few cities is one thing, but being in meetings full of government water geeks from around the state is quite different than sitting around the table with visionary activists. It's a different ecosystem, culture, language, and mindset. As important as it is to understand the challenges in the grassroots, we need to understand the challenges of operating in big bureaucracies that can limit creativity and innovation, burying people under piles of paperwork and regulation. While the reality of working across vastly different ego systems can be daunting, building such bridges, relationships, and understanding is vital.

Another important niche is environmental or justice groups advocating for policy change. Coming from a nature-inspired, community-based approach that is focused on hands-on solutions and collaboration provides a different perspective and relationship with government. We need advocacy groups AND those on the ground implementing solutions. In the next section, we'll look at how these things integrate, innovating people-powered policy while supporting government partners.

There's discomfort and misunderstanding when leaning into our edges, but this is where the richness is. We need the wisdom and leadership of all communities. This means building relationships and trust. Part of this is understanding the profound impacts of colonization, structural racism, and even micro-aggressions, and the thousand little cuts a dominant White culture inflicts on people of color, even if unknowingly. Another part is getting to know how governments and grassroots work.

Learn the strengths and challenges of spaces dominated by a particular mindset, be it decentralized community groups that lack resources and management capacity but are innovative, integrated, and adaptive, or centralized government spaces that can be siloed and slow to change but have the resources and influence to play a big role in making communities more healthy, equitable, and climate resilient.

All this is about developing an inside-out strategy. It's getting to know the strings that control the system so we can transform it with the least resistance. There are so many pathways and levers to pull. Just find your fit, a beneficial diversity of partners to play with, and engage through time and at a range of scales. Working with these edges evolves our sense of who we are and of community, growing us more whole and powerful. And hopefully more kind and understanding.

Key Concepts
• Nature's wisdom: Design philosophies that help reconnect us to the wonder and wisdom of this precious planet so we can better design our lives and communities while caring for life.

Key Points
• Listen to, study, and act from nature's wisdom at home, in the garden, and in life.
• Nurture the power of small groups and networks for big change.
• Share your group's inspiration and practical examples of your vision.
• Continue to step into the moment with more partners, fun, and a bigger, bolder vision.
• To handle tough issues, be kind, encouraging, and compassionate with yourself and others.

Questions to Ask If You're Looking to Get Engaged
• Which issues are you deeply passionate about or interested in learning more about?
• What scale do you want to work at? Locally, regionally, or larger?
• Which groups most inspire you with their vision, people, and activities?
• What skillsets do you love sharing that you can offer to groups?

Questions to Ask if You're in a Group and Want to Grow Your Impact

• How can you amplify your impact and joy while strengthening your group and community?

• What actions can you take to embody your vision, get a win, and build momentum?

• How can you better strengthen your collective voice, vision, and impact?

Steps to Take

• Personal

  o Identify which issues and groups deeply inspire you—talk to friends and attend talks, events, and activities to explore your interest and develop connections.

  o Reach out to groups or people in them to connect, learn, and get involved.

  o Join a local board or city commission that influences issues you care about.

• Groups

  o Find the mentors, resources, and reference points your group most needs.

  o Reflect on and hone your vision, values, voice, and desired impact.

  o Find ways to partner in collective action with groups and networks.

  o Work to bridge differences and find common ground for collective good.

> "My heart is moved by all I cannot save:
> so much has been destroyed
> I have to cast my lot with those
> who age after age, perversely,
> with no extraordinary power,
> reconstitute the world."
>
> —Adrienne Rich

Photo: Robb Hirsch

Resilience

Adapt and Thrive

Beautiful and edible? Yep. Chrysanthemum flowers.

Chapter 16

When It All Goes Pop

As the world comes unhinged, resilience is on the tip of many tongues. It applies to everything from personal perseverance and surviving trauma to organizations, communities, and ecosystems. As David Orr, professor and author, writes, "The goal of resilience…is an ongoing adjustment to changing political, economic, and ecological conditions. In practical terms, resilience is a design strategy that aims to reduce vulnerabilities." In short, when faced with adversity, resilience is the ability to adapt and spring forward.

It's time we listen to our world as it speaks in the language of ever more extreme fires, floods, droughts, and pandemics. Returning to the unconscious ways that got us here is not an option. Restoring nature, reversing climate disruption, and healing the injustices our society is built on is paramount. We must transform how we live in and with this beauteous world. We do this by unleashing the reverent, resilient spirit at the heart of human genius and by reconnecting to the long lineage of survivors who got us here.

When Things Click and It All Goes Pop

In *Gaia's Garden*, Toby Hemenway writes about a point in an ecological garden when the whole place suddenly goes pop and surges with vitality. With the right elements in place, the garden accumulates a richness that's able to sift, sort, and transform any bit of sun, rain, or nutrient into a thriving community of critters, plants, and people. It starts with healthy soil able to store each drop of water. Then add a diversity of beneficial plants and animals and some human stewards. At the same time, green the structures that shape what flows through the landscape.

By mimicking natural plant communities and accelerating nature's succession, a self-replenishing oasis emerges. The direct transmission from entering a garden like this changes lives.

As we reconnect to and regenerate nature, we learn the skills to mobilize and transform our communities. It's in our DNA to build fertility and recycle everything, to reward cooperation, operate on sunshine, and create conditions conducive to life. Nature's core impulse, to *help life flourish*, is in us because we are nature.

Cyberpunk author William Gibson wrote, "The future has already arrived. It's just not widely distributed yet." So how do we distribute more vibrant, life-changing solutions and models? How do we grow a culture of reverence and resilience that connects people to their genius—the spirit of this place and time? We get our lives, gardens, and small groups to all go pop as we turn magic backyard moments into organizations that spread models, build coalitions, and strengthen movements to change the world.

This starts with each of us. The path and practices of living our inspiration in a way that cares for self, nature, and community is what makes our inner garden go pop. You just start small and build. What comes next is rebuilding our relationship with the living world, right in the garden.

When the Garden Goes Pop: Growing Food, Medicine, and Beauty

The beauty of getting to know your place, be it urban or rural, rented or owned, is that we start to rebuild the intrinsic richness of our atrophied relations and relational capacities. We can grow food, medicine, and beauty and regenerate the biological wealth of our lives, landscapes, and neighborly relations. While I didn't have words for what I stumbled upon in that first garden, it woke something in me. It grew as I experimented on a redwood hillside, created pockets of wonder at a shady rental, and then when Mary and I moved to 8th Street in Petaluma. True to the season's abundance, everywhere you turn are harvests to be shared, as we come together to recreate a culture that values every drop of water, scrap of carbon, and act of living.

Swarm

Within months of moving into our new home on 8th Street in Petaluma, we began to host Daily Acts workshops at our house. As Janine from our first sustainability tour whipped up a batch of clay paint, original daily actor Gavio was out back with attendees talking eco-design geekery. Suddenly the air filled with thousands of swarming bees.

Honeybees beat their wings around 230 wingbeats per second or over 13,000 flaps per minute.[25] Following an urge, I moved to the center of this buzzing cloud. I was in a sea of 10,000 bees, bathed in the sonic vibration of over two million wing beats per second. Standing there in a T-shirt and shorts with a gentle bee breeze blowing across my skin, I felt a sudden shift. I felt it in every ounce of my being before I knew what "it" was. It was this instant when 10,000 buzzing bees came into cadence and said, "We're landing on that branch there." In over a decade of beekeeping and catching swarms, I'd never experienced anything like this.

It was a feeling deep in my cells of community coming into cadence. I couldn't help but take notice of the moment—transforming a new space while empowering people, creating habitat, and regenerating nature. When the dust settled on the swarm of the first couple of years on 8th Street, I saw that the whole thing had been a series of pops, of community coming into cadence. We planted almost two hundred fruit trees, berry bushes, vines, and medicinal and habitat plants and grafted more varieties to existing trees. We installed rainwater and greywater systems, and a cob bench/pizza oven. Bees were swarming, chickens roaming, and harvests popping. This was all tied to a lot of grassroots action. It was creating homegrown oases through workshops, helping change state greywater policy, installing neighborhood food forests, and dabbling in larger mobilizations. By following our inspiration and nature's operating instructions, all the elements for a larger set of pops were falling into place. It's a potent tonic for

the times to know that such models are emerging everywhere, turning dreams, seeds, waste streams, and constraints into bright, tasty beacons of hope.

Now two decades in, the deeper *why* has never let up. As the urgency of an increasingly stormy world has grown, more people have recognized the need to create safe, nourishing, resilient spaces.

Soil

In *Gaia's Garden*, Toby Hemenway outlines the elements that get your garden popping. The first element, he writes, is soil. This precious thin skin that blankets the Earth is the foundation from which life's flourishing wonderment springs forth. When you start to nourish the mother of life's fecundity, instead of taking 500 to 1,000 years to grow an inch of soil, we can quicken nature's regenerative recipe. On 8th Street, we used moving boxes, gleaned wood chips, recycled coffee grounds, horse manure, local compost, and most anything we could find, adding over 40,000 pounds of organic materials in the first few years to rebuild the wealth of our 6,200-square-foot lot.

Beyond adding organic matter, there's growing your own—mulching green waste, making worm tea, and composting scraps. Even untended piles let nature work her magic. To lift up a clump of decomposing weeds and see a crawling, creeping mass of critters is astonishing. Once you feed the soil in a range of ways, the whole thing comes alive.

Plants

A well-fed soil system can grow beautiful, tasty, nutritious plants for food, fuel, fodder, fun, farmaceuticals, and more. While you can geek super deep on knowing plants' needs, yields, and how they fit together, you can also just find some multi-beneficial plants with the colors, scents, and flavors you love and experiment. Once you get a range of functions in place that cover fruiting, pollination, producing mulch, and harvesting nutrients from earth and sky, the system starts to pop. Layer in a diversity of plants that produce year-round yields from root to ground cover, herb, shrub, small and large trees, and a vining layer, and the whole thing gets super juicy.

Then there's the seasonal meditation of when winter's browns are joined by that first hint of color as swelling flower buds become a cascade of blossoms. Who can resist burying their face in a fragrant bouquet of jasmine petals? Soon spring's blossoms are joined by a verdant emergence of bright, tender green shoots that scream of newness. Then they harden, darken, and fill in the landscape, covering winter's boney branches

as the plethora of heaven-scented petals becomes a tasty procession of berries, plums, apples, grapes, and the like. Soon the beauty of fall signals the Earth's need for rest and renewal. Foliage turns yellow, orange, and red, and leaves drop to feed soil and critters. Then to close the show, a freeze and a breeze hit, and a symphony of mulberry leaves drop to blanket the earth.

Of course, it's all happening at once—whiffing blossoms, harvesting tangerines and greens, grafting plum trees, making compost, and tuning into whatever the moment calls for. It's how one thing leads to the next in a connected system, like when harvesting Goumi berries leads to finger pruning, fruit thinning, and cleaning away leaf blight. Oh, and there's garlic to harvest and tomatoes to get in the ground. And on you go in a productive putter, tuning in, tinkering, and exploring the wealth of relations in a garden ecosystem.

Water

Water is life. As we grok the privilege and rarity of fresh, clean water, we must treasure it. There's the simple pleasure of rain on your skin. Noticing how it amplifies the vitality in a landscape does the same in you. Then there's playing in rain garden puddles and getting giddy over those first drops echoing off the bottom of your rain tank. Not to mention the luxury of a bath that becomes soooo much more when you pull the plug and, instead of going "away," it pulses through a wetland that feeds a forest of food, medicine, and beauty. Water renews life, soil, and spirit alike.

As the pied piper of all things water, Brock Dolman says, "Slow it, spread it, sink it, and store it." Instead of letting that sky water drain away, once we welcome it onto our land and into our lives, the magic starts to happen. With your structures set up to recycle your laundry, bath, and sink water and to store the rain, the ecosystem starts to feed itself. Healthy soil holds water better and grows stronger plants, which in turn hold more water in their roots, photosynthesizing sunshine, carbon dioxide, and water into bark, fruit, and leaves. These leaves shade and later feed the soil when they drop. Then when that out-of-season rain comes, the tanks, downspout, and soil are ready to receive and store the unexpected harvest to keep the system

thriving. Meanwhile, you can pause to appreciate the moisture in the air and the brief return of the leaves' luster. For emergency preparedness, it helps to have rain in the tank if the water quits coming out of the tap.

With two greywater systems, five catchment systems, and drip irrigation, we are a decent step towards catching and cycling water through our landscape. But once you start, you're hooked. We have plans for more catchment and greywater, getting our laundry tied to the rain tank and squeezing in a habitat pond. Since tanks fill up fast and the landscape may not need the rain in winter, offsetting indoor use is a great opportunity to use the rain and reduce outside water use.

An inch of rain on our roof is about 600 gallons of water. On our property, it's 4,500 gallons. In the city of Petaluma, it's 240 million gallons. Percolate on the potential of small, slow, decentralized water systems and green infrastructure solutions at scale. They can rehydrate our soil carbon sponge, regenerate our watersheds, and transform our lives and communities from ridge to river, with each property a micro watershed in a reverential rehydration revolution. In an era of extreme weather with both increasing drought and deluge, these solutions get all the more critical at all scales.

Structures

In the arc of human history, we've spent very little time inside. Part of the pop is having structures that feed your spirit, meet your needs, and pulse with life, all while harvesting rain and sun. It's greening our homes so they are healthy for us and cause no harm in the making.

One of my great joys is the art of creative reuse. Making or fixing stuff out of what's lying around, has been given to us, or was grown in the garden is ridiculously satisfying. Many things in our home and garden are from recycled or homegrown materials, be it reused clothes and kids' stuff, wood chips from the neighborhood, kindling, bottles, jars, or garden furniture. Or stuff that just shows up, like when a neighbor drops off a pile of oak flooring scraps for firewood, and we upcycle it into a table top.

Critters

Another part of what gets things popping is the critters. There's tending bees, chickens, ducks, or rabbits for nectar, food, fertility, and pest protection. There are the critters in the soil food web and the pollinators and predators that show up once there is ample food and habitat. This ranges from insects to native bees, birds, raptors, rats, and raccoons. It's creating space to connect with the nonhuman world, tuning into the hive mind when you keep bees and appreciating the loudly clucking pride of a chicken's first eggs of the season. It's the baby birds, big birds, and circling hawks that sometimes talk to us if we listen. Growing healthy soil, food, medicine, and habitat in a nontoxic environment sends a message to nature that you are valued here. Which is good since we are nature and we need this connection for emotional well-being and to pollinate and fertilize our food and soil.

It also creates conditions conducive for surprise encounters, like the night I stood on the sidewalk at dusk and got my mind blown when some crazy prehistoric-looking creature zipped up and dipped its long tongue into an evening primrose flower for a sip of nectar. Turns out it was a night-pollinating sphinx moth. Or when we hosted a class under our Asian Pear tree and a cicada joined the circle, ditching its exoskeleton on someone's backpack. In fourteen years and many thousands of hours in this garden, I rarely hear, let alone see, a cicada. And this one rocked up to our first ever personal ecology circle to ditch its old self, when we are literally talking about personal transformation and how community, a circle of support helps this? Nature is full of magic and mystery and hungers for us to tap into the regenerative powers of gardens, lives, and communities going pop.

Relations—Fences, Edges, and Burnt Tortillas

When these models start to spread and connect, a relational pop happens as a mosaic of eco-oases emerges, sharing inspiration, meals, plants, laughter, snails, and celebration. I couldn't say the number of times I opened our door to see plant starts, garden harvests, or recently a bottle of homemade limoncello. Our landscape is alive with stuff from other landscapes—plants, trees, pots, bricks, our chicken coop, recycled rain tanks, and more.

How we relate to fences and edges says a lot about how we relate to life. Are we walling off from the world and neighbors in privacy, a clean separation of me from you, us from them? Or are our boundaries more like nature—pervious, fluid, and conducive to connection? Do our edges invite others in to pause, appreciate beauty, or strike up a conversation? Share fruit over the fence? Maybe harvest your neighbor's roof water if they aren't using it?

Putting food, a free library, or a bench in the front yard creates a whole gamut of new interactions that lead to nourishing connections. Of course, I can no longer put a tortilla on the stove and run out for fresh greens to fill it. After many a burnt tortilla because of a passerby engaging me as I dashed out to harvest, I've learned to turn the stove off until I return. There's the time I was bent over picking basil and heard a gentle voice say, "Excuse me, sir." I turned to see a woman in a suit after a long work day, who sweetly said,

"I just wanted to let you know your garden makes me happy."

From happy strangers to converging neighbors for spontaneous happy hours, these gardens create good human habitat, too.

Then when crises hits, as they do more frequently, all these relations mean so much more. A study after Super Storm Sandy showed that a core quality of neighborhoods that were more resilient and bounced back quicker was social cohesion, or neighbor-to-neighbor connectedness.[26] It's having food in the ground and pantry, rain in the tank, your own seed bank, some energy resilience, and the skills, connections, and stuff to meet local needs.

Helping Roger bottle homemade wine from the grapes that shade his house.

Roger

One day this spicy old fella walking by starts sharing all the ways we could use our giant red leaf mustard for a meal. Little did I know a longtime friendship and mentorship was beginning. Long before we planted eco-anything, Roger was grafting thirteen varieties onto his driveway plum, keeping bees, and making wine from grapes that shade his house from the summer's heat. Roger was like a medicinal plant that could taste bitter but was good for you. Each bit of wisdom he imparted came with a few pokes, prods, and sighs. But under it was a heart of gold. We shared homegrown meals, homemade wine, and ample laughter. He always looked out for neighbors and commented when something needed attention in the garden or neighborhood. He just noticed more. He knew when to plant and harvest everything and could fix anything. I am frequently reminded of Roger, and after his passing, we became friends with his son Nate's family.

The Bonaguras

While I love my family, I didn't have much hope for eco-change in my close relations. But at some point, on family visits, my brother-in-law Rob started geeking out in the garden with me. Soon, every visit we were digging up herbs, flowers, and berries for him to take home. Before long, his front lawn was a third edible, then half, then the full tilt food forest boogie! There was the year a family of birds took up residence on his family's front door, making a nest in his wreath. Holidays got more fun as we'd head into the yard to see what plants he'd added, to prune and graft his fruit trees, install rain barrels, dry persimmons, and generally revel in inspired visions. Then Rob kicked it up a notch with beehives on the roof of his chicken coop, raising the holiday turkey, and becoming the neighborhood homestead store, selling honey, turkeys, jam, pomegranate juice, and more.

Handling Failures and Setbacks

Some folks think our permaculture oasis is a problem-free land of easy living, but there's always a to-do list with piles and projects. Sometimes I'm tired and just want to chill. It can feel like a constant struggle with life and schedule to get to what matters. There are times when the hives need a refresh, the chickens are getting old, and the rats and deer too comfortable. I think we've canned, jammed, planted, and processed everything a homegrown life could, but we rarely do it all or as much as I'd like. There are years when the sowing or harvest gets missed, and there's no canning, jamming, or kraut made. I've never had a great harvest for dilly beans or pickles and have let 1,500 gallons of rain drain from the tank by mistake. I've watched a faucet drip for a month until I measured it and found it was as much water as in

The Bonaguras' front
yard edible ecosystem.

our giant rain tank. Our greywater system shorted out our laundry machine. Plants have died. Young branches I've spent years tending have snapped because I didn't thin enough fruit. I've known the pain of cutting a blighted pear tree back to a stump after years of painstakingly grafting and training it into a beautiful espalier.

Like the death and decay that renews life's fertility, we must honor and learn from our failures and setbacks. As with the seasons and cycles, you just begin again. Rain tanks refill, you fix drips, give dilly beans another try, and graft and train anew. Just keep planting and returning with reverence. There's always a reframe to harvest, plants to share, or you turn clearing a weedy path into compost, food, or medicine. Batch of cider soured? That's a decade's worth of vinegar. Pile of debris? Habitat it or make a *hügelkultur* bed. Sometimes there's a community solution to your problems, like when a friend upcycles your unsightly piles into another garden's dream just when you hoped a spring breeze might whisk them away.

At times you may feel disconnected, overloaded, or just need a recharge. In most anything, it's amazing what just getting started can do. A walk around the garden quickly turns into sniffing, nibbling, and geeking out on whatever's buzzing about. Before you know it, you're on your knees weeding, pruning, and chatting with neighbors passing by, refreshed in connection and inspiration. Or maybe you just grab some soothing herbs, put 'em in a sock, toss it in the bath, and let your stresses melt away.

Weaving It All Together—Pops Big and Small

As with a peak experience, a garden going pop comes in many shapes and sizes. There are grand ones like that first spring, special bee swarm, or when my baby girl arrived in the middle of a workshop. There are timeless ones full of wonder, with a glistening raindrop, swooping hawk, or tree full of fragrant blossoms. There are small ones like growing something new. It's the spontaneous neighborhood happy hour or garden feast with the bounty of what everyone pitches in.

The excitement of first harvests or a trickle of rain in your new tank becomes the familial feel of seasonal visits from cherished friends. It's the daily meditation of breathing in the subtle shifts between big moments, like the slowly changing angle of the sun as it moves through the sky and, with it, the pulse of warmth, light, and life. Or my baby in diapers foraging for blueberries and bathing in a five-gallon bucket of rainwater, weaving willow fairy gardens and growing with the seasons. Sometimes it's the tingling aliveness of anticipating a pop, like in early December when the lemons are laden, but you're still patiently waiting because they're not quite ripe, not quite like the plump orange persimmons hanging naked on leafless trees. Or the pineapple guavas practically rolling down the street because we no longer see the subtle shifts or seasonal surplus. It's like when I speak to Mark

Cohen, who shared that first permaculture spark with me decades before. It never matters the time of day or year. I always feel his sense of wonder as he recounts whatever project or harvest he's in the middle of, the jams, sauces, and meads or the seasonal flavor shift in his winter garden greens.

As we rapidly move into an era with fewer resources and a moral imperative to leave a livable future for those to come, why not descend this peak resource moment with wholeness and our ethics intact? Contrary to lack or an "I gotta get mine" paradigm, a garden ready for harvest begs to be shared. Homegrown living is all the more amazing when you know the true cost of agribusiness dinners and car trips for imported fruit. Aside from declining resources and ecosystems, with people in debt to their eyeballs and dollars that don't go as far, it's wise to use less. We can do this while growing the real wealth of healthy, skilled, and prepared relations as well as rich, resilient lives, neighborhoods, and communities that are more lush, productive, and sustaining.

The gift and challenge of tuning into the seasons is that it pushes against the busy schedules and habits of a consumer culture that has grown disconnected from the living world. Our attention is occupied by a maelstrom of distractions and individually wrapped plastic crap. But what a delight it is when we make space for what brings us alive and nourishes our connections. We do have enough time for what matters when we prune what doesn't meaningfully contribute to our lives, loved ones, and world.

Why not make tuning into the seasons, tending our relations, and living in rhythm our culture and future? Why not feed and infect friends, family, and strangers on the street with a well-loved life? With proper placement in heart, mind, and taste buds, these conditions conducive to life can thrive.

From Garden to a Glimpse of Scaling

Working at this small scale is relatable, accessible, and achievable. It's returning power to the people by decentralizing our systems of energy, food, water, health, economy, and politics. This spreads a lived-in eco-literacy of care, connection, and regeneration throughout a community one person and one garden at a time. Such regenerative mini-ecosystems can nourish at the deepest levels of human motivation. And what better way to change your life and world than by recentering in your inspiration and nature's operating instructions?

Inspiration is a divine wind that flows through us.

When we listen, we know how to find it. It's like raptors riding a thermal; that invisible current of uplift that puts wind in their wings. When we tap into the flow, the pop, the genius of where our inspiration meets nature's wisdom, much is possible.

The lessons learned in a garden can then be applied to drive systemic change in organizations, coalitions, and networks, to build collective power for social change. In the garden we infect people—from neighbors to mayors and lawmakers—with an alive, tasty, palpable vision of what's possible. Then we make it so by growing more gardens, people, and groups who feel the uplift and start propagating the programs, partnerships, and policies to spread these things. In short, we move from understanding the garden as a network of communities to recreating community as a network of gardens. That's what's next.

Planting community. Sebastopol City Hall. Photo: Jay Swetech

Inspire
Educate
Activate
Transform
daily acts
because every choice matters
SRJC PD

Chapter 17:

When Small Groups Go Pop—
Coming into Cadence

That day years ago, when I picked up the phone to hear Senator McGuire's inspired hot damn salutations, it was more than a gathering. I was finalizing details for a government and grassroots panel at the first combined North America Permaculture Convergence and Northern California Building Resilient Communities Convergence. This merged convening came out of a conversation the year before at the International Transition Towns Gathering.

I'm still a bit amazed at how partnering with local government has been a pathway to transformative change that increased Daily Acts' joy, capacity, and impact. These relationships have been essential in going from installing one permitted greywater system, to five in a day in a neighborhood, to thirteen in two cities in a weekend, and later a 100 Greywater System Challenge while helping to shift California state policy. Through city and community partnerships is how we went from one yard to dozens of landscapes at libraries, parks, schools, churches, and city halls while helping to innovate a city program to transform over 500 lawns, saving tens of millions of gallons of water per year. The power of community and civic collaborations took us from the scary-to-mention goal of planting 350 gardens in a weekend to catalyzing tens of thousands of resilience-building actions and projects.

Underlying our evolution was the deeper *why* of inspiring transformative action through the power of small actions, gardens, and groups. People showed up to learn about water conservation but were actually hungry for connection to like hearts and minds. Programmatically, our *what* evolved from inspiring people with a vision through educational tours to skill-building workshops to transforming chemical, resource-intensive lawns into eco-oases. Once we transformed one landscape, given the times, we naturally pondered, how can we do LOTS more? This led to community mobilizations and shifting civic programs and policies for wider change.

A *why* and *what* capable of unleashing the power of community to spread transformative solutions needs an effective *how*, that is, collaboration and co-creation. Asking "What would get others to play?" naturally moves you from ego to eco. Like in the maturing complexity of a garden ecosystem, coalitions, alliances, and networks form the next level of relationship and engagement on the pathway to change at scale. A simple tour can change lives, empowering people with a vision and pathway. Once exposed to a compelling idea, people need the skills, relationships, and confidence to take action. Start small with inspiration, good relations, and a practical example to build from.

We Plant Gardens

With so much hurt and uncertainty, ethical and ecological principles that are timeless and true are grounding, guiding, and reassuring. Gardens rooted in such principles can teach us about transformation and about community coming into cadence.

Like the succession of natural systems, our first food forest at the Cavanagh Center evolved through time, adding complexity and richness to the landscape, neighborhood, and community. Seasonal workshops have taught people to prune, propagate, install rainwater catchment, and build with the Earth. We've had permaculture and leadership courses here. Signage and a beautiful mural painted by students inspires and educates passersby. A local organization serving systematically disenfranchised youth planted themselves here. Neighbors have hired our business partners to install landscapes modeled after this garden. It has been a catalyst for love and remembrance with first date rainwater workshops ending in marital bliss

We Plant Gardens

In response to drought, fire, and flood, we plant gardens.

For food insecurity, homelessness, COVID, and climate emergency, we plant gardens.

We plant gardens to grow food, medicine, habitat, and beauty.

We plant gardens to save water, catch water, recycle water, and recharge stormwater.

We plant gardens to save money and emissions, to harvest carbon, and to

sequester atmospheric inspiration out of strangers and thin air.

We plant gardens to change landscapes and lives, hearts and minds, diets and values.

We plant gardens to build relationships, build businesses, and build power.

We plant gardens to grow organizations, coalitions, and movements.

We plant gardens to change policy and the structures that govern us.

We plant gardens to bring people together, from grandmothers and kids to

eco-warriors who cloak their superhero garb beneath professional attire.

We plant gardens because tapping into the regenerative powers of nature and

community is a nourishing, kick-ass bucket of fun.

and neighbors who've passed away but live on through their contributions to this garden. On the corner, a young inspired do-gooder showed up and soon became a volunteer, then staff (where his coworker became his wife) before leaving to direct a permaculture program, start a cider company, and later return to join our board. I love watching kids wander through, sucking the nectar out of flowers, checking for ripe figs, apricots, and plums, and I love the seasonal swarm of humans harvesting elderberries for medicine. While the countless positive ripples have been astonishing, it has all felt familiar to that first backyard immersion, that first tour, special swarm, and so many other experiences of community coming into cadence.

And these are just a few stories from one of thirty-seven public demonstration gardens we've planted, saving over 6.2 million gallons of water in addition to creating numerous other benefits. If you factor in civic policies and programs influenced, and action campaigns, dozens of landscapes become thousands. Like in a garden, a strong guild of partners is what makes each project flourish. It's local and regional agencies, landscape professionals, businesses, and engaged community members. From here we spread these models through neighborhoods, cities, and counties, waking people to their potential while regenerating nature and community. We grow more inspired, connected, and unstoppable leaders and groups and a more eco-literate and engaged citizenry. Together, these things build the social infrastructure of powerful, connected organizations and movements able to change lives and communities. Taking an integrated eco-design approach with holistic gardens can start to rewire the siloed, disconnected way in which people, organizations, and agencies think. This is the biggest shift in the paradigm or thinking that informs society's rules, structures, and culture.

We Mobilize Gardens

Start small with an example of your vision and get a win. This builds skills, relationships, confidence, and momentum. Then just keep stepping into the moment. This got us from transforming a teeny patch of police station lawn to a modest city hall landscape to creating a neighborhood food forest to transforming a 25,000-square-

Planting the Petaluma Library Living Learnscape. Photo: Leslie Curchack

foot city hall lawn in a day to mulching more turf and saving more water in months than in years of programs, all while in the height of a drought. These projects ranged from working with a youth crew to convert thirty lawns in thirty days to transforming 60,000 square feet in a day with mulch, music, and massage tables, ultimately saving 1.6 million gallons of water while winning awards for our local business partner. Every ounce of this came from an incredible array of partners and sometimes unexpected ones.

The right action campaign at the right time with the right goals and allies can align and unleash diverse stakeholders in astonishing ways. It's heartening and empowering to feel and be a part of something larger. Given the times, we NEED this. We need to experience setting audacious goals and unleashing the power of community to achieve and exceed our dreams. What started with the outlandish idea of planting 350 gardens in a weekend swelled to near 100,000 resilience-building actions and projects, well over 200 times what was a scary-to-speak goal. This morphed into other campaigns, some more successful, some less. While imperfect, all in all, such campaigns are an elegantly simple, low-cost way to empower communities and spread collaborative models.

Engaging the wisdom and skill of many people and communities is critical to addressing the climate crisis. Dream big and boldly throw yourself at living your vision. Find mentors and partners ready to share insights and connections and rally together to make things happen.

We Throw Parties…in Gardens

One warm summer night, I stood in the garden surrounded by food, beauty, and one hundred friends, leaders, and allies. Pizzas flew out of the cob oven, and beverages flowed as we celebrated Daily Acts' top supporters. I noticed Nancy visibly bubbling as she started to tell me this story of her family's Community Resilience Challenge project and how they transformed their front yard into a beautiful water-wise garden with a community bench and a free library. This led to a swarm of activity ranging from young girls sitting on their bench eating strawberries from the landscape while reading books from the free library to cars stopping in the street. Nancy and Jim felt like movie stars. Then Nancy shared something crazy. Since installing their garden, they have met more neighbors in three months than in the three decades they've lived there. I couldn't believe my ears. This was one of over 7,000 local Community Resilience Challenge actions that year. They were saving 10,000 gallons of water per month in the summer while creating beauty, food, habitat, and community. Plus, by partnering with Weaving Earth, the students who installed the garden were learning eco-design skills.

This all started with Nancy sitting at Ripple the World and hearing Judy tell the

Mary Heckman serving up tasty cob-oven pizza.

Daily Acts team and friends prepping to celebrate our relations. Photo: Deb Wilson

story about how, since getting involved with Daily Acts (at the Cavanagh garden), she had transformed her front yard and, in the process, met more neighbors in a year than in twenty years in her neighborhood! Even better, she hired a daily actor, who built his landscape business off teaching for Daily Acts.

How we went from a mostly unfunded organization to taking low-cost, low-tech, nature-inspired, and people-powered solutions to scale was by starting with an inspiring vision, getting a win to show what's possible, partnering widely, and then continuing to level up with a bolder vision, bigger wins, more partners, and more fun. Like building soil to help a garden flourish, the fruit of success came from tending the stuff below the surface. This brings us back to the core values that make an organization's inner garden go pop. It's starting with reverence, reclaiming the power of our ripples, and nurturing our relations. We did all this while adapting and persevering with joy.

Chapter 18

Tending the Stuff Below the Surface

Growing and sustaining organizations, networks, and movements is tough. But like getting the right elements in place for the garden to pop, we can do the same in our groups. Over two decades in Daily Acts, and all the coalitions we've been part of, it has mostly come down to this: deepening our values and refining our operating principles, practices, and cultural norms, aka modeling how to take heart and take action while nurturing our relations. This becomes the shared pathfinding of working with others to hone a vision and voice through consistency of action and wise self-management. It's how we act with each other—with compassion, consideration, and courage. Taking action to nurture relationships with your constituents and with the wider world is a constant call and response that builds resilience and requires it.

Sweet Spot—What You Love, What You Are Good at, and the Resources to Sustain

The difficult work of finding and following one's North Star gets more complicated at an organizational scale. You must find your sweet spot, which is a deep understanding of three intersecting circles: your passion, what you are good at, and what sustains you. Honing your organizational compass by reflecting and envisioning from a heart space takes place in a variety of ways. From personal modeling to shared pathfinding with a team and partners, it happens in all manner of meetings, retreats, and inspired conversations. Once clear on vision and values, align your goals and how you measure success. Then remove barriers and provide the support for people to act. This looks different in a volunteer-powered startup phase versus with staff, a governing board, coalition partners, or when working across sectors and movements.

Dreaming big and setting goals commensurate with your challenges is vital, but what sustains through time is commitment, process, and consistency of effort. Take heart, take action, assess, recalibrate, repeat. And pay constant attention for when to change. This includes knowing what to do, what not to do, and having the discipline not to do the stuff that creates negative impacts.

Over the years, Daily Acts has evolved a lot in how we set direction and recalibrate. There have been many missed marks and imperfect tools, from jotting our vision and goals on scraps of paper and in journals to spreadsheets and polished thirty-page plans. What has worked through time is consistently setting a vision, turning it into a plan and schedule, and regularly checking in to recalibrate and adapt. But getting your group to pop and to keep it popping is also about culture.

Creating Culture Change

Culture is how people do things. It defines who and how you are, your outlook, values, and the customs that inform how you see the world. Culture derives from the Latin *colere*, which means to tend the earth, to cultivate, and grow. At its best, culture is a protective force that cares for and shelters us. It helps us make sense of things and deal with difficulty. Culture shows us how to behave and what's not okay. When they are successful, leaders, organizations, and movements naturally create cultural change.

To contribute their best, people need to feel safe, connected, cared for, and a part of something larger. Organizations need clear agreements on behavior, attitude, and performance. It's being compassionate and supportive and having courageous conversations when issues arise.

Through time, it became clearer what contributed to a healthy culture and our impact and what didn't. It was investing in the development of our people and a re-view process to provide support and accountability. Where tension exists, especially in small groups working with whoever shows up, is leaning into the truth of getting the right people on the bus. A community-nurturing approach can make it hard to have courageous conversations when people are acting in a way that's damaging to them, those around them, and your group. As you have honest conversations, unhealthy aspects of your culture start to change, but it can be painfully slow.

Courageous Conversations

Courageous conversations are authentic, honest discussions on difficult topics. They are often associated with race, class, and power dynamics. It means talking about real stuff with family, friends, coworkers, and even strangers. But the most important conversations start with ourselves. Am I living my truth? Am I looking with honest eyes and an open heart at this bigger moment? Am I pointing fingers at others and the world around me without owning my part? Am I giving my power away? Such reflections can help us live more aligned with what we are here to contribute.

It can be scary and uncomfortable to have such conversations. Working in the grassroots with volunteers and small groups, it's easy to think, "Take it easy on the poor, overworked, and underpaid do-gooders." But it's critical to have such conversations in organizational and movement work and even in everyday living. With rapidly increasing crises, fear, and political division, there's a lot to talk about. It's messy and hard. But meaningful dialogue is an important part of how change happens and issues get addressed.

Early on I thought success meant that people would stay forever as one big happy family. I felt sadness and failure when this wasn't the case. Waiting too long to have courageous conversations creates unnecessary stress and discord, often for both parties. Ultimately, being a pushover on poor behavior or performance isn't good for anyone or for the critical work of remaking the world. I've seen too many groups, coalitions, and projects lose good people because of not being able or willing to address difficulties and damaging behaviors. It creates tolerance for behavior that drives people away and isn't conducive to healthy, inspired people who are empowered to live and give their best. This is about holding each other and ourselves accountable to how we show up from a place of love, compassion, and respect for the urgent work that too often gets sidetracked by ego drama.

This is difficult stuff, even more so when working across scales, values, and leadership styles. To truly transform our communities and world, we need a mosaic of connected leaders, groups, and movements who understand and value difference, be it cultural, institutional, or whatever. We need to invest in the social infrastructure of groups, networks, and alliances in the way we invest in the physical infrastructure of roads and buildings. This involves training in leadership skills, mind-body medicine practices, and developing the cultural humility to work across difference and in a trauma-informed way. We must recognize that many people have deep layers of trauma in their lives and histories and aim not to re-traumatize each other. For the many challenges we face, it also means there are a BAZILLION ways to make a difference.

Centering Transformative Practices

Finding personal practices to help you sustain in the work is ongoing. At an organizational scale, this is even more challenging. It wasn't until Daily Acts centered these practices in our strategic priorities, culture, and common activities that this ability to stay nourished and inspired, even in the face of ongoing difficulty, became more consistent across the organization. This is where our collective inner garden started to pop, where we became a community of practice that could help the whole recenter and reconnect to our power, supporting team members to carry this work into other parts of their lives.

Providing space for mindfulness practices before meetings can go a long way to help people get present and bring their best. Personal check-ins help a group sense where each person is. This builds care, connection, and safety, all critical to teams

Fresh jasmine flower altar during team Mind-Body Medicine Training. Photo: Sarina Consulter

and organizations, especially where there is lots of change. It also matters because people's personal struggles easily carry over into their work.

Beyond regular practices, deeper dives help teams calibrate and build skills and meaningful connection. This could be monthly, seasonal, or as needed. Ours begin with meditation, reflection, and journaling on key compass questions. There's often a deeper check-in and educational or skill-building element like addressing emotional triggers and self-assessment tools for personal wellness. We are always experimenting and evolving these practices. We've done two-week *Be the Change Challenges*, an eight-week mind, body, medicine program, and a series of trainings that integrated anti-racist education with mind-body practices to increase self-awareness for navigating unconscious reactivity, bias, and historical trauma in our bodies.

Daily Actors making pizza: Liz, Marie, Nichole, Brianna, Susan, and Sarah

It's tough enough to solve the world's problems. Why make it more difficult with the small stuff? By developing a shared understanding and language about things like emotional triggers, we can better know ourselves and each other and address problems in a proactive way, whether it's the big stuff or knowing that speaking with food in your mouth REALLY triggers a coworker. Such practices create opportunities to build trust, understanding, and good communication in nonurgent situations. So when things get difficult, the basis to voice and resolve issues is present.

Even with great practices, people still get stressed and overwhelmed. But there's something powerfully different when, at an organizational or group scale, you invest in clarifying and living your values and in helping teams develop deeper personal connections and when, through time and effort, you make this your culture. When you do, people have greater resilience and ability not to get lost in the noise, hurt, or hard work. Or they recenter more quickly. There's more often a soft acceptance and detachment, not getting overtaken by one's problems or triggers. Handling difficulty with grace empowers others to see they can do the same. On the flipside, having the psychological safety for folks to express vulnerability is equally powerful.

There is an array of benefits to getting teams skilled in transformative practices. Like the synergy of getting the right elements in a garden, such efforts feed and reinforce each other, supporting people to contribute their best. Learning these skills helps people maintain health and happiness, develop as stronger leaders, and stay grounded, effective, and even grateful in tough times. It also helps people more quickly recalibrate when stress and overwhelm do take over.

Choosing to stay awake and engaged in this moment is no small thing. It's easy to want to pull the covers over your head, to numb, distract, and disengage. To truly transform ourselves and our communities, developing such practices and communities of practice in our lives, organizations, and movements are vital. While these are internal to Daily Acts, they are also embedded in our messaging, programs, coalitions, and leadership training programs.

From Relations to Your Resource Engine

Once you are producing inspiring results centered in your passion and purpose while nurturing your people and honing your systems, things start to pop. This creates conditions to unleash the genius of your community—the physical, financial, and emotional resources that enable growth and transformation. While passion and purpose are the currency that drives many a do-gooding group, a viable resource model is critical to long-term success. Three primary resources are time, money, and commitment. Time is attracting people who will contribute to your cause for free or at a reduced rate. Money is, well, money. Commitment is how well your organization cultivates a deep emotional bond with supporters.

Like a garden needs water, the work needs financial resources. Frustrated by greed and a money-focused material society, small groups can unconsciously repel money or just not prioritize developing a strong resource engine. Start with your relationship to money. As fundraiser extraordinaire, Lynn Twist, has written, what we appreciate appreciates. Even in urgent times and with your piled high to-do list, make the

time to tend to relationships and build long-term commitments. To inspire people to contribute and be a part of your work, you often need to *speak to the heart but satisfy the head*. This means establishing a connection to your purpose, vision, and values while articulating your impact. Raising money is not something separate from what you do; it needs to be your mission in action. Whether at a program, when fundraising, or in how you thank donors, build this muscle of embodiment through more of your activities.

There are a range of ways nonprofits sustain themselves. Daily Acts has developed numerous funding streams through time, from program fees to business sponsorships, grants, contracts, fees for services, and donors. The three legs of our financial foundation have been donations, government contracts, and grants. For many small groups, developing a strong base of donors can be critical to all aspects of your resource engine, from volunteering to donating and inspiring others to connect to your work via their passionate commitment.

Most importantly, don't be afraid to ask. Most people don't want to ask for money. But you are serving a larger purpose and gifting people the opportunity to be part of this. It's a chance to move through your fears, move important work forward, and embody your mission.

Evolution through Time of Donor Care and Cultivation

While Ripple the World, our annual 600-person fundraiser, is a bright, shining beacon that raises money, reinvigorates our team, and builds community, fundraising is not a once-a-year thing. Just as that big fall garden harvest is a part of a year-round cycle of stewardship, cultivating the relationships that help organizations flourish is too. It takes a while to understand and act on this when you are trying to figure it all out. But through time you can create a richer, more complex, fruitful, and resilient ecosystem. By applying the right principles, we can rapidly accelerate the natural succession in gardens and the grassroots.

Changing your relationship to money while developing financial streams and an ecosystem of supporters can take years. At the start and end of the day, it's about relationships, results, and improving your systems. Cultivating and caring for your people and partners is important to all three of these things. At Daily Acts, we initially learned about the idea of a system of year-round donor care and cultivation through Benevon, a mission-centered fundraising model. It took years to evolve this. Our annual 600-person gala led to smaller events to thank and celebrate donors and keep them connected. This led to donors creating other fundraising and program activities, which further strengthened their engagement and commitment and brought more donor-volunteer-advocates.

As we deepened our donor care and connection, we committed to tending to the donors we had. I remember being excited to get a $1,000 donation from a longtime participant. While we had a handful of donors in this range, I hadn't prioritized connecting with them to let them know the impact their support would have. So I met with this donor to enthusiastically thank him. The next thing I knew, he donated $32,000 from his family foundation. I was astounded by what this gift meant to a small organization. It was a big lesson in remembering to appreciate and care for who you have. All those years, I was busily on to the next thing. You only have so much time. Spend it wisely. Finding and caring for major donors can be important to sustain and grow the work.

Nurture the hell out of your people in a way that is beautifully true to you. In the early days, I'd sprinkle flower petals in donor envelopes. This led to other creative touches, like love notes on letters, immediately calling and thanking volunteers and donors after an event, and sending hundreds of thank you letters and cards. It's sitting around a table together to stamp hearts, draw flowers, or write words of gratitude for donors big and small. In a world of disconnection, automation, and lack of human touch, I want people's hearts to melt when they open their letter or card. I want new major donors to be astounded when they get a call within hours of a huge event that started and ended on time and was packed with love, inspiration, community, and hope for the future.

While calls, meetings, and notes became important to our culture of care, connection, and gratitude, so did throwing big, fun parties that oozed our mission in action. Who would think thanking people could be so damn fun? It was like that first time stepping into a permaculture garden oasis, except with one hundred top supporters, pizzas sizzling in the oven, music, and tasty local food and beverages. Sometimes we'd sprinkle in a neighborhood garden tour or sustainability scavenger hunt, with folks running the streets looking for food forests, chickens, rainwater catchment, and other eco-savvy goodies. There was the year our mayor walked into the garden amidst a buzz of activity with a smile of surprise on her face as she saw our state assembly member playing guitar. It was now Congressman Jared Huffman's first public performance, rocking out in a backyard garden.

Earlier I told the story Nancy shared with me about how transforming her landscape as part of the Resilience Challenge led to meeting more neighbors in three months than in three decades. After their experience, her family became long-term committed donors, leading to more garden parties that eventually inspired them to host a house party. That party was Mary McCammon's first Daily Acts event. When she saw Nancy's little library and heard the stories of neighborly connection, she took action, repurposing an old baby crib into a little library box. Weeks later she wrote, "I am not going to lie; we expected vandalism due to past actions in our neighborhood. However, quite the opposite has happened. So many neighbors

The legendary Julie Young writing love notes to Daily Actors.

(who have NEVER spoken to us in the seventeen years we have lived here) have now come out to ask questions, make donations, and leave encouraging notes of thanks! People have slowed their cars and shouted out their support! Wow! So it really does work!"

This is the kind of transformation that comes from simple ripples, starting with Judy showing up at the neighborhood food forest and then transforming her garden, which inspired Nancy, who then inspired Mary. All three of them have inspired hundreds, maybe thousands of others, all while getting connected to community in a way that hadn't happened in decades and strengthening their relationship to and support of Daily Acts. Whatever slice of world-changing goodness you seek to grow and spread, nurturing your relations is key to a viable operating model and resource engine as well as to a richer, more resilient community.

The drought-busting crew that transformed thirty lawns in thirty days.

Chapter 19

When Movements Go Pop—Nurturing Networks

The better world being born is richly messy and emergent. But we can learn to dance well with the chaos. Here are some systems change strategies from the Center for Ecoliteracy to help do so:

- Foster community and cultivate networks.
- Work at multiple scales.
- Make space for self-organizing.
- Seize breakthrough opportunities when they arise.
- Facilitate, but give up the illusion that you can direct change.
- Assume change is going to take time.
- Be prepared to be surprised when a small ripple turns into a wave of transformation.

There is an iterative action learning that occurs as you put vision into action and build relations in a community ecosystem. By engaging your people and those in power, you get to understand how systems work and can adapt and hone your approach. As Daily Acts evolved from tours to workshops, gardens, and action campaigns, we moved toward understanding a larger whole and our part in affecting it. This is where networks, alliances, and coalitions come in, where we start to build structures of shared leadership and collective power.

Gatherings as a Systems Change Catalyst

Gatherings act as a catalyst for a number of these systems change insights. Engaging in multiple gatherings through time can seed a further emergence and evolution in and between movements, bridging difference and scale.

The evolution in the permaculture and Transition Town movements over a five- or six-year span is an example of how movements can evolve and intermingle. In 2011, two years after joining the board of Transition US, I attended the International Transition Towns Conference in Liverpool, England. I was in a session for groups outside of the UK, with transitioners from around the world pouring in. While most groups were from the UK and Europe, the movement had spread with a growing contingent from most continents. Like a pot of water set to boil, there was a buzz in the air. As I glanced at our host, movement co-founder Ben Brangwyn, I saw surprise in his eyes as he reoriented to a bigger-than-expected crowd. So I offered support. By the end of the hour, we'd scheduled another session later in the day, after which, sensing the need to seize the moment, a small group of us kept the conversation alive into the night. Then with a burst of enthusiasm, a fellow attendee named Filipa volunteered to coordinate Transition in other countries. We approached the founders with the idea, and with the decentralized "accept all offers" ethos of the movement, they agreed. I can't say we were thinking about systems change strategies like supporting self-organizing, fostering networks, and working at multiple scales; we were just following our inspiration.

Two years later, another movement space was about to boil. This time it was 400 activists from sixty countries at the International Permaculture Conference. Since permaculture is said to be revolution disguised as gardening, it fits that we were at the Hotel Habana Libre where Fidel Castro launched Cuba's revolution. Two things from that conference stood out. The first was when the room erupted after members of Movement Generation passionately spoke about centering justice in our collective work. The second was seeing a map of Permaculture UK's formal network of farms, gardens, and demonstration sites. When I saw the image, instantly, a disparate bunch of sites became a big, connected, powerful network. Suddenly I saw a greater whole. THIS was how to spread models and empower and engage many more folks, sharing resources and communications. We were already part of this rapidly growing Transition Town movement as well as local networks, but this was the next level of potential.

Two more years passed, and this international stew of world changers was at it again. This time the permaculture and Transition movements scheduled back-to-back gatherings for overlap. As I stepped into the rural, South England sunshine, I felt a sense of heightened joy and possibility. I spent the morning connecting with fifty grassroots leaders from twenty-five national Transition hubs around the world. Things had come a long way in the four years since four of us sat around that late-night Liverpool table envisioning what could be, and the founders chose to dance.

Over the weekend in that same sunny spot, a few of us were again sensing into the moment when an idea sprouted. What if we combined the biannual North American Permaculture Convergence with the Northern California Regional Resilient Communities Convergence? Two years before, this regional convening was itself a merger of separate annual permaculture and Transition Town gatherings.

The next year saw this first combined national and regional gathering. At it came gains in bridging differences between grassroots and government, between social justice advocates and Earth stewards, and the launch of the Norcal Resilience Network.

Big things happen
in small moments
of inspired connection.

Movements emerge and evolve as intimate groups engage in late-night strategy sessions around a table, a fire, in a hot tub under the stars, or between workshop sessions. It's about showing up, connecting, and leaning into what seeks to emerge. The intrinsic richness of such gatherings has many of the self-rewarding aspects of a flow state or the infectious feel of a garden going pop and can have a transformative effect, building stronger, more connected movements.

Movement Evolutions

Between occasional bright spot experiences like gatherings that hatch grand insights and nourish connections, there is a ton of work to growing organizations, networks, and movements. While there's no one-size-fits-all approach to systems change, here are a few examples of how movements emerge and evolve. Each has a different growth strategy, including the role of organizations that influence and support these evolutions. As we've touched on with permaculture and throughout this book, recognizing patterns is important for learning. This feels good and drives focus because it releases dopamine in our brains. So, as we turn unknowns and abstractions—like nature's form and function and the intricacies of social change—into things we can relate with, our brains release more feel-good chemicals that further drive motivation, focus, and understanding.

It's amazing what a teacher and a handful of students can do to spark global movements. Rob Hopkins, who wrote the *Transition Handbook* that seeded the Transition Movement, was teaching permaculture at a small college in Ireland when he worked up the Transition ideas with his students. Before becoming the largest climate-focused organization on the planet (at the time), 350.org had a similar start. It began with author Bill McKibben and a group of college students he was teaching. Recognizing that no climate plan stood a chance without public will, they went about mobilizing action and building a global movement. This spurred the next generation of youth organizers in the fossil fuel divestment movement, which helped launch the Sunrise Movement and other efforts.

Permaculture and Transition Town groups have grown by casting seeds in organic, decentralized ways. A natural emergence of national Transition hubs supported this growth, which further evolved through developing the international hub network. At the same time, growing clusters of local permaculture and Transition groups led to the above-mentioned regional gatherings that eventually merged.

As the climate movement grew, a small wing of it inserted a powerful one-word intent into its center: justice. The Climate Justice Alliance (CJA) and allies changed the narrative and focus of the climate movement. Different than a seed dispersal strategy, CJA targeted their growth, slowly and thoughtfully brought groups in, and focused on the analysis and strategy needed to build power, change narratives, and influence movements.

One pattern in network organizations is the power and influence of strong local groups on a larger network or movement. It's the Bright Spot strategy of *see what's working and then learn from and implement it*. Movement Generation, a thought leader in the Climate Justice Movement and one of the founders of the Climate Justice Alliance, helped bring justice to the center of the larger climate movement, influencing leaders, funders, and wider thinking.

An additional pattern in movement ecosystems is the role of support organizations in training and providing backbone services or thought leadership. Occidental Arts and Ecology Center is an example that supports communities and movement organizations, as they have with Movement Generation, Daily Acts, and many others. They do this in a range of ways—from providing retreat space to permaculture trainings, group facilitation, mentorship, and even facilitating connections to funders who have supported movement-leading organizations.

Another example is how 350.org supported the 2019 global youth climate strikes in 185 countries. They provided backbone support for this emerging movement, managing logistics, organizing volunteers, doing trainings, and connecting strikers with a coalition of hundreds of organizations. Like with the dancing fool, it's knowing when to jump in, to encourage self-organizing, seize opportunities, mobilize, and nourish this collective immune response.

Movement Challenges
—Field Notes from the Jungles of the Egosystem

While we can regenerate nature and change the world with the lessons from gardens and dancing fools, to grow strong networks and movements, the real work is with the messiness of us humans. A key lesson from nature and networks is about connection. As has happened so often over the years, once we start noticing and acknowledging such things, the living world responds to us at key moments. Just as I wrote this insight about nature connection, a bird flew so close to my head that I could feel the breeze from its wing beats through a thick hood.

When we're repelled by the dominant cultural paradigm destroying our people and planet, it's natural to want to change the values of self-interest, wealth concentration, and hierarchical power structures, focusing instead on shared-interest and decentralized structures. But money, hierarchy, and self-interest aren't inherently bad. They do a lot of good when in service to Earth care, people care, and ensuring a fair share for all.

Something that seems to influence the types of organizing structures and strategies that groups employ is our relationship to privilege and power. I've relished listening to friend and ally Davin Cardenas, the co-founder of North Bay Organizing Project (NBOP), speak about self-interest as a core organizing principle to build power. He talks about how self-interest is a process of self-discovery and discovery of others, getting in touch with the motor that moves you while understanding the needs of others. Davin and NBOP came out of the Gamaliel Foundation network lineage. I've heard this lens echoed listening to Mary Gonzales of Gamaliel nearly tear down the walls of a hall with the thundering force of her words about building organizations that build power—as opposed to the sentiment I've felt in

more White, eco-focused movement spaces where leadership and power seemed like dirty words.

Too often we aren't comfortable with our own power. We may even wield a power greater than we know. As a White male coming from a regenerative permaculture perspective, it's easier for me to focus on solutions. I was born with power and privilege in a way I didn't understand for a long time. I haven't been oppressed because of my skin color or gender. Our country's wealth wasn't built on the stolen land or labor of my ancestors. I have a different, more privileged relationship to power.

Power shows up in many forms within how organizations organize themselves. In eco-social organizing circles, flat and "leaderless" groups and shared leadership are often a spoken ideal, and hierarchies have a bad rap. But you can as easily have dysfunctional, ego-driven, flat organizations, or servant leadership hierarchies. Regardless of your structure, if people don't have agency and voice on important matters, that is, if they don't feel safe, heard, and valued, you probably won't be as happy or effective. This doesn't mean dancing on eggshells around issues or egos; it means more courageous conversations. In grassroots spaces, I've heard idealistic activists talk about nonprofit industrial complex in regards to small organizations that barely have two nickels to rub together. I've seen a board of directors nearly come undone because people thought they were doing the work of the movement's founder in arguing against fundraising and that the organization would magically sustain itself. Ego-driven power grabs can come under the banner of decentralized, leaderless organizing. Movements lose good people because they don't want to deal with this dysfunction or can't afford to volunteer all the time. To rise to this moment, our groups and movements need to quit shooting ourselves in the foot with our unprocessed issues around money and power. We also need to compassionately and collectively heal our traumas and embrace a healthier relationship with money and power.

Yes, we need to decentralize and spread power and resources through communities, to nurture networks, self-organize, and all the rest. But to really drive systems change, to sustain gatherings and nourish movements, we also need to centralize some power and resources in our organizations and networks. To effectively engage and transform existing power structures, we have to invest in the social infrastructure of our movements and leadership.

Activist/author, Naomi Klein, has defended the right of young movements to choose amorphous structures and later come to realize that "the rebellion against any kind of institutionalization is not a luxury today's transformative movements can afford." Similarly, leadership author, Meg Wheatley, has noted the need for some hierarchy, a structure not usually associated with self-organizing systems, because while networks don't have hierarchy, self-organizing requires sane leaders. We need volunteer-based groups and decentralized movements that can rapidly spread ideas and action, and we need organizations and networks that can pay people a living wage and provide training on things like self-care, emotional intelligence, cultural humility, and building shared power.

Call it grit or what you will, but what seems to move things forward the most is unrelenting folks who keep showing up and stepping up. They have a high threshold for pain, frustration, and complexity. They are focused but open, balance self-interest and shared interest, and bring their strengths while tapping into their Spidey senses to think and act from the whole. It's a matter of sharing power, building the power of others, and importantly owning your power…and privilege. This all demands cultural change.

"We are entering an age in which leaders of the future will face a series of disruptions, breakdowns and turbulence that will be unparalleled by anything that has happened in the past.

So what matters now is how we prepare the people who will end up in key leadership positions over the next decade or two, how well they are networked across systems and sectors, how well they listen, how creative they are in turning problems into opportunities."

—Otto Scharmer, Katrin Kaufer

Returning to the Garden

Since thinking and acting on all of this nearly melts my mind, I frequently return to my source for clarity and connection, aka my garden and stool. Here it's simple— it's all connected; it's all alive. Life is emergent and simultaneously operates at a range of scales. A flower or bee doesn't lose who it is or what it does. You don't have to overthink how systems change happens because the garden naturally moves you from ego to eco by reconnecting you to nature's operating instructions. The garden can be a muse, mentor, and source of wisdom in working with complex systems. Part of it is just being present and responding to the season and need at hand, be it harvesting fruit, peering in wonder at a baby chick in the bushes, or at a rarely seen cicada that decides to ditch its exoskeleton on your backpack. It's exciting to explore and embrace what's emerging as you tune into the living, breathing landscape. We are physically wired to wonder, with our survival instincts helping us find fulfillment in the new and embracing uncertainty.

Even the human networks that can be so confusing and challenging make more sense in the garden. Often between sowing, harvesting, and whatever calls for attention, I'm taking calls with allies, officials, and leaders at a range of scales. There are meetings, interviews, kids' parties, dinner parties, donor parties…and can we just have more parties? I'm working with the emergence of neighbors or strangers who stop by to say hi, strategize, or are just drawn in by the richness and want to say, "Your garden makes me really happy." This includes tours, workshops, personal ecology circles, team retreats, and digging up a big cluster of Goji berry plants for permaculture students to bring home, all of which hits numerous systems change levers. So much happens in the garden that it's tough to distinguish who I am and what I do from the garden. Whether it's working through life and leadership struggles, writing, preparing talks, or most anything else, life is an intimate, ongoing conversation with the materials and the moment.

Redefining Self—Identity as Organizing Principle

Pulling any of these systems change levers requires rethinking our sense of self. Meg Wheatley writes, "We always and only organize around identity; a membrane or boundary that distinguishes us from everything else. Without identity there is no life…no possibility for evolutionary change. Yet every change is motivated by an attempt to preserve a self." Our small, disconnected sense of self that we currently organize around is destroying our world. But being hyperaware and overwhelmed into inaction does as much good as putting your head in the sands of complacency and distraction.

We can't fix it all, yet it's a survival imperative to think beyond a too-narrowly defined sense of self, family, group, or country. So how do we dance with emergence, sowing the beneficial thoughts, actions, and values that help us stay open and adaptable while both practicing self-care and valuing our interdependence? This is tough as a person. Doing it in organizations, coalitions, and movements is a whole other level. But it starts with a clear identity, rooted in values and principles that guide how we respond to change. Though our identity also evolves through time. For example, White would not have been something I would have identified myself as ten years ago. Now it is.

Leadership is needed to keep an eye on your group's identity and to ensure people are using this guiding compass to determine actions. There needs to be enough decentralization for creativity and engagement but enough centralization for consistency, quality, and sane leadership. Courageous conversations are needed. As is the courage to change who we are.

Getting It All to Go Pop

Like learning the invisible elements that get a garden to pop, we can do the same in our lives, organizations, and movements. Understanding systems change strategies and seeing practical examples can help us respond and evolve in ways the world calls for. The garden and nature help us see that life is made up of nested systems, like a cell in an organ, in a body, in a community, in an ecosystem. What makes a *be the change* lens so powerful is that changing one system affects a series of larger systems. Facing climate reality can change our minds, emotions, and values and thus our actions, homes, and families. It can increase our civic engagement to start or support a small group of world changers or put a little more wind in the sails of larger movements. Celebrating small wins as we go feeds our joy and commitment and helps us persevere for the long journey.

To nurture community and cultivate networks is in our DNA. Relationships are fundamental to how our brains work. Think of your body, work, school, church, friends, or where you volunteer. All networks frequently self-organize to solve problems or celebrate a birthday. Gatherings big and small nourish connections, ideas, and dreams, be it a conference, book club, or dinner with friends. These are the things that create conditions for movements to grow and evolve, whether it's a teacher and some students, a few folks dreaming in the garden, or scheming around a table at a local café. Find your spot: as a dancing fool, first follower, or part of the gaggle gaining steam. And yes, we can and should use these insights to grow stronger organizations and movements, but they can be leveraged at any scale, in most any part of your life to feel connected to the world in a richer way and to feel and feed more frequent pops in your life, your garden, and the bigger change you are inspired to support. When we start with our hearts, reclaim the only power we have, and focus on nurturing life's relations, it's easier to deal with the difficulties along the way and to act with compassion and encouragement.

This builds in us the grit and determination to persevere with joy. Experiencing many types of pops through time—and occasionally where they harmonize—changes you little by little. It builds a faith in your path, a clarity, and resolve. As many a high-level leader, athlete, artist, or spiritual devotee knows, conscious or not, you can start to dial up the neurochemistry of joy, drive, focus, compassion, and whatever it is you need to contribute your best.

One morning I was sitting on my stool in the garden as a little white flake fluttered down out of the dark, pre-dawn sky, captivating in its quiet, eerie beauty. Hours before, I was woken from a deep sleep by a knock on our back door. I turned the light on to see our good friends, Hanna and Chris, standing there with their kitties in their arms. Living on the edge of Santa Rosa, close to where the Tubbs fire began, they made it out of their house just before the flames came. We were their second stop. First, they evacuated to Coffey Park, the community on the cover of the *New York Times* that was wiped out after the flames jumped the freeway. Something fires didn't use to do.

We knew there was a fire but had no idea of how bad it was or would get. Three days in, with firefighters pouring in from around the state and beyond, when I heard the state fire chief say it's gonna get worse before it gets better, I could barely comprehend his words. Unknowingly, we entered a new era of devastating fires.

Gonna Get Worse Before It Gets Better

With eco-social disruption on the rise everywhere, Sonoma County and Northern California have been hit extra hard by repeated crises in recent years. What follows lays out examples in the evolution of repeated emergency response, transforming government as a pathway to a living democracy, and why investing in the grassroots and building social infrastructure are so critical.

I used to be in the camp of *don't scare people because they won't act if overwhelmed by reality.* But endless fires and disasters, a constant stream of more alarming reports, and the fierce moral cries of the climate youth has changed me. Daily Acts is still focused on nurturing community, and collaborative solutions, but we are doing our best to work with both greater urgency and presence, with stronger demands, deeper engagement, and more understanding. This moment calls for bringing political pressure and community expertise to inform and craft bold, transformative approaches. This means building stronger organizations and movements that can mobilize hearts, minds, and action; get climate champions in office; and expand democracy to include more voices.

With increased crises, more complexity, and greater demands, it's important to frequently recharge and anchor into one's vision, values, and who we seek to be.

We need to double down on our patience, compassion, and empathy even as the urgency rises.

Claiming space for rest, renewal, and joy helps us pay attention to who we are becoming in unending emergency. Aligning with our passion and purpose, our community, and the wisdom of the Earth connects us to a greater joy and power. This leverages potent neurobiology and nature's operating instructions to lift our efforts to the next level and spread this infectious energy to wider communities.

The secret formula has always been about balancing inspiration and urgency without losing one's sense of eternity, of the magic and mystery. A notion that has long stuck with me are the words from Eckhart Tolle, who said that acceptance of the unacceptable is the greatest form of grace on this earth. When our hearts break, the cracks let the light in. This is how we heal and grow strong, with a more profound sense of love and belonging. This is why we start with our hearts and with reverential pathfinding, connecting to a power beyond our own. When shut down in fear and "self" protection, we close our hearts, minds, and borders to the world we've created. We "other" people, groups, and agencies, reducing empathy and compassion. Instead, we must open, embrace heartbreak, and lean into our interconnectedness.

Fire Response and Recovery

There is an aliveness to crisis. When the North Bay was on fire in 2017, signs popped up that read "The Love in the Air is Thicker Than the Smoke." And it was true. In a culture of disconnection and distraction, the life-threatening urgency had our full attention. People's lives and actions were infused with a higher purpose, like the helper's high that powers many a do-gooder. However, in twenty years of organizing, I've never seen anything like it on this scale, community-wide.

Even in a place known for bold leadership like Sonoma County is, there was still the business-as-usual approach of concentrating power and privilege and the systemic injustice that disadvantages many to the benefit of the few. But disaster is a chance to reset, to build civic engagement, bridge difference, and transform systems, even evolving who we think we are. With more frequent and varied disasters, we need to be prepared to address immediate suffering but also to organize for bigger change. We must lean into the emerging future by listening to nature, those systemically excluded, and the truth of who we seek to be in this time.

Before the fires hit, Daily Acts was again stepping up to meet more of our community's needs by bringing The Leadership Institute for Ecology and the Economy, a struggling local nonprofit, into our organization, starting an Environmental Health network to support vulnerable populations, and helping launch a regional resilience network. The weekend before the fires, we were at the Northern California Building Resilient Communities Convergence organizing for this emerging network, facilitating workshops, and bridging divides.

By Monday everything changed as flames wiped out whole neighborhoods and communities. Emergency services were maxed, and though we were collectively unprepared, an incredible array of efforts emerged. With our largest fundraiser of the year scheduled that week in a hall now filled with fire survivors, our own organizational survival felt at risk. We called a full team meeting to assess our risks and needs and to align behind going all in on emergency response.

Within weeks we'd partnered with dozens of groups, businesses, and agencies to launch three network initiatives to raise money for underserved communities, protect the environment from toxic fire debris, and bring equity and community voices to the table. In those early months, we were like an old-school switchboard operator, making connections, hosting meetings, and presenting and organizing at conferences. This gave way to re-gardening the rebuild by helping create the community-informed, scalable landscape templates utilized by 46 percent of rebuilders who submitted plans. The templates saved time, money, and stress while installing more sustainable, drought- and fire-resistant landscapes. We engaged hundreds of fire survivors in developing the templates and installing landscapes. Within a year, the Just and Resilient Future Fund had raised and distributed over $300,000 to undocumented workers, family farmers, and grassroots organizations while the Watershed Collaborative had created the Living in a Fire-Adapted Landscape report to inform county watershed resiliency efforts. We helped launch additional initiatives for the exasperated housing crisis and addressed mental health issues through mind-body medicine practices.

By the next fall, we were again called to evolve by the difficult truth of how quickly business as usual reasserts itself. A deeper feeling of *oh shit* came with the Intergovernmental Panel on Climate Change's (IPCC) most alarming report yet, released on the one-year anniversary of the fires. These two realities clarified the need for stronger advocacy and led to mobilizing our community to ask the new Office of Recovery and Resiliency to do three things: 1) prioritize a preventative approach to climate action; 2) place equity at the center; and 3) invest in collaborative structures and community networks because operating in silos cannot solve complex, interconnected problems.

This level of advocacy was an edge for us, but we were called into the space by a request from an agency director and county supervisor to comment about what was missing from the recovery framework. While it felt like a well-done, inclusive effort, the Office of Recovery's draft report was mostly about how to recover from this disaster and prepare for the next one with little mention of addressing the climate crisis fueling such disasters, the inequities caused by them, or that the community needed to be engaged differently. We spoke with residents, leaders, agency staff, and elected officials about the challenges they faced, once again getting to know different parts of the system and pulling our levers better together.

Vision and strategy emerge out of need by bringing people together and listening. In the span of a year, we learned that we are collectively not set up to respond to disaster, let alone frequent, intensified, compounding disasters. The solution is the power of community—when people and groups across society connect, learn, and lead together. As the fires turned everything upside down, they also created an opening, a more heart-centered field of possibility with heightened awareness, social bonding, and concern for all community members. In being forced to self-organize, barriers were broken and siloes bridged, spurring innovation and helping the system learn and evolve. Ultimately our focus came down to increasing community connections to support self-organizing that bridged difference, brought community voice to the table, and got stuff done on the ground.

2019—All In on the Climate Emergency

The last few years had been tough, but it felt good to step into the moment. Still, after eighteen years of growing Daily Acts and responding to larger and larger needs, I craved space for a deeper reset and for family, with my daughter Ella coming of age in a tough world. I had also been leaning into the escalating climate crisis and facing my excuses. Daily Acts worked on climate but never centered on it. It was too big, too challenging. We weren't experts and didn't want to feed divisive politics. Plus, our hands were full growing and sustaining a small group that already did a lot.

My body and spirit begged to pull in. But my grief and concern said it was time to go all in on the climate emergency. Even as the director of an organization with privilege and positional power, big change doesn't come easy. There are lots of barriers with fear, unknowns, busyness, and the functional denial of an existential threat. But with spring being the season of newness and action, like in the fires, we sowed a lot of seeds. In a matter of months, Daily Acts helped found Climate Action Petaluma (CAP) and a campaign to prioritize equitable climate action in our city. We partnered with the Regional Climate Protection Authority to launch a county-wide action campaign, and we started plans for a fall climate concert to turn fear and apathy into action. We were also bringing the climate emergency to the forefront of conversations with dozens of community and agency leaders pushing for it to be central in wider, county-scale initiatives.

That spring was my first exposure to the Sunrise Movement when I took Ella to a local climate strike led by high school students. It was heartening to hear how bold and articulate they were, even speaking the same Margaret Mead quote about the power of small groups that I shared on Daily Acts' first tour seventeen years before. Aligned with the rapidly emerging youth movement, the spring flurry of stirring grief into action led to a quicker, more positive response than CAP could have imagined. Within a month, Petaluma became the first Sonoma County city to declare a climate emergency, which rapidly spread through other municipalities. Within three months, our city council approved our request to create the county's first Climate Action and Policy Commission. Within six months, I was slapping high fives with council and community members and hugging it out with our city manager after a packed house listened to a record number of applicants speak in the city's first ever public commission interview process. Everyone was joyfully over-whelmed by the civic engagement, the heart, and the skill that showed up.

Every step of the way, there was a conversation, a negotiation, and taking a *we're in this together* approach instead of only pointing fingers and making demands. This is what we need more of—tapping the genius in our communities to drive change. It was a climate action crescendo of community coming into cadence with global strikes, our concert, a packed house forum on equity and climate organized by Climate Action Petaluma, commission interviews, and emergency resolutions going before more city and county officials. All in a matter of weeks. It was about leveraging and aligning with the bigger moment while giving people ways to en-gage locally.

The concert pierced the bubble of silence and denial by acknowledging climate grief, using art, beauty, and music to turn quiet, tortured awareness into bold action. We had powerful speakers from climate youth and justice activists to a county supervisor. We signed climate emergency petitions for other cities and mobilized people for the upcoming County Climate Emergency Resolution proposal. Like in Petaluma, this led to unanimous support and guidance for the Regional Climate Protection Authority to develop a bold ten-year climate emergency mobilization plan.

Climate Action Petaluma started with the courage and conviction to push for bold, inclusive climate goals aligned with an urgent, fast-changing reality. We knew that government alone wasn't going to do this and that we needed to build positive pressure to quicken awareness and action. This is the space where grassroots and government fit well together. At the city scale, we had a small, diverse, and connected group rallying our people from young leaders to local businesses, organizations, and concerned residents. We took a *we're in this together* approach, working closely with our mayor, council, and city manager. Having a former Daily Acts staff who was a trained permaculturist and Leadership Institute fellow as a climate champion on city council was significant. Then we made a series of sprints to get the next collaborative win, building confidence, trust, and momentum. It was an ongoing process of making the case to agency partners for building this collaborative muscle, working across difference and in new ways.

Things are going to get more difficult. We have to invest in building relationships and trust. This is what's needed for the complex, interconnected challenges of now: being open to and encouraging community input and thinking differently. From an equity perspective, for historically marginalized communities, it takes a lot more to heal and rebuild trust. This openness to input from the edges is critical in any organization, agency, or community.

Once there was an example of a city passing a climate emergency resolution, other municipalities were interested. Other groups pushed for similar measures. This

Eighth graders on the mic firing up the crowd with some morning chants at the Climate Emergency rally outside the City of Petaluma's goal-setting session.

added pressure for the county to take a bold, more inclusive and comprehensive approach. At all scales, having allies from elected officials to senior staff in key agencies helped us work better together.

While the urgency of the fires spurred widespread engagement, the climate emergency was something people and leaders could still deny or avoid. It required building public and political will by getting folks in the streets, at concerts, and forums, signing petitions, packing council chambers, and pushing emergency resolutions. Our approach to fire and climate emergency was lots of conversations, convening, and connecting. This led to a flurry of projects, coalitions, and gatherings to build awareness, alignment, and engagement. Such activities naturally leverage a range of systems change strategies already introduced. The foundation was relationships and listening to what sought to emerge. Even stronger advocacy was informed by partners in all parts of the system. It was sensing into the change needed and how to pull our levers better together.

In the end, 2019 was the year of climate reckoning with *climate emergency* and *climate* strike being the words of the year for Oxford and Collins Dictionaries. It felt like a giant breath of hope and momentum. Finally, a movement was emerging to address the climate crisis.

2020—WTF? Rising to the Moment with Gardens, Youth, and People-Powered Policy

Then COVID hit…and the brutal, systemic taking of more Black lives…and more climate-fueled extreme weather, wreaking devastation across the country and world. A derecho ripped through the Midwest, record hurricanes on the Gulf Coast, the biggest fires in history on the West Coast. Not to mention toxic political leadership. With so much struggle, some folks called this the worst year of their lives while others wondered if we'd look back on it as one of the last good years.

It's a lot to be with.

This is why we start with our heart.

We center in our power.

We nurture our relations, all our relations.

We must double down on learning to live and lead well, creating islands of sanity in the chaos. As we collectively reinvented organizational processes to work from home, Daily Acts centered on our team, to listen, connect, and provide self-care support. In some ways, COVID brought many of us back to the power of small and local, to gardening, homeschooling, walking our neighborhoods, baking and making for entertainment.

Early in the pandemic, hearing the needs in our communities, Daily Acts launched a Be the Change campaign focused on self-care, growing food, saving resources, and civic engagement. By late spring, we'd partnered to give out 1,000 apartment-friendly and culturally relevant food garden kits for Latinx community members.

On the climate front, we were heartened by the city's new Climate Commission and chosen commissioners. The commission was based on criteria CAP helped develop and became the city's most culturally diverse. The record number of applicants and increased cultural diversity were both the result of CAP's engagement and a community forum we hosted. The commission also added a new level of complexity. In the previous year, roles were clear as CAP worked closely with city partners to implement our original requests. But with a newly appointed body, there were new relations and a new structure in the ecosystem to orient around. While COVID turned most things upside down, we had to keep the climate response moving forward. So CAP members and Daily Acts helped the new commission form working groups and mobilize dozens of volunteers to draft a community-powered climate emergency framework. It had a lot of things that were missing from most climate plans, centering on equity, bold zero emissions targets, carbon sequestration, and addressing consumption-based emissions. We started with the science, our total emissions, and an equity lens. It happened because it was community-led, which benefited an already stretched city staff dealing with COVID. Because the city worked with the public, new resources and expertise were brought to the table in the formation of the commission, recruitment for it, and digging up dozens of additional expert volunteers. This is the work of expanding democracy. Imagine what we are capable of when we align and unleash the full wisdom and skill of our communities.

By 2021, in barely a year and a half, what started with a small group rallying our people and working closely with the city changed the North Star and compass of our community. An emergency declaration led to a new climate commission, which led to the community-powered climate emergency framework now guiding the city. This resulted in further engagement and in coalition members and allies running for office and unseating two incumbents. This led to Petaluma becoming the first city in the country to ban new gas stations and set one of the boldest all electric codes to remove natural gas from new buildings. Paired with growing momentum on city staff and council, new initiatives emerged such as Releaf Petaluma with a goal of planting 10,000 native trees for the many community and climate benefits.

Just as Releaf was forming, Daily Acts partnered with Equity First Consulting to address a critical unmet need by piloting the Petaluma Equitable Climate Action Coalition. This created a space for building relationships and trust while funding BIPOC residents to learn about the Climate Emergency Framework, host community listening sessions, and provide the city with policy recommendations. With few examples in government of doing deep, authentic community engagement, it was important for us to model a different way to involve people, especially from underrepresented groups in shaping our shared future. As Alegría De La Cruz, Director of the Office of Equity shared at the presentation of policy recommendations, "You have truly created a new standard for high-quality community engagement with complex bureaucratic documents."

As if all this bold, inspiring momentum could get any better, when the opportunity arose to compete for a million-dollar Cool California Climate Challenge grant, CAP members D'Lynda Fischer and Natasha Juliana mobilized again with many others chipping in. When the dust settled, Petaluma finished top in the state, registering a whopping 300 block captains to help our neighborhoods become more planet friendly, disaster resilient, and community rich. For context, Petaluma is about 56,000 peo-

Petaluma Equitable Climate Action Coalition cohort 1: Celeste, Luis, Ri, Lisa, David, and Kymberly, with Kerry, the author, and Ella.

ple and that's 50 percent more block captains than the other two winning cities of Los Angeles with 3.91 million people and Irvine with 328,000. The power of small. Though it's not a competition, as all three cities are working together.

In the span of a few short years, Petaluma went from being a climate laggard in the county to a local, state, and national leader. For Daily Acts and most core founders of CAP, it took a decade or more of relationship-building and work in the community. It took an amazing new city manager, a shift on city council, aligning with the bigger moment, and a lot of folks doing their part, mostly through small acts and groups.

It has been a phenomenal amount of action and change at all scales, building momentum each season and year with more and bigger wins. AND still, it's difficult to comprehend how far away we are from achieving zero emissions by 2030. So, we dream bigger, bolder, more inclusive, and sweeping dreams, we share with and inspire others. Then we roll up our sleeves and make it so.

To continue our 100x thinking and action, from one fall to the next Daily Acts went from writing a $25,000 grant to pilot PECAC to negotiating a $4.5 million grant with the state to start scaling decentralized water and climate solutions like rainwater catchment, greywater, rain gardens, and lawn transformations. We are building momentum to launch a climate action network as called for in the city's climate framework to help coordinate civic and municipal action towards our 2030 goals while creating a structure to build community leadership capacity and prioritize missing voices.

Cool Petaluma has a pathway to reaching every block in our city in a few years if each neighborhood captain gets just one more captain for the next round. The Climate Commission has formed small groups to lay out policy and action pathways to zero emissions, zero waste, and zero excuses as we regenerate the earth, repair past harms, and reclaim our future. This upwelling of civic engagement and climate leadership has reframed the city's thinking and approach to updating its General Plan, the long-term vision and blueprint for our future.

Small adds up.
Momentum builds.
The unimaginable comes
into reach as gardens, groups,
neighborhoods, and communities go pop.

Like in a garden, creating conditions conducive to life has a regenerative effect that builds interest, excitement, and momentum. While I think I'm often one of about six people on our monthly climate commission calls, they're must-see TV. All eyes are glued to the screen as the drama unfolds. It's seeing the many difficulties and barriers there are to driving bigger change, but also the amazingness in the real-time experience of how culture shifts and momentum builds, little by little, meeting by meeting, month to month. How small acts and small groups intermingle and wrestle with finding alignment, recovering from the latest devastation, and not getting overwhelmed by it all. And together cohering a path to the better world being born with each milestone and problem solved.

For years I had nudged local climate leaders about key elements missing from our climate plan. But then I mostly left the complicated science and issues to "the experts" until the urgency became too great. With other folks feeling the same, we organized and advocated. We worked with our city to create new tables, expand democracy, and help spread emergency resolutions around the county, leading to Sonoma being the first county in the US to have all municipalities declare a climate emergency. Together we started writing policy and shifting culture, on city staff, on the council, and in the community.

This is complicated, tough stuff for anyone to step up to, let alone those who are systemically excluded and told their voices don't matter or aren't valued at every step of the process. Whether you have climate and policy expertise or not, we all have something to contribute. We all need to advocate for our collective good. It's about learning how to lead as we go while creating space for more historically ignored voices. There is no time to waste, and our purpose and potential are great. As you rise again and again, you get better at sniffing out those invisible currents of collective uplift. You learn to better sense and find the inspiration that informs your action, and puts wind in your wings. It's that thing that gets your butterflies flying together, your garden and group popping, and your community coming into cadence.

Daily Actors circling up to connect and stretch before the outer transformation begins.

Chapter 21

Together We Rise—Grassroots, Government, and Gatherings

Crisis is an opportunity to reset and level up our shared potential. Across the planet, we are seeing the rise of social movements, purpose-driven corporations, and more folks finding and contributing their part. Locally, we've had a lot of opportunities to respond to disasters and have taken steps on a bigger reset. We've gotten better organized and connected, bridged differences, built new coalitions, and deepened our partnership with local government. Across the land, this has led to changing how government works, who's in office, and who's at the table.

As grassroots organizations, movements, and government agencies propel our communities into climate emergency mode, it means more urgent, evolving priorities that integrate a range of strategies, issue areas, and left-out groups. Emergency preparedness and response is a critical part of our resilience-building, and all of this has to be done while addressing systemic inequities and prioritizing the voices and perspectives of front-line communities.

Leveling Up the Grassroots

To create a tipping point in addressing the climate crisis at speed and scale, grassroots groups, networks, and movements have a critical role to play. We do this by acting as ecosystem catalysts to align and unleash the power of community and a wide array of partners to take action, build public and political will, elect climate champions, and enact bold policy. Four interconnected strategies to do this are model, spread, build, and transform.

First comes **modeling**, which means living your vision even in the face of heartbreak and difficulty. Individual modeling becomes shared pathfinding at the organization scale. Strong personal practices need to be embedded in our culture, part of who we are and what we do. It's relentlessly staying tuned to your compass and doubling down on building the physical, mental, emotional, and organizational reserves to face continued emergency. More time listening, reflecting, and checking in with folks helps address some of the rubs between being adaptive by stepping into the moment and being consistent to sustain for the long haul. We need to act and advocate for fast change while moving slow enough to build relationships and inclusivity. This requires our full presence. We must stay connected to our joy, power, and compassion and to the living Earth and each other.

Next is **spreading** solutions and models. This includes both spreading on-the-ground climate solutions and the self-care practices to stay sane while living and leading in chaos, uncertainty, and rapid change. Wanna step up further? Do this at multiple scales from home and neighborhood to your school, church, work, and even other places.

Then it's **building** stronger, better connected and aligned organizations, networks, and movements. We do this by training and growing leaders and fostering networks and coalitions. Read, study, take trainings, and develop your inner capacities and your ability to play well with others.

These three strategies are interconnected and needed at all scales. As for the fourth strategy, while we need to **transform** it all, government is an important set of institutions to evolve. The synergy of bringing together the first three approaches in partnership with municipalities at a range of scales leads to greater, more systemic transformation.

Expanding Democracy—Power to the People

We've allowed democracy to become small, undervalued, and divisive. Outdated, siloed structures, a business-as-usual approach, and a disconnected, disengaged citizenry no longer works for complex, fast-emerging, interconnected disasters. While it can be frustrating to see a lack of leadership from government on our greatest existential threat, we need to understand how government works, their challenges, and how to help them work better. Leadership can come from within agencies, but the culture and structure often fail to encourage it. Direction comes from the top with elected officials balancing the needs of diverse constituents, trying not to get too far in front of the community, and minding special interest groups with wealth, power, and influence.

More integrated, decentralized approaches that engage the full wisdom of our organizations, agencies, and communities are needed. Community engagement is a common buzz phrase. But current government thinking and systems aren't designed to encourage inclusivity and engagement from the whole community. This can come from busyness and overwhelm, from not seeing how to do different, or not having the support to try new things. It can be from fear of change and not wanting to give up power and control. These things are as true for organizations, businesses, and people in general as they are for government. We need to embrace the wisdom and difference of perspective from all parts of society, especially the edges.

While filling the streets and council chambers is important to build public and political will, we also need to work with government up close to transform it. Partnering with agencies (or anyone) is a delicate dance of understanding needs, concerns, and barriers while working to accelerate critical change in societal systems that are not moving quick enough.

There's an increasingly recognized need for working in integrated ways across siloed departments and agencies. Less understood is the need to invest in new leadership structures and a social infrastructure that strengthens and connects the organizations, networks, and alliances on the ground. This is how we bring the needs and expertise of our full communities to the table. It is important, complex work. It must be properly valued and funded. While we need more volunteering as civic engagement, we can't just rely on tapping community leaders and experts to serve on ever more volunteer-based commissions and advisory boards. Government can't do this alone. And we can't leave it to small, under-resourced groups to create and sustain the critical social infrastructure to rapidly build resilience, decarbonize society, draw down emissions, and address the mental health crisis of living in these times. We also can't expect systemically excluded community members, who may rightly have enormous distrust in government, to show up on their own time and dime to inform and drive this change, especially when the larger dominant culture continues to devalue their stories and lived expertise. To bring the wisdom of the community into addressing the climate crisis while helping heal and repair the historical traumas of frontline communities requires a focused investment of time, intention, and resources.

Part of why new leadership structures are needed is because many hands and hearts make for better engagement, more resilience, and lighter work. It's a seat at the table to support decisions that reflect the needs of all. It's also new tables, powered by the community and written into policy, like commissions, networks, and citizen assemblies. This expands our democratic structures and ultimately supports what many agencies are craving: more and better community engagement that leverages new perspectives and expertise and increases buy-in.

Establishing partnerships that meet an agency's resource conservation and engagement priorities helps build trust and understanding. When an organization works in a networked way, this can bring diverse expertise and perspectives to the table. Collaborations like installing a garden or mobilizing an action campaign expand and strengthen the informal social infrastructure of connection and collaboration. The next tier out is for a municipality to foster, engage with, and support coalitions, which bring a range of stakeholders to the table around issues like climate, health, emergency preparedness, the food system, or fire resilience. These strategies create a foundation for more innovative, inclusive approaches to program implementation, policy development, and expanding democracy. This builds the relational muscle to reweave the tapestry of community. It creates the social coherence needed to engage in the rapid transformations required.

Government Partners Leveling Up

Starting small and working with inspired consistency to achieve bigger and bigger impact creates more ripples and more opportunities. Another thing that happens is that allies gain influence. The young writer and organic farmer covering the 350 Garden Challenge becomes a county supervisor with a fierce commitment to changing how government works and a great partner in response to fires and climate emergency. The former nonprofit leader becomes the head of the water agency. The spry young school board member joins city council, becomes mayor, and then county supervisor, and before long, he's your senator. People in higher positions of power still need trusted relationships to achieve their goals and inform their direction for the greatest good. This means more and different levers to pull together in a more intricate garden ecosystem.

Then there's recruiting candidates and creating conditions conducive for everyday people to rise to the moment. The volunteer-turned-Daily Acts-staff member becomes an amazing climate champion on city council. The climate justice organizer with no intention of being in government gets inspired by the community rising up and becomes the vice chair of the climate commission. The young, engaged, climate activist feels supported and inspired to run for office, and before you know it, is the vice mayor. As civic engagement builds, more folks run for council and commission seats, start new groups, and plug into existing efforts to meet evolving needs. Like in a garden, the right elements going pop create conditions conducive to bigger and deeper change.

As climate chaos touches every corner of our planet, this brings up a lot of concern for people. We must feel ourselves as part of a larger whole and get comfortable with fear, complexity, and unknowns. This requires faith, a good compass, and trusted relations. It means regularly putting the pieces back together to make sense and connect with who and what grows you whole.

For the rest of forever we'll need groups who act as ecosystem catalysts and connectors, advocating for bolder change, evolving our response, expanding democracy, training leaders, and developing pathways to solutions at speed and scale.

To rise up, we must pull in.

Coming Together

Part of the magic of this planet is the renewing power of cycles. The end of a day, week, month, and year are important times to pull in, reflect, and reconnect. As this book comes to a close, so does our time together, unless you highlight, take notes, and otherwise use this as a tool for personal and planetary betterment. As I finish these words, fall is in the air, signaling another cycle of life pulling in to rest and renew. Then there's the bigger shifts afoot as we close an era of climate stability, of business-as-usual politics, and planet-destroying gluttony. There's lots to make sense of in finding our way to a more just, reverent, livable future.

Fall is a time of gathering together to get reinspired and reconnected, to nurture networks, evolve, and level up. It's when movements have emerged from the Arab Spring to Occupy Wallstreet, 350.org's first global action, and the youth climate movement in recent years.

For Daily Acts, fall is both when we began, catalyzed by hurt and loss, and when we historically gather 600 daily actors to get inspired, connected, and to resource the work. Three of the last four years, we've had major fires the week of our big event. For our community, fall has become a time of fear, devastation, and choked lungs. That happens with a backdrop of contentious politics and our humanity and civilization seemingly on the line. But still, we need to connect and make sense, to take heart, take part, and take action.

With so many difficult moments, we must relish the lit ones, where small groups come together to fuse efforts or dream anew. It's the folks who can't stop, won't stop, who keep leaning in after a workshop or remember that laughing, dancing, and even some late-night starlight strategy sessions feed our evolution while nourishing body and spirit.

There are the moments of *arrival* to celebrate, like when after years of work to make the NorCal Building Resilient Communities Convergence a more inclusive and courageous space, in reference to the cultural diversity of attendees, local community leader Wanda Stewart says, "This isn't even light brown; this is a legit dark shade." Gatherings can provide a richness of visions, cultures, and perspectives, informing who we are as people, groups, and movements intermingle.

There's also much to learn from the difficult moments, be it courageous conversations about not letting differing views blow up an important network or addressing power, privilege, and racial bias to create more inclusive spaces. A post-conference happy hour can mean dealing with the real-time emergency of someone whose town just burned down asking for help a few feet and minutes from a consultant who's managing the creation of a major city's climate adaptation plan asking for experience with a planned retreat.

From relishing lit moments, to celebrating wins, and leaning into the complexities of converging disasters, this moment calls on us to cultivate new capacities. For this, we reverently recenter; we reclaim our ripples, and we nurture our relations.

Key Concepts

• Transformative action: creating shifts in awareness, patterns of thinking, and habits of action at multiple scales for positive personal and social change.

Key Points

• When we get the right elements in place in our lives, gardens, and groups, we can unleash the reverent, resilient spirit at the heart of human genius to transform our crises.

• Lessons from a garden can help drive social change. In the garden, everything is connected; life operates at a range of scales and through networks; people and groups can learn to handle complexity and find inspiration to solve challenges and better relate with others.

• Find your group's sweet spot at the intersection of what you love, what you are good at, and the resources to sustain you.

• What sustains through time is commitment, process, and consistency. Take heart, take action, take feedback, assess, recalibrate, and repeat. Pay attention to when change is needed.

Questions for Activists, Organizers, Those Interested in Taking Action

• Where do you fit? What gatherings should you plug into? If you can't find this space, how might you create it?

• Where do you have power, privilege, and influence? How can you use it for greater good?

• How do you prioritize sustaining for the long haul? How can you support this change in your institutions?

Steps to Take to Get Yourself and Your Group Popping

• Personal

  o Reflect on and highlight the insights in this book that speak to you.

  o Relentlessly recommit to finding and living your inspiration day after day.

• Groups

  o Tend the culture you are creating by working on your group not just being in it.

  o Deepen into your values while refining operating principles, practices, and norms, aka modeling how to take heart and take action together.

  o Have courageous conversations, and use practices, such as deep breathing, meditation, journaling, visualization, and being in nature to support this.

Dave and Scotty ambling down Bear Creek Watershed, Sierra Nevada Mountains.

Conclusion

Return to What Grows You Whole

Putting the Pieces Back Together

Waking to, feeling, and feeding this emergence is living in the grip of a haunting hunger that won't let go. You can sense it in your breath and bones, in the air that somehow seems more aware, readying for a shift. This feeling persists and grows, like the atmospheric pressure before a rain, a pending release, like how fall's leaves know just when to let go. It's a thing beyond comprehension, which is fine because the thinking mind is only part of how we divine.

I first got rocked by permaculture at an herb conference, leading to a Bioneers immersion and through a backyard gate into an alternate world—life as a thriving oasis. I was infected by repeated glimpses of a deeper why, connecting the dots between lots of breadcrumbs on an emerging path of living and sharing my inspiration in a way that regenerates self, nature, and community. This led to a lot of years of working in and with small groups, highlighting bright spots to grow more of them, turning inspiration and education into application and transformation.

Bright spots act as beacons in the dark to show what's possible and light the way.

Mobilizations harness our collective power to be that change.

Gatherings nourish our connection to each other and the better world being born.

These strategies enhance our ability to dream and achieve the impossible, feeding our joy, flow, and interconnectedness. They help us tap into the spirit of shared potential, creating conditions conducive for new efforts and consciousness to emerge.

Following our beacons and regularly listening for guidance provides lots of small glimpses and reference points. Then every so often a magical encounter might rewire our hearts and minds, providing a different way of seeing and being. Such bright spots embody new frameworks, secret formulas for how to transform our lives, gardens, groups, and communities. While such experiences may come in a flash—from an article, a tour, or enchanting encounter—they may take years to live into. But the power of their signal can help us map the path and more frequently get back to it.

Of course, seeing our North Star doesn't excuse us from the difficulty of following it. This still lands us at the doorstep of each day, navigating life to make something worthy of the materials and the moment. It means more courageous conversations and self-care, recognizing when we need a break or maybe a cry to reset and center on our best next steps. Given the times, there will always be more suffering and loss. We will never know less. Accept this. Focus on the hurt you are called to heal and what you are called to contribute.

Begin with reverence. By starting with our hearts, we can embrace the heartbreak that opens us to greater healing, aliveness, and possibility.

Reclaim your ripples. Following our hearts starts us on the path to greater purpose. Taking action to live what we love taps us into the most powerful human motivators. Developing ourselves through movement and self-care practices hones our signal, providing sustenance for the journey.

Nurture life's relations. Time in nature heals, and studying life's lessons can gift us a lived-in literacy of this precious planet that we can apply to ourselves, our gardens, and growing eco-efficacious organizations and groups. Doing so on a foundation of

passion, purpose, and eco-literacy, while
tending our relations puts the keys to the
universe in our hearts and hands.

Flow—the Next Rewiring

Several years ago, another paradigm rewiring came to me through reading about
flow, a state of consciousness where you feel and perform your best. This led me
back to snowboarding, my original source of flow, and then to recenter on
all the other places in life that lit me up, ones I had let slip because of
more leadership responsibility, maybe writing them off as indulgences.
But as I came to understand the neurobiology of joy and performance, I saw
that flow is a critical aspect of the transformative change we need. In hindsight, it
was the feelings of flow that I was chasing all along. It was recreating my experiences through programs of embodied environmental education that engaged multiple
senses and my sense of connection to community, nature, and a larger purpose. In
learning how to tap into and share these powerful human motivators with others,
I was figuring out how to elicit group genius or collective flow state. It's the hive-
mind of coming into cadence that can then drive bigger change (with more fun and
purposeful action, of course).

Part of the problem is that awake do-gooders get so overloaded by the immensity
of the problems and hurt that we lose, give up, or even feel guilty about indulging
in pure beauty and joy. But we need this to give our best. We need to claim space
to be in nature, with friends, doing what we love, and glimpsing the best version of
ourselves. That means taking the time to slow down and connect with that deeper
source of inspiration and insight.

Living in impossible times with an urgent, larger-than-life need, there's much to learn from the action sports community, which has been wildly successful at achieving the impossible. Be it in snow sports, big wave surfing, kayaking, or free climbing, athletes have succeeded by living their passions and creating a fun, infectious culture of constant progression, of personal and collective flow. It's in part about how living your light can elevate you into your potential. In *Stealing Fire*, Steven Kotler and Jaimie Wheal speak to how these athletes pack their lives with flow triggers and flow in packs, leveraging powerful neurobiology to build tighter communities and foster innovation and then outsource this to larger communities.

Why not pack your life with delight and meaningful connection?

Why not pack your life with delight and meaningful connection as you rock the kind of world-changing shit that this moment desperately calls for? You can do it all while melting hearts, minds, and paradigms, inoculating others with a deep, unquenchable desire to find and live their part. From here you can't help but want to spread this to a larger community of world changers. Of course, life is more than moments of flow. It's a long, complicated journey with heartbreaking difficulties. But fear, challenge, and stress will not get us where we need to go. Though we can make fear our friend, embrace challenges, and use stress to grow stronger, we also need to tap into our joy.

While we can't ensure the future, we can always be the change we wish to see. We can inspire hearts and minds with how rich we live, how much love we give, and how much we can transform by starting with ourselves, our small groups, and our gardens. Even among the unraveling, we can persevere with joy, bettering what we can while navigating the disruption locked in.

Living it Day to Day

I think about death a lot. This comes from losing my parents at a young age and the pain of what's being lost each day. But it's mostly about how I want to live. A folded scrap of paper in my wallet has goals for the next two, five, and fifteen years. It starts on my deathbed with what I want to see when looking back over my life. As I approached the age of my dad's death, forty-six, I started this practice of questioning, what if I had a year to live? Six months? Just today? It clarifies what matters.

For a more regular recentering, whether in smoke or COVID, drought or deluge, it's back to the garden, to breathe, listen, and give thanks. This while tuning my compass and seeking guidance from the earth below my feet, bird chirps, or the sway of trees. We just keep putting the pieces together, from making sense of the uncertainty, to healing our grief, owning our highs, and staying tuned to our companions on the path. Living our visions day to day by the ongoing reverential process of tuning into the materials and the moment is long, hard, rewarding work. Reverence helps us hold the paradox of vulnerability and strength, of letting our hearts break so we can find the light to guide us. From here, it's developing the commitment and conviction to live our best.

For this, periodically tuning into where we are on the larger path in our lives is a helpful practice. It's been over twenty years since 9/11 and my mom's death, which catalyzed the start of Daily Acts. Twenty years of gatherings, reference points, and relations to guide the unfolding. For most of those years, backpacking has provided renewal and insight on navigating difficult territory with others. There's something special about walking a path into the mountains to find our way together. It's astonishing how far we can travel in a day or week over rugged terrain. Such pilgrimages reconnect us to a deeper source of sustenance as we stare in wonder at lakes, meadows, and streams. We remember how rich we can live with so little, and that the breathtaking beauty of fiercely twisted trees and deep-spirited people are made so by tough conditions. Deep time in nature nourishes. Here we remember that the truth of who we are is richer and vaster than we know. And that with good company, a good compass, and reverence in our hearts, we can travel far fast, across unsteady ground.

This is important for every committed changemaker to know, but especially for the generation coming up, feeling urgency and despair about their futures. Years ago, I remember watching in utter joy as my four-year-old daughter Ella ran down the trail at dusk looking for fairies on her first backpacking trip. For a range of reasons, I've made a lot of effort to get her in the garden and on camping and backpacking trips but especially for nature connection. Hopefully when climate grief hits her, she will have accumulated enough experiences and connections to help her with the skills and support to find her place and way, to hear and trust her voice and also the one in the breeze, falling leaves and hawks that talk to her thoughts, if she listens and believes.

There's a connection between joy, flow, and a large accumulation of peak experiences. A key characteristic of flow is clarity of focus, the pursuit of a goal. This brings order to consciousness. As does developing a faith in finding and walking our paths. It

Ella, Mary, Mason, and Sharon scoping for fairies.

doesn't mean we're not wired for the struggles of being human. But sheer persistence with a good heart and intent goes a long way. Just keep leaning into the big questions and living the answers that come.

Claiming Space

An ongoing theme is the need to claim space—for joy, rest, family, nature, and everything that gets squeezed out when rising to the times. Humanity and life on our planet are facing a big decade. To go far in a decade, we need to make the most of each year. To make the most of each year, we need to tend the seasons, months, weeks, days, and hours in it. Given what we know about flow, our state of optimal joy and performance and the power of time in nature, with loved ones and doing what we love, why not revision how to radically expand our impact without sacrificing what grows us whole?

Like many of us, I need time for family, friends, and impromptu happy hours on the porch. I need to laugh and play with my daughter and get her skilled up as a nature-connected Earth warrior coming of age in a big moment. I need to garden my ass off and nourish our carbon-sequestering, tastiness-producing soil food web. I need to fly down big snow-covered mountains, through trees and chutes and off snowy kickers into great puffs of fluff while my fifty-year-old body still lets me. I need to dip my head in raging streams, to hike peaks, and drink high country margaritas with good friends, made from that last patch of snow up some beautiful granite pass. I need to stand at the edge of the Earth, staring at the horizon and breathing from the sea of possibility itself. I need to be in the garden with friends, partners, and policy makers, laughing, dreaming, and scheming how to regenerate the hell out of it all. I need to regularly stick my finger in that light socket of aliveness that Sark's words helped me find so long ago.

> **What do you need to live and give your best?**
>
> **What sets your heart afire and rekindles your flame?**

This is the stuff that fuels our inspiration and creativity to wake up and step up each day and to heal our beauteous, broken lives and world. It's staying focused but free, living beyond fear and hope, guided by an internal compass that knows your small but essential role. It's all the small bits, daily habits, and practices, regularly recentering, cultivating that determined intent to contribute something worthy of the materials and the moment.

While the distances one can cover in a single day across high mountains can seem miraculous, it's tougher to feel such accomplishment in life's daily commute. This is where mindfulness and heartfulness come in, building a fierce commitment to infuse majesty into our daily moments.

Claim space from the torrent of your schedule to rest, renew, and play, to dip your head in wild streams and stay true to your unbound dreams. Take time to clearly see and feel your vision. Then schedule and live it. After, appreciate what went well, gently learn from where you fell short, and begin again, a little wiser, a little more experienced, a little more connected and infected by the better world being born and your part in it. Craft your compass, your practices, and the systems that help you stay true. Do it regardless of how imperfect and inconsistent they feel.

Standing at the edge of a new age and the most important decade humanity has faced, we are embarking on a great journey through uncharted territory. For this we need a good compass, good companions, and the skills of shared pathfinding. We start with our hearts because hope is not an option. It's a biological necessity, a state of being that nourishes our strength and resolve to dream bigger and act bolder, aligned with the times. We do this by returning to the only power we have: our small daily actions. We tend and mend what is within our reach while nurturing the hell out of our relations. When we consistently do these things, we can build the richness and resilience to stay awake and engaged in the great work of remaking our lives and world.

You are amazing and whole and were born for this time.

Live and love accordingly.

You are amazing and whole
and were born for this time.

Live and love accordingly.

Photo: Gayio

Acknowledgments

This book, Daily Acts, and the whole of my life have been shaped by so many hearts and hands. Through the first twenty to thirty revisions, these pages were full of many more mentors and co-conspirators. For those unnamed who have been part of our path, know I feel immense gratitude for you.

Inspirations, Mentors, and Friends

In addition to everyone already mentioned in the book, I want to thank the folks who have put wind in my sails and provided bread for the journey. Stephanie Valdez-Kominsky started it off, sharing her values in a richer way at the right time. After stumbling along for years, much of what has influenced my life and Daily Acts' work was seeded in a weekend gathering where Mark Cohen's spark got me on the permaculture path, Kenny Ausubel introduced me to Bioneers, and Paul Strauss embodied how to regenerate forests and farms from a deep reverence. Penny and James Livingston-Stark who first showed me you can regenerate the world in a garden. Brock Dolman and the crew at Occidental Arts and Ecology Center who so deftly model sustainable hedonism, I mean post-patriarchy regenerative we-do-nism. To Scotty, Heavi, Meucci, and Sam, my companions on many high-country pilgrimages to replenish my spirit and reset my compass. Brad Lancaster, Mark Lakeman, Andy Lipkis, Mateo Nube, Pandora Thomas, and Bernie Langan.

Daily Acts Staff, Board, and Community

After twenty-plus years of community-powered daily acting, I could fill a book with the names of relations who helped bring our eco-efficacious dreams into being.

For our original and longtime daily actors on staff, board, and in the community—

The Holders of the Groove aka HOG who turned Daily Acts into an organization—Julie Young, Marty Falkenstein, Gavio, Sarah Wright, and Loi Medvin. Sheryl Webster, Erik Ohlsen, Rick Taylor, Janine Bjornson, Scott Mathieson, Kevin Bayuk, Pride Wright, Chas Moore, Judy Mazzeo, Christopher Peck, Stacey Meinzen, Suzanne Mackey, Larry Robinson, hot knife Carl Schuller, Erin Axelrod, Eve Goldberg, Ellen Bicheler, Gretchen Schubeck, Jim Shelton, Natasha Juliana, Jessica Vibberts, Cate Steane, Miriam Volat, Ryan Johnston, Dan Bleakney, Kait Schroeder, Brianna Schaefer, Susan Price, and our most dedicated daily actor since the start, Terry Church.

To the countless allies working to transform government from the inside: Senator Mike McGuire, Congressman Jared Huffman, Supervisor Lynda Hopkins, Supervisor James Gore, Oscar Chavez, Ellen Bauer, Dave Iribarne, D'Lynda Fischer, Peggy Flynn, the Petaluma Climate Commission, and so many more. To longtime municipal partners—the cities of Petaluma, Sebastopol, Cotati, Windsor, Santa Rosa, and the Sonoma County Water Agency.

To the ecosystem of coalitions and convenings that have evolved our work and identity. Climate Action Petaluma who continues to show how crazy kick ass a coalition can be, changing the trajectory of a city while having fun, connecting, kvetching, and getting it done. Localizing California's Waters, the Sonoma County Food Systems Alliance, the Just and Resilient Future Fund, the Alternative Water Resources Working Group, Transition US and the Transition and permaculture movements. To the often unfunded or underpaid folks who against all odds, herd purposeful cats and bring coherence to the messy emergence of the better world being born. Thinking of you Susan Silber, Carolyne Stayton, and Regina Hirsch.

Because good deeds can't run on love alone, big thanks to Daily Acts' many financial supporters, in particular: The Elizabeth R. and William J. Patterson Foundation, Nick Colby and the Appleby Foundation, Rick Theis and Carolyn Johnson, Sohrab Nabatian, and Kalliopeia Foundation, Marcy Pattinson, Jim and Sandy Shelton, Hidden Leaf Foundation, Bancroft Foundation, the Yavanna Foundation, and Guayaki Yerba Mate.

Those Who Made This Book a Reality

Gavio for heavy lifting on edits and graphics, not to mention his worthy efforts at taming my verbosity for so many years. Andrew at Bisbee Creative for the beautiful layout and design of the book. Ronda Fleming, Kerry Fugett, Connor Devane, Marie Kneemeyer, Sarina Consulter, and Rachel Kaplan who provided invaluable editing and/or graphics support. To Leslie Curchack, Scott Hess, Robb Hirsch, Kerry Fugett, and Gavio for the beautiful images. Since images were pulled from twenty years of running programs, if I missed attributing an image you took, I apologize and let me know! To the team at Scribe who were a joy to work with, especially Mikey Kershisnik, Kat Dixon, and Miles Rote.

My Family

Mom and Dad, though I lost you too soon, I was well-blessed by the time I had. To my daughter, Ella, you will always be my little girl, foraging for berries in your diapers, bathing in a bucket of rainwater, and flying down a mountain path at dusk, covered in dust and looking for fairies. Mary, I couldn't imagine my life without you. You are my foundation, and though you rather dislike the term, you truly are my life partner on this path.

As I reviewed dozens of acknowledgments from favored and bestselling books, there was a startling lack of appreciation of the nonhuman world. So, an extra big shout-out to the hawks, raindrops, hot springs, cicadas, bees, ice cold streams, mountain meadows, peaks and trees who have nourished my dreams and this work. Lastly, I give thanks to my garden stool. Though you had your own life as a tree long before we met, for these last twenty-plus years, you've been there each day as I meditate, write, reflect, watch the stars and seasons come and go, and endeavor to reverently make the most of the materials and the moment.

"There are simply no answers to some
of the great pressing questions.
You continue to live them out, making
your life a worthy expression
of leaning into the light."

—Barry Lopez

Additional Resources to Inspire, Path-Find, and Mobilize

Are you inspired or motivated by what's in these pages?

- **Spread the love!** Lend your copy or gift a book to a friend, organization, or government ally working to create change.
- **Share the first chapter of this book for free!** It's available on the Daily Acts website, https://www.dailyacts.org/takeheart. We also offer group/bulk ordering discounts.
- **Write a review on Amazon.**
- **Share** with your local paper and change makers to spread the word.
- **Get involved** in your local community and grassroots movements. Use the leverage points you learned about in this book, and make your voice heard and your actions ripple!

Want More Resources, Motivation, and Connection?

We hope you become part of the Daily Acts community and network of partners driving transformative change commensurate with the scale of the crises we face.

Please join us at Daily Acts website to:
- Share your reaction to this book, what inspired you, what steps you plan to take, and get the support you need to live and give your best.
- Donate to help us help more people, groups, and communities turn small acts into big change.
- Access great resources, additional content, and trainings.
- Visit: https://www.dailyacts.org/takeheart.

About the Organization

Daily Acts unleashes the power of community to address the climate crisis through three connected strategies:

• Building community leadership by training leaders and fostering networks.
• Spreading on-the-ground solutions and models that strengthen local resilience.
• Working with government partners to accelerate equitable climate programs and policies.

In Petaluma and Sonoma County, we are working to align a wide array of partners to create and implement a climate emergency mobilization road map. At the regional, state, and national level, we partner with agencies and nonprofits to build people power as a critical pathway to healthy, just, resilient communities.

To learn more, get engaged, or make a donation, please join us at https://www.dailyacts.org/takeheart.

The author's proceeds from *Take Heart, Take Action* are being donated to Daily Acts Organization; a 501(c)(3) nonprofit organization. You are also invited to support this work with a tax-deductible gift by visiting https://www.dailyacts.org/donate/.

About the Author

Trathen Heckman is an award-winning nonprofit leader with over twenty years of experience cultivating grassroots groups and community networks. He is the founder and Director of Daily Acts Organization, which specializes in unleashing the power of community to address the climate crisis. Before this, his passion for the mountains led to frequently flying through trees and off cliffs and jumps as a sponsored snowboarder.

Trathen's life and leadership are deeply informed by time in the garden and wild places and with inspiring people. He utilizes his skills and resources to empower communities toward reclaiming the power of their actions to regenerate self, nature, and community. He lives in the Petaluma River Watershed where he grows food, medicine, and wonder, while working to compost apathy and lack.

End Notes

[1] Todd Kashdan, "Wired to Wonder," Greater Good Magazine, September 1, 2009, https://greatergood.berkeley.edu/article/item/wired_to_wonder.

[2] Rollin McCraty, Science of the Heart: Exploring the Role of the Heart in Human Performance, HeartMath Institute, accessed May 3, 2022, https://www.heartmath.org/research/science-of-the-heart/.

[3] Doc Childre, Howard Martin, and Donna Beech, The Heartmath Solution, (New York: Harper One, 2011).

[4] Jill Suttie and Jason Marsh, "5 Ways Giving Is Good for You," Greater Good Magazine, December 13, 2010, https://greatergood.berkeley.edu/article/item/5_ways_giving_is_good_for_you.

[5] See note 1.

[6] Clarissa Pinkola Estés, A Letter to a Young Activist During Troubled Times, Maven Productions, accessed May 3, 2022, https://www.mavenproductions.com/letter-to-a-young-activist.

[7] Bruce Allyn and Mike Amaranthus, "Healthy Soil Microbes, Healthy People," The Atlantic, June 11, 2013, https://www.theatlantic.com/health/archive/2013/06/healthy-soil-microbes-healthy-people/276710/.

[8] Marianne Williamson, A Return to Love, (New York: Harper One, 1996).

[9] Courtney E. Ackerman, "28 Benefits of Gratitude & Most Significant Research Findings," PositivePyschology.com, April 12, 2017, https://positivepsychology.com/benefits-gratitude-research-questions/.

[10] Richard Whittaker, "Godfrey Reggio: A Call for Another Way of Living," Works & Conversations, February 18, 2006, https://www.conversations.org/story.php?sid=91.

[11] The leadership intent to model, pathfind, align, and unleash is based off similar ideas in Stephen Covey's book, The 8th Habit.

[12] David Suzuki, The Sacred Balance, (Greystone Books, 2006), 62, and Ken Ausubel, Restoring the Earth: Visionary Solutions from the Bioneers, (H J Kramer, 1997).

[13] Ken Ausubel, Restoring the Earth: Visionary Solutions from the Bioneers, (H J Kramer, 1997).

[14] See note 2.

[15] Greg Sarris, "The Last Woman From Petaluma," KCET, September 29, 2016, https://www.kcet.org/shows/tending-the-wild/the-last-woman-from-petaluma.

[16] Marco Margaritoff, "Medieval Peasants Worked Less And Vacationed More Than Modern Americans Do," allthatsinteresting.com, April 20, 2022, https://allthatsinteresting.com/medieval-peasants-vacation-more.

17 Marcus Lu, "These 3 studies point to the mental health benefits of working less," World Economic Forum, February 19, 2020, https://www.weforum.org/agenda/2020/02/shorter-workweek-people-happier/, and Tim Smedley, "How shorter workweeks could save the Earth," BBC, August 6, 2019, https://www.bbc.com/worklife/article/20190802-how-shorter-workweeks-could-save-earth.

18 Laura Cochrane, "'DIY is an Instigator of Community': Dale Dougherty Chats with Etsy," makezine.com, March 8, 2013, https://makezine.com/2013/03/08/diy-is-an-instigator-of-community-dale-dougherty-chats-with-etsy/.

19 Masashi Soga, Kevin J. Gaston, and Yuichi Yamaura, "Gardening Is Beneficial for Health: A Meta-analysis," Preventative Medicine Reports 5, (November 2016), https://doi.org/10.1016/j.pmedr.2016.11.007.

20 A fibershed is a geographic region that gives boundaries to a natural textile resource base. It's about re-localizing our fabrics in an equitable and regenerative way. In this case Suzanne was drying flowers to use as natural dyes for cloth. Check out www.fibershed.org.

21 An excerpt from Sandor Katz's book Wild Fermentation: The Flavor, Nutrition, and Craft of Live-Culture Foods can be found in an article hosted by Chelsea Green Publishing here: https://www.chelseagreen.com/2012/cultural-rehabilitation-the-health-benefits-of-fermented-foods/.

22 In The Carbon Farming Solution, Eric Toensmeier writes, "homegardens have been characterized by leading agroforestry scientist P.K. Nair as 'the epitome of sustainability' for their social and environmental impact, in the areas of 'biodiversity conservation, gender equity, social justice, environmental integrity, appreciation of indigenous knowledge, preservation of cultural knowledge and so on.'"

23 Hop Hopkins, "Racism Is Killing the Planet," Sierra Club, June 8, 2020, https://www.sierraclub.org/sierra/racism-killing-planet.

24 Annalee Schafranek, "What's the Difference Between an Ally and an Accomplice?" ywcaworks.org, December 21, 2021, https://www.ywcaworks.org/blogs/ywca/tue-12212021-1103/whats-difference-between-ally-and-accomplice.

25 Sara Goudarzi, "Scientists Finally Figure Out How Bees Fly," Live Science, January 9, 2006, https://www.livescience.com/528-scientists-finally-figure-bees-fly.html.

26 Emma Green, "It Helps to Like Your Neighbor During a Disaster," The Atlantic, April 3, 2014, https://www.theatlantic.com/business/archive/2014/04/it-helps-to-like-your-neighbor-during-a-natural-disaster/360139/.